Shame Matters

Understanding shame as a relational problem, *Shame Matters* explores how people, with support, can gradually move away from the relentless cycle of shame and find new and more satisfying ways of relating.

Orit Badouk Epstein brings together experts from across the world to explore different aspects of shame from an attachment perspective. The impact of racism and socio-economic factors on the development and experience of shame are discussed and illustrated with clinical narratives. Drawing upon the experience of infant researchers, trauma experts and therapists using somatic interventions, *Shame Matters* explores and develops understanding of the shameful deflations encountered in the consulting room and describes how new and empowered ways of relating can be nurtured. The book also details attachment-informed research into the experience of shame and outlines how it can be applied to clinical practice.

Shame Matters will be an invaluable companion for psychotherapists, clinical psychologists, counsellors, social workers, nurses, and others in the helping professions.

Orit Badouk Epstein is an attachment-based psychoanalytic psychotherapist, supervisor, teacher and member of The Bowlby Centre, London. She is also the editor of *Attachment: New Directions in Psychotherapy and Relational Psychoanalysis* and co-edited *Terror Within and Without: Attachment and Disintegration: Clinical Work on the Edge* (Routledge, 2013).

The Bowlby Centre Monograph Series

A series of books taken from the annual John Bowlby Memorial Lecture, produced in association with the John Bowlby Centre, London.

Terror Within and Without
Attachment and Disintegration: Clinical Work on the Edge
Edited by Judy Yellin and Orit Badouk Epstein

Shattered States
Disorganised Attachment and its Repair
Edited by Judy Yellin and Kate White

Trauma and Attachment
Edited by Sarah Benamer and Kate White

Unmasking Race, Culture, and Attachment in the Psychoanalytic Space
Edited by Kate White

Sexuality and Attachment in Clinical Practice
Edited by Kate White and Joseph Schwartz

Touch
Attachment and the Body
Edited by Kate White

Shame Matters
Attachment and Relational Perspectives for Psychotherapists
Edited by Orit Badouk Epstein

For further information about this series please visit https://www.routledge.com/The-Bowlby-Centre-Monograph-Series/book-series/KARNBCM

Shame Matters

Attachment and Relational Perspectives for Psychotherapists

Edited by
Orit Badouk Epstein

Routledge
Taylor & Francis Group

LONDON AND NEW YORK

First published 2022
by Routledge
2 Park Square, Milton Park, Abingdon, Oxon OX14 4RN

and by Routledge
605 Third Avenue, New York, NY 10158

Routledge is an imprint of the Taylor & Francis Group, an informa business

British Library Cataloguing-in-Publication Data
A catalogue record for this book is available from the British Library

Library of Congress Cataloging-in-Publication Data
Names: Epstein, Orit Badouk, editor.
Title: Shame matters : attachment and relational perspectives for psychotherapists / edited by Orit Badouk Epstein.
Description: Milton Park, Abingdon, Oxon ; New York, NY : Routledge, 2021. |
Series: The Bowlby Centre monograph series | Includes bibliographical references and index. |
Summary: "Shame can be one of the most paralysing of emotions and seems to emerge as a consequence of early or contemporary attachment traumas. Understanding shame as a relational problem, this book explores how people, with support, can gradually move away from the relentless cycle of shame and find new and more satisfying ways of relating"— Provided by publisher.
Identifiers: LCCN 2021014870 | ISBN 9781032007779 (hardback) | ISBN 9781032007755 (paperback) | ISBN 9781003175612 (ebook)
Subjects: LCSH: Shame. | Attachment behavior.
Classification: LCC BF575.S45 S548 2021 | DDC 152.4/4—dc23
LC record available at https://lccn.loc.gov/2021014870

ISBN: 9781032007779 (hbk)
ISBN: 9781032007755 (pbk)
ISBN: 9781003175612 (ebk)

DOI: 10.4324/9781003175612

Typeset in Times New Roman
by codeMantra

Contents

Illustrations

Contributors

Aileen Alleyne, Ph.D., is a UKCP-registered Psychodynamic Psychotherapist, BACP-qualified Counsellor and Clinical Supervisor in private practice. She is based in East Sussex and South East London. Alongside her private practice, she consults to organisations on Working with Issues of Difference and Diversity, and is also a visiting lecturer on various counselling and psychotherapy trainings. Aileen is the author of several book chapters and journal papers exploring themes on black/white dynamics, shame and identity, and working with issues of Difference and Diversity in the workplace.

Elaine Arnold, Ph.D., qualified as Psychiatric Social Worker and went on to research the often-traumatic effects of broken attachments, separation, and loss on children and parents as a result of immigration from the Caribbean to Britain. Utilising the theoretical framework of Attachment Theory, her research also explored the impact of foster care, adoption, and bereavement within this already-fractured community.

She has more than twenty years of experience within the statutory and voluntary sectors, provides assessments and consultancy to students from colleges researching loss through immigration, and facilitates workshops, seminars, and conferences for the organisation she was central in founding, Supporting Relationships and Families (SRF) (formerly known as the Separation and Reunion Forum). Based on her research, she has written a book, *Working with Families of African Caribbean Origin: Understanding Issues around Immigration and Attachment* (2012), and contributed to many other books and journals.

Orit Badouk Epstein is a UKCP-registered Attachment-based Psychoanalytic Psychotherapist, a training supervisor, and a training therapist. She trained at The Bowlby Centre, London where she is the editor of the journal *Attachment: New Directions in Psychotherapy and Relational Psychoanalysis.* She specialises in attachment theory and trauma and regularly lectures, teaches, writes, and presents papers on these topics and consults worldwide on attachment theory. She runs a private practice and works relationally with individuals, couples, and parents. Orit has a particular interest in working with individuals who have experienced extreme abuse and trauma and have symptoms of dissociation. She is a co-editor of *Ritual Abuse and Mind Control: The Manipulation of Attachment Needs* (Badouk Epstein, Wingfield & Schwartz, 2011, Routledge) and *Terror Within & Without* (Yellin & Badouk Epstein, 2013, Routledge). She was the co-editor of the European Society for Trauma and Dissociation (ESTD) newsletter for ten years as well as being a regular contributor of articles and film reviews. In her spare time, Orit enjoys the cinema, reading philosophy, and writing poetry.

Richard Chefetz is a psychiatrist in private practice in Washington, D.C. He was President of the International Society for the Study of Trauma and Dissociation (2002–2003), Co-Founder and Chair of their Dissociative Disorders Psychotherapy Training Program (2000–2008), and is a Distinguished Visiting Lecturer at the William Alanson White Institute of Psychiatry, Psychoanalysis, and Psychology. He is also a faculty member at the Washington School of Psychiatry, the Institute of Contemporary Psychotherapy & Psychoanalysis, and the Washington-Baltimore Center for Psychoanalysis. He is a Certified Consultant at the American Society of Clinical Hypnosis and is trained in Level I and II EMDR. Dr. Chefetz was the editor of *Dissociative Disorders: An Expanding Window into the Psychobiology of Mind* for the Psychiatric Clinics of North America, March 2006; Neuroscientific and Therapeutic Advances in Dissociative Disorders, *Psychiatric Annals*, August 2005, and Multimodal Treatment of Complex Dissociative Disorders, *Psychoanalytic Inquiry* (20/2, 2000), as well as numerous journal articles on psychodynamic perspectives on trauma, dissociation, and clinical process. He recently published a book with Norton (2015), in their Interpersonal Neurobiology series, *Intensive Psychotherapy for Persistent Dissociative Processes: The Fear of Feeling Real.*

Elizabeth Howell, Ph.D., is on the faculty of the NYU Postdoctoral Program in Psychotherapy and Psychoanalysis; faculty and supervisor for the Trauma program, Manhattan Institute for Psychoanalysis; Past Co-Director and Faculty, International Society for the Study of Trauma and Dissociation (ISSTD) Professional Training Program on Dissociative Disorders; and on the Editorial Board of the *Journal of Trauma and Dissociation*. In addition to many professional articles, her books include: *Trauma and Dissociation Informed Psychotherapy: Relational Healing and the Therapeutic Connection*; *The Dissociative Mind*; *Understanding and Treating Dissociative Identity Disorder: A Relational Approach*; *The Dissociative Mind in Psychoanalysis: Understanding and Working with Trauma* (Howell & Itzkowitz); *Psychoanalysts, Psychologists & Psychiatrists Discuss Psychopathy and Human Evil* (Itzkowitz & Howell); and *Women and Mental Health* (Howell & Bayes).

Elizabeth Howell is the recipient, from ISSTD, of the Cornelia Wilber Award for outstanding clinical contributions in the field of dissociative disorders, and the Lifetime Achievement Award. She is the recipient, with Dr. Sheldon Itzkowitz, of the Author's Recognition Award from the National Institute for the Psychotherapies (NIP), and is a Gradiva Award nominee for both *The Dissociative Mind in Psychoanalysis* and *Trauma and Dissociation Informed Psychotherapy: Relational Healing and the Therapeutic Connection*. She has lectured nationally and internationally. She is in private practice in New York, where she works with clients, does consultations, and runs consultation and study groups.

Adriano Schimmenti, PhD, DClinPsy, is Professor of Psychopathology at Kore University of Enna, Italy, where he is also the director of the Master's course in Clinical Psychology. He is deputy director of the Italian Society of Psychological Assessment (SIPDC – Florence), research director of the Italian Institute of Psychoanalytic Psychotherapy (IIPP – Palermo), and research director of the Specialist School in Clinical Psychology at the University of Turin – SSPC. He also teaches an advanced course in post-Freudian models in the training program of the Italian Society of Psychoanalytic Psychotherapy (SIPP – Catania). He has been trained in the administration and scoring of the Adult Attachment Interview, the Attachment Style Interview, and the Childhood Experience of Care and Abuse assessment, and has extensively published in leading journals on the topics of attachment, childhood trauma, dissociation, and addictive behaviours. He has received funds in 2012 and 2014 from the EU for his research on online sexual abuse of children, and has been scientific advisor to social research centres and clinical treatment programmes. He is also an editorial board member of the APA journals *Psychological Trauma* and *Psychoanalytic Psychology*, and is the Editor in Chief of the Italian book series on *Psychotraumatology* published by Fioriti Editore (Rome).

Ulrich Schultz-Venrath is Professor of Psychosomatics and Psychotherapy, University of Witten/Herdecke, Germany. He is Head of the Clinic of Psychiatry, Psychotherapy and Psychosomatics Evangelisches Krankenhaus Bergisch Gladbach, University of Witten/Herdecke. He is a member of the DPV (IPA), GASi, D3G, DGPM, and DGPT. He is Chair of the Group Section and Board Member of EFPP. He is a recipient of the René Spitz-Award of the German Psychoanalytic Association 1994. He is a Founder Member of the International Society for Neuro-Psychoanalysis 1999, DATPPP (German Association for Day Hospital Treatment in Psychiatry, Psychotherapy and Psychosomatics) and of the D3G (German Society of Group Analysis and Group Psychotherapy) 2006. He is the author of nearly 150 publications on psychoanalysis, psychosomatics, group analysis, and mentalization-based treatment in groups. He is the Editor of the Journal *Gruppenpsychotherapie und Gruppendynamik – Zeitschrift für Theorie und Praxis der Gruppenanalyse*.

Judith Solomon is internationally recognized for her pioneering research and theory-building on attachment and caregiving, including her discovery, with Mary Main, of the infant disorganized/disoriented attachment category. She conducted the first longitudinal study of infants in separated and divorced families and developed key representational measures of caregiving and child attachment, including the Caregiving Interview and the Attachment Doll Play Projective Assessment. She is the first editor of *Attachment Disorganization* (1999) and *Disorganized Attachment and Caregiving* (2011). She was recently a Fulbright Visiting Professor at the University of Vienna. Currently she is a Visiting Researcher in the Department of Public Health and Primary Care, Cambridge University, UK and an Adjunct Professor at The Institute for Parenting, Adelphi University, New York.

Colwyn Trevarthen, a New Zealander born in Auckland, is Professor (Emeritus) of Child Psychology and Psychobiology at The University of Edinburgh, where he has taught since 1971. He trained as a biologist at Auckland University, studied ethology and physiology at Otago, and then travelled to California for a PhD in psychobiology at Caltech. After post-doctoral work in France, he was a Research Fellow at the Center for Cognitive Studies at Harvard, where his infancy research began fifty years ago. He has published extensively on brain development, infant communication, and child learning and emotional health.

He is interested in the innate creative and cooperative motives of children that lead them to make friends in society, wanting to learn what other people know. This has led to his interest in the effects of neglect and of disorders, such as autism and depressive illness, and to research on how to help parents, teachers, and therapists give the best care and companionship to young children who feel alone and unsafe.

His current research concerns how rhythms and expressions of "musicality" in movement help communication with children and aid their development and learning.

He has an honorary Doctorate in Psychology from the University of Crete, and is a Fellow of the Royal Society of Edinburgh, a Member of the Norwegian Academy of Sciences and Letters and a Vice-President of the British Association for Early Childhood Education.

He is co-editor of two books: *Communicative Musicality: Exploring the Basis of Human Companionship* (Oxford University Press, 2009) with Stephen Malloch, and *Rhythms of Relating in Children's Therapies: Connecting Creatively with Vulnerable Children* (Jessica Kingsley, 2017) with Stuart Daniel.

Acknowledgements

The conference which preceded this publication owes its success to the enthusiastic help of the conference organisers at the Bowlby Centre: Orit Badouk Epstein, Carol Tobin, Mark Linington, Yvonne Forward, Andrea Graff, and Natasha Roffe (who always helps us add pride by delivering the most beautiful flower arrangements!).

This monograph is yet another book in the series produced by The Bowlby Centre under the skilful leadership of the series editor, Kate White. A special thanks to Kate whose helpful comments and sharp eye has made this book more than just a report of a conference.

My thanks also to my husband, Lee who continues to be a source of support and immense help through all my writing projects. In addition thank you to all the contributors for their creativity and perseverance and to their colleagues and families who have supported them as we have worked on this project together.

Thank you to Elizabeth Howell for her gracious forward and to Jennifer Leighton for the artistic image she has donated for our use on the cover of the book.

Finally, thanks to everyone at Routledge who helped publish this book, especially to Alexis O'Brien and Susannah Frearson.

Foreword

Elizabeth Howell

This new volume of essays edited by Orit Badouk Epstein is aptly titled in two ways. As a title, *Shame Matters* designates a category, i.e., matters of shame. But as a declarative sentence, it states its mission: Shame certainly does matter! Long overshadowed by the psychotherapy field's preoccupation with guilt, shame is now the topic du jour. Despite the current recognition of shame's importance, discussions of shame's relationship to, even its dependence on, attachment have been frequently lacking. Nonetheless, shame often hangs on attachment, as many of the essays in this collection clarify. *Shame Matters*, in which all of the essays address shame as related to attachment, is a gem of a volume, gleaming with new theoretical insights, models, and knowledge. Contributors include many well-known experts in the fields of attachment, psychoanalysis, mentalization, and trauma/dissociation.

Although solidly entrenched as a vitally important topic now, shame "has been a long time coming." As several of the authors in this volume note, shame has been sparsely documented in much of the early literature, such as in Bowlby's or Freud's work, even though it was often implied. Perhaps the fact that most theorists were simply not thinking in a focused way that much about shame contributes to the fact that it has not often been linked to attachment.

In addition, shame has been overshadowed by guilt, which was too long considered a superior affect to shame. Perhaps it has been more palatable in the mental health field, as in ordinary life, to contemplate guilt because only the thing one *did* is bad, not the overwhelming feeling of oneself as *being* bad. In contrast, shame is about the self, about one's own sense of badness and deficiency. In shame, one is painfully and acutely aware of the self. Shame goes to the core of one's identity and can be unremitting. To make matters worse, while in guilt, the person is still an agent, in shame the person is helpless. Furthermore, guilt can often be remedied by an act of penance. In contrast, one cannot "do something" to make shame go away.

In intense shame, a person may feel their worth is being estimated in the eyes of the attachment figure. This experience of being shamefully held in the other's judgement can be excruciating. As Helen Lynd (1958), a lone shame scholar in the mid-twentieth century noted, a significant part of shame's power derives from the fear of being excluded, banished from one's attachment figures. The need for attachment and redemption from shame can be so great that "in the midst of a situation in which one is overwhelmed by shame, one may confess to a crime of which one is innocent, inviting punishment in order to re-establish even through condemnation, communication with others" (Lynd, 1958, p. 66).

Another pioneer in work on shame who notably linked shame and attachment was Helen Block Lewis (1971, 1981, 1990). Despite being a Freudian, she was an early devotee of Bowlby's work (even publishing an important essay of his in the very first volume of *Psychoanalytic Psychology*, of which she was the founding editor). Emphasizing the innate capacity for attachment, she wrote: "Human beings are social by biological nature and... shame and guilt are 'givens' whose function it is to maintain the basic affectional bonds." The papers in this volume are richly diverse, many offering new insights, and ways of thinking, even new models. In her groundbreaking essay, Judith Solomon, the well-known attachment researcher, proposes a convincing new model – a construct of a shame behavioural system comparable to Bowlby's attachment behavioural system. Noting the homeostatic aspect Bowlby's construct of the attachment system in which the set goal would be physical safety (later understood by Lyons-Ruth (2003) to be a release from fear) and proximity to the attachment figure, she outlines a similar and related construct for shame. Tracing shame inducing situations with secure, avoidant, ambivalent, and disorganized children, she focuses on the repair. She notes that "Until or as long as there is no parent to make reparation self-generated shame is irresolvable." So, what resolves shame? She notes that "both attachment and shame are assuaged by acceptance and physical contact from primary attachment or powerful social figures." She follows by reminding us of 'Helen Block Lewis' (1987) profound observation that shame should be understood "as a means by which people try to preserve their loving relationship to others." That is, shame may function as a "conditional attachment strategy" (Main, 1990) which permits the child to keep the parent "close" in actuality or psychologically, by taking the blame for misdeeds or imperfections rather than attributing them to the other (Solomon, 2021, p. 6)."

This theme, of the preferability of being bad to being banished, has been widely echoed in the mental health literature, stated so well by Ronald Fairbairn (1944/52), that "It is better to be a sinner in a world ruled by God than a saint in a world ruled by the Devil." (Fairbairn, pp. 66–67). And to paraphrase Fairbairn, it is better to be bad, and to internalize that state of shame, if that is how one stays in the attachment relationship. Such internalized shame is the topic of Adriano Schimmenti's chapter on "The aggressor within: attachment trauma, segregated systems, and the double face of shame." He discusses internalization of the aggressor and the resulting segregated shame states.

Also highlighting internalized shame and the shame of being viewed as "less than" are two essays that deal with shame and race. Elaine Arnold vividly describes her journey and those of many other African Caribbean people who have experienced ongoing social stigmatization and shame in social, health, and educational systems, all of which can be punishing. In addition, these systems often ensnare children's attachment systems as collateral damage, e.g., the way out is education, yet to acquire education, a mother must leave her children. All of this results in internalized racism and internalized shame. Another related essay by Aileen Alleyne also connects the woundedness of race, with its background of colour-coded slavery, with the internalized shame of internalized oppression. Her connection of shame to unresolved grief points to mourning as a way out of unresolvable shame.

In his highly scholarly essay on mentalizing shame, shamelessness, and shame by proxy, Ulrich Schultz-Venrath raises the important issue of shamelessness. Emphasizing the importance of mentalization, he notes that whereas shame arises with the ability to mentalize, shamelessness arises from the inability to mentalize the other's position as a subject with feelings and a separate mind. Thus, shamelessness is connected to violence. He highlights how shamelessness is often behind the scapegoating that too often occurs in groups.

As he does in other papers, Colwyn Trevarthen describes infants' innate capacities for purposeful imitation and collaborative, joyful communication. But in this article, as he observes the baby's (and the adult's) pride in joyful self-expression in communication, he emphasizes the emergent shame at not being understood or accepted.

Orit Badouk Epstein, in both of her essays included here, gives us the gift of writing from the heart. In "Primary shame: needing you and the economy of affects", she makes a plea for acceptance of the validity of attachment needs and for de-shaming them, noting that needing the comfort of an attachment figure is still considered shameful and taboo, even in psychotherapy mores. In one fascinating section, she traces through the variety of shame affects that coincide with different attachment patterns. Emphasizing dependency as a primary human need, she powerfully states: "...... the word dependency, in its pejorative sense, has become a shaming noun and a sign of inherent weakness, ensuring that society at large remains dismissive about our basic attachment needs. This down-regulation and affect avoidance has contributed to the ossified world we have had to adapt to, where many of us have experienced shame whenever needing the proximity of our attachment figures" (Badouk Epstein, 2021, p. 53).

In his essay on "Attackments" Richard Chefetz eloquently presents us with new concepts as he makes the important distinction between acute and chronic shame, noting that in the experience of acute shame, one has the hope of repair of the disrupted relationship. In contrast, in chronic shame, the "person is like a bird plucked clean of its feathers while still alive: naked and unrecognizable, completely vulnerable, devalued, unable to flee, unable to hide." Echoing Badouk Epstein's plea for de-shaming attachment need and dependency, he says, "We are all patients, really. We're just at different points on the trajectory of healing."

Shame that is too severe or too prolonged can be overwhelming. Overwhelming shame can be traumatic – and therefore dissociogenic. Philip Bromberg (1998) wrote, "Shame signals a traumatic attack upon one's personal identity and typically calls forth dissociative processes to preserve selfhood" (p. 295). Survivors of traumatic abuse often report that bodily injuries are not as painful as the emotional pain of feeling so denigrated, so shamed. Often a significant part of the dissociative post-traumatic damage of abuse and neglect stems from the unremitting, unendurable, and inescapable shame involved. The dissociogenic power of shame is one topic that Badouk Epstein addresses in her final chapter, "Suicide Addict": the sovereignty of shame in the dissociated mind.

The psychotherapy relationship is an attachment relationship, and it is also a shame-infused one, by the very fact that attachment longings are elicited. Wisdom from contributors to this volume is highly relevant to one of the psychotherapist's important tasks: that of de-shaming shame.

Elizabeth Howell

References

Bromberg, P. (1998). Staying the same while changing: Reflections on clinical judgment. In P. Bromberg (Ed.), *Standing in the Spaces: Essays on Clinical Process, Trauma, and Dissociation* (pp. 291–308). Hillsdale, NJ: Analytic Press.

Badouk Epstein, O. (2022). Primary shame and the economy of affects. In: O. Badouk Epstein (Ed.), *Shame Matters: Attachment and Relational Perspectives for Psychotherapists*. London: Routledge.

Fairbairn, W. R. D. (1944/1952). Endopsychic structure considered in terms of object relationships. In *Psychoanalytic Studies of the Personality* (pp. 82–136). Boston, MA: Routledge & Kegan Paul.

Lewis, H. B. (1971). *Shame and Guilt in Neurosis.* New York: International Universities Press.

Lewis, H. B. (1981). *Freud and Modern Psychology, Vol. 1: The Emotional Basis of Mental Illness.* New York: Plenum Press.

Lewis, H. B. (1990). Shame, repression, field dependence and psychopathology. In J. Singer (Ed.), *Repression and Dissociation: Implications for Personality Theory, Psychopathology and Health* (pp. 233–258). Chicago, IL: University of Chicago Press.

Lynd, H. (1958). *On Shame and the Search for Identity.* New York: Harcourt Brace.

Lyons-Ruth, K. (2003). Dissociation and the parent–infant dialogue: A longitudinal perspective from attachment research. *American Psychoanalytic Association, 51,* 883–911.

Main, M. (1990). Cross-cultural studies of attachment organization: Recent studies, changing methodologies, and the concept of conditional strategies. *Human Development, 33,* 48–61.

Solomon, J. (2021). Shame as a behavioural system: Links to attachment, defence, and dysregulation. In: O. Badouk Epstein (Ed.), *Shame Matters: Attachment and Relational Perspectives for Psychotherapists* (pp. 6–20). London: Routledge.

Introduction

Orit Badouk Epstein

Shame matters a great deal. It can be one of the most paralysing of emotions and most withering of relational experiences. It can be unbearably painful and corrosive, attacking one's body and identity. It threatens to freeze the self and can have a significant long-lasting negative impact on the quality of attachment relationships. Shame seems to emerge as a consequence of neglect, alongside criticising and humiliating caregiving and other attachment related traumas. In the context of our clients' experience in the therapeutic relationship, the feeling of shame may relate to current events, actions and negative responses as well as memories of these from the past. The human need to keep proximity, to be respected and feel cherished is universal, all of which constitute secure attachment. In the absence of meaningful relationships and connections, shame can also trigger the terror of aloneness and dissolution.

John Bowlby, alongside an ever expanding body of empirical research, has taught us that secure relationships are the bedrock of affect regulation and reflective functioning, creative exploration and robust wellbeing. Often a greater pressure for survival envelopes these relationships. The shameful deflations we encounter in the therapeutic dyad, can immobilise both the therapist and the client's capacity to move on. By understanding shame as a relational problem, the client can gradually learn to move away from an overwhelming cycle of unbearable shame affects. Once we recognise shame affects presented by the person sitting with us, we are better equipped to respond with compassion and nurture new ways of relating.

For the twenty-fourth John Bowlby Memorial Conference, the planning group at The Bowlby Centre in London, decided to make *Shame Matters* the title of the conference and to use this theme as an invitation to the speakers and participants from the field of psychotherapy to explore and understand the multiple layers which this topic demands that we consider.

In this monograph, we have gathered perspectives from infant researchers, trauma experts and socio-political writers from around the world, so that we can expand and connect with our own experiences of shame as well as with those of our clients.

DOI: 10.4324/9781003175612-1

The book opens with Judith's Solomon's ground-breaking paper on shame as a behavioural system which is comparable to Bowlby's attachment system. Solomon notes the gap in attachment studies which she puts down to the fact that shame is only manifest in the second year of life once the attachment system has become established rather than earlier on when the child is becoming aware of themselves as a person. Although Bowlby hardly mentions the word shame in his writings, he did however perceive it to be the catalyst in the creation of segregated systems – a concept he elaborated on in his later work. Thus, Solomon links shame to dissociative processes and relational trauma. She expands her understanding of the prevalence of shame in normative and at-risk attachment caregiving relationships. Solomon revisits the research which she had carried out with Carol George into the fear and helplessness found among children with disorganised attachment patterns and looks at it with a fresh attachment lens. With this new perspective, she describes how she can now see the mother's shame and also the child's shame reflected in the mother's experience of her own shame. In addition, she sheds light on the long-lasting effects of self-generated shame which she aptly calls "Irresolvable Shame". In the absence of an attachment figure, the child will learn to blame herself whenever she can't understand the reason for the separation from her primary caregivers. She claims that shame, by its nature, wants to hide itself, making it difficult to spot, particularly when fear and other defences are so salient.

Colwyn Trevarthen, whose research on the neonate's mutual engagement with caregivers focuses on their sharing with joy the imitation and observation of their environment, requires a new scientific understanding about how we come into life as a moving self in a community of other active selves. He also looks at how we share and compare experiences sympathetically. In his chapter "Caring for the human spirit in pride and shame", Trevarthen joyously illustrates the pride and shame of young infants in their responses to the attention of other persons of different ages. He looks at how caring about the emotion of shame comes with the hope of a less analytical and more responsive relational therapy in order to reduce the loneliness and isolation of shame and how correcting our understanding of shame can be shared with pride. This chapter narrates as a story of "shared knowing" of shared minds, relationships and seeking to discover and enjoy life with or for the other people in our lives.

In her chapter "Primary shame: needing you and the economy of affects", Orit Badouk Epstein follows on from Bowlby and Ainsworth's observations of the impact of early separation of the infant from her caregiver. Additional links are made between separation and shame as an affect that the child learns to defend against, and which is expressed through the specific and varied attachment patterns. She calls it "primary shame". Badouk Epstein locates primary shame within the larger societal context: how traumatic events during previous centuries have taught us to economise our feelings of dependency, encourage self-reliance while forcing young children to grow up prematurely. Even if it is not always possible to meet the infant's as well as the client's needs optimally, rather than blaming, or denying but acknowledging the existence of these needs with authentic empathy and tenderness will only improve human relatedness. Badouk Epstein also explores Suttie's contribution to the importance of responding to feelings of vulnerability with tenderness in contrast to shaming.

In his moving and elegantly written chapter "Attackments: subjugation, shame, and the attachment to painful affects and objects", Richard Chefetz describes his long-term work with a very traumatised client and the desperate feelings of nakedness which shame leaves her struggling with. It is "like a bird plucked clean of its feathers while alive". He coined the term "attackment" as he comes to understand that shame is at the core of attacking the close relationship this client develops with her therapist. On the client's part, it is an attempt to preserve proximity while at the same time avoid the collapse or terror resulting from separation. Shame is at the core of this double bind. In his search to understand what is the opposite of shame, Chefetz also introduces us to the relational representation of the word "beloved", a word that knows the dignity of a confirmed, enduring, positive and growth promoting relationship which is to be cherished.

"Shame and black identity wounding: the legacy of internalised oppression" is a powerful and timely chapter written by Aileen Alleyne. In seeing shame as a positive tenet of humanity, Alleyne states that it keeps our humanity in check. However, shame is also highly problematic and its wounding of black identity, through the transmission of intergenerational trauma from slavery and colonisation has left black, indigenous and people of colour as always experiencing themselves as "less than". This is in addition to the mass macro aggression of racism that black people endure. Alleyne also writes about the micro aggressions of racism white societies inflict upon generations of black individuals which is often so hard to prove. She utilises the term "intersectionality" to explain these dynamics most effectively. What's more, when historical wounds compound the racism in the present but are not being recognised, the forgotten trauma of slavery, even though it's everyone's shame, is left isolated for black people to endure. Perceiving this shame as unresolved grief, this is what needs to be shared and mourned. Her poignant distinction between the "internal oppressor" and internalised oppression and how we should acquire the "reflexibility" that will land us in a state of grace is fundamental to the understanding of ourselves as a whole diverse community.

The chapter "Mentalizing shame, shamelessness and Fremdscham (shame by proxy) in groups" is a deep and generous chapter which brings together the different modes of shame experienced in social groups and within individuals in dyads. As a group analyst, Ulrich Schultz-Venrath tells us how from a mentalising point of view, the ability to be ashamed is an important psychological development achieved by a higher order of mental representation. He explains the difference between shame and shamelessness and how both can occupy specific body expressions as well as how both can inhibit mentalisation. Shame is also a culturally embedded social construct that changes over time. Reflected in the body, shame makes the body want to hide or shrink while pride leads to expansive physical movement. Schultz-Venrath places shame within an historical and a social context and recognises its relational and subjective qualities as central to the development of group dynamic processes. The phenomenon of scapegoating in groups is one example of a non-mentalised shame driven act which creates the illusion that by removing the scapegoat from the group, the group will be able to function better. In a group therapy setting, the challenges the leader of Mentalising-Based Therapy (MBT) faces when leading a session is to facilitate and navigate the tension created through the modes of intense emotions which often result in shame or missed emotions that then lead to shamelessness. The wealth contained within this paper means that reading it once will certainly not do it justice.

Adriano Schimmenti discusses the multi-layered organisation of shame within the context of attachment trauma by weaving attachment theory, trauma and dissociation theories together, in his most informative chapter "The aggressor within: attachment trauma, segregated systems, and the double face of shame". He sees shame as being self-conscious, represented in segregated mental states as well as being a protective mechanism against fear and helplessness. He aptly calls it "Double Faced Shame" which first threatens the individual's self-esteem and secondly fosters a sense of unworthiness. In his clinical vignettes Schimmenti illustrates, with sensitivity and skill, how "segregated core shame states" occur as a result of traumatic identification with neglecting and abusive attachment figures that sometimes leads to identification with the aggressor. This is when the client will think that something is terribly wrong with her rather than that something terrible was done to her. But for the survivor, shame is a way out of unbearable feelings, it organises and simplifies what is overwhelming. It represents internal solutions to an insoluble dilemma, namely using dissociation to protect the attachment bond at any cost.

In the chapter "Personal and professional reflections: shame and race", Elaine Arnold, who becomes a teacher, a social worker and a psychotherapist working in the UK, intimately shares her moving story as an immigrant from the Caribbean. Her journey includes a first-hand witnessing of the multiple traumas inflicted by slavery, colonialism and dislocation on the first generation of migrants to the UK. It has left many of them struggling with severe mental health issues compounded by exposure to appalling episodes of racism both structural and personal. The shame attached to the stigma of mental health from this period left many immigrants isolated, homeless, poor, and too ashamed to return to their home country. Elaine, concludes, being made to feel shame is a core problem in a racialised society and the time is rightly overdue for change.

Finally, in "'Suicide Addict': the sovereignty of shame in the dissociated mind", Orit Badouk Epstein explores the different meanings of suicidal ideation through an attachment and trauma lens. The client's wish to die is also her will to live. It is through the paradox of attachment and dissociative processes that the client expresses her attachment cries, chronic shame, anger and her plea for separation from her "scaregiver". Through polyphonic dialogism and affective responsiveness, Badouk Epstein finds creative ways of communicating with the client's dissociated despair, eventually leading to more regulated affects and a significant reduction in her suicidal ideation.

We are delighted and take pride in bringing together all the contributions to this book, in the hope that it will enable the helping professions to come closer and fill the gap between the private and public self and to reduce the crippling impact of shame on people's lives through a deeper and more compassionate understanding of its origins and thereby support change.

Chapter 1

Shame as a behavioral system

Its links to attachment, defense, and dysregulation

Judith Solomon

Shame is the silent, unacknowledged companion to attachment and caregiving. At least, until now, it certainly was under-appreciated and unacknowledged by me. In the last twenty or thirty years, a great deal has been written about the experience of shame in the context of clinical phenomena and trauma. Erikson (1980), Kohut (1971), Lewis (1987), and contemporary thinkers about the infant-parent relationship such as Schore (1994) and De Young (2015) all have argued that shame originates in perturbations in the early parent-child relationship. Yet, despite my background as a comparative psychologist, attachment researcher, and child-parent psychotherapist, and before embarking on the preparation for this chapter, I was largely unaware of the inevitability of shame as a constituent of attachment relationships. I am not alone. There seems to be very little research examining the links between shame and attachment security in young children (see the work by Lewis for an exception, e.g., Lewis et al., 1989).[1]

I do not think that this gap in attachment studies is merely due to the fact that shame behavior does not appear until the second year of life, after the attachment system has already consolidated. It seems to manifest around the second birthday, at about the time the child is capable of awareness of himself as a person, or as the expression goes "an object" in the mind of another, and begins to comprehend that he is not achieving some standard or expectation that the child perceives his parents or others to value (Lewis et al., 1989). Perhaps, it is not surprising, given the late development of shame, that in John Bowlby's published writing, the word "shame" rarely appears—there isn't a single entry for the word "shame" in the index of any of the Bowlby trilogy—1969, 1973, 1980.[2] Bowlby clearly understood, however, the importance of shame in the development of relationship-related pathology. In his important essay *On knowing what you are not supposed to know and feeling what you are not supposed to feel* (1988) in which he considers the contradictory mental or representational models of their attachments that children develop he wrote:

> The scenes and experiences that tend to become shut off, though often continuing to be extremely influential in affecting thought, feeling, and

DOI: 10.4324/9781003175612-2

behaviour, fall into at least three distinct categories: (a) those that parents wish their children not to know about; (b) those in which parents have treated children in ways the children find too unbearable to think about; (c) *those in which children have done, or perhaps thought, things about which they feel unbearably guilty or ashamed.*
(Bowlby, 1988, p. 114). (Author's emphasis in italics.)

Here we see that Bowlby clearly pointed to shame as a potential catalyst in the "onset" of segregated systems, which I and my colleague, Carol George (Solomon & George, 1999) as well as Giovanni Liotti (2004), and others have equated with dissociative processes. Thinking about dissociation as a product of shame leads directly to relational trauma, which we know from many other sources to be strongly associated with shame. Nevertheless, it seems to be the case that attachment research has not given due weight to—or made clear enough—the role of shame in attachment phenomena. I hope to begin to remedy this in this chapter.

My goals are, first, to consider the ways in which Bowlby's ethologically informed methods can shed light on our understanding of the experience of shame, that is, to explore how what I propose to call the shame behavioral system compares to Bowlby's description of the attachment behavioral system. This will help us clarify the nature of this complex state. Second, I want to highlight the prevalence of shame in normative and at-risk attachment-caregiver relationships.

I'd like to begin by applying Bowlby's general ethological approach and control systems model to the phenomenon of shame. I do not mean necessarily to suggest that the mind is, as it were, a collection of behavioral systems, but I have always found this aspect of Bowlby's analysis of attachment behavior to be a helpful heuristic, at least. At a minimum, it provides an intellectual structure. It focuses our attention on what should be the key elements in our understanding. Additionally, by its nature, it helps us to disentangle the normative from the pathological varieties of the behavior under consideration. This is because in a homeostatic or well-regulated system, such as the mind apparently has evolved to be, we can expect that there will also have evolved neurophysiological and behavioral *adaptations or strategies* resulting in individual differences, types, or processes that facilitate a flexible accommodation to variations in the natural or social environment. From these, we can also derive the variants that characterize strain or pathology in the system. What I am assuming here, of course, is that shame, like attachment, is a product of natural selection—this was once a controversial view but now is no longer (Gilbert and Andrews, 1998)—and may, perhaps, be understood to function analogously to the attachment system.

A behavioral system is a *construct*—no one should expect an attachment or caregiving or, now, a shame model to be found in the nervous system any more than one would expect nowadays to find an ego or superego. (We might eventually, however, be able to trace the dynamic pathways of this system in the brain.) In developing a systems model, Bowlby was positing that change in one element of the attachment system necessarily results in corresponding changes in the remaining elements—this is how any system, natural or mechanical, remains responsive to changing circumstances (see Figure 1.1).

He was also presuming that attachment is organized with respect to a "set-goal" with adaptive importance to the organism, that is, a behavioral or state goal. Finally by conceptualizing attachment as a system, Bowlby was assuming that behavior and internal regulation function in such a way as to achieve approximate homeostasis. As clinicians we are going to be especially interested in what happens when conditions are less than optimal and what happens when the elements of the system are under severe strain, for these are the conditions in which we expect to see a heightened risk for pathological functioning.

Bowlby's (1969) control system model of attachment enumerates the many behaviors that are associated with the infant's bond to a particular person and the evolutionary or selective advantages of this bond in the environment in which humans evolved, which Bowlby believed to be physical safety. The set-goal of attachment behavior, that is, the homeostatic sweet spot that the system is designed by natural selection to achieve, is physical contact or proximity with the caregiver. Once this goal is achieved, Bowlby proposed that the system is temporarily at rest, attachment behavior is said to be terminated, and the individual can then turn to other activities, such as play and exploration. Attachment behaviors are activated by particular conditions: when a threat is perceived, when the infant is ill or weak, and

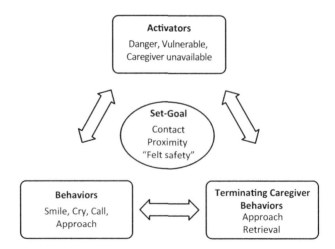

Figure 1.1 Bowlby's model of the attachment behavioral system.

when the caregiver is physically unavailable or psychologically absent. Once activated, attachment behaviors bring the infant close to the caregiver or the caregiver close to the infant, which terminates or "down-regulates" the system again. This, in essence, is how Bowlby envisioned the functioning of the attachment system. In the course of development, we know that this system becomes integrated with and regulated at the level of representation.

What would a control systems model of the shame system look like? The formal definition of shame included in the American Heritage Dictionary (2020) is "a painful emotion caused by the belief that one is, or is perceived by others to be, inferior or unworthy of affection or respect because of one's actions, thoughts, circumstances, or experiences".

There are also many shades and varieties of shame, as indicated by the many terms we have for it (e.g., embarrassment, humiliation, disgrace, chagrin, loss of face), at least some of which have been operationally or empirically distinguished (Lewis & Ramsey, 2002). These various states have in common a desire to hide or cover one's face, escape, sink into the ground, and a feeling of being at least temporarily stuck in place. We have all experienced these states and, indeed, there is commonality among artists about how to depict them an example of which is shown in Figure 1.2.

Two points are worth mentioning here. First, note how natural it is to describe shame *behavior*—what we do or want to do when in that state—when seeking to capture the experience of shame. This seems to correspond to the *wordlessness* that characterizes shame states (Lewis, 1987). Perhaps this state of wordlessness is related to the underlying neurophysiology of shame. The experience of shame is controlled, according to Porges (2001) and Schore (1994) by activation of the parasympathetic nervous system through the dorsal vagal nerve. The same evolutionarily ancient motor pathway activates stilling and freezing responses, physical collapse, and immobility—when a frightened individual perceives that neither fight nor flight will lead him away from danger. Thus, shame is associated with a defensive shutting off or shutting down of behavior and thought. The activation of this ancient neural pathway may also account for what we often experience as the quality of automaticity or rapid kindling of shame, the sense that shame responses are sudden, involuntary, with an all-or-none quality. Not surprisingly, shame is accompanied by feelings of helplessness and vulnerability. Significantly, these states—feelings of helplessness and vulnerability—are also among the main activators of the attachment system. *This suggests that the experience of shame simultaneously, consciously or unconsciously, activates the attachment system and a desire for proximity to an attachment figure.*

There seems to be widespread agreement that shame evolved from behaviors used to regulate social rank and status—that is, the loser's side of that equation (Gilbert & McGuire, 1998). Within the primate order, though there are species differences in facial expression associated with submission or appeasement, there is commonality in posture—averting the eyes, looking

Figure 1.2 Eve on the Rock, August Rodin, Musée Rodin, Paris.

down, turning away, even crouching down. In essence, the submitting animal emits behaviors that are the negation of threat or power displays.

In a troop of monkeys, it is essential that young animals require no
training to display submission behaviors to higher ranking members of the
troop. There is a clear selective advantage to displaying shame behavior
(and possibly experiencing the affect of shame) for the individual's long-
term reproductive fitness. The price of failing to do may be injury, or, even

worse, ostracism or exclusion from the group—a fate that sometimes befalls juvenile males who may be harassed by other males and even other females until they actually leave the group (Keltner and Harker, 1998). Although the shame system seems to have evolved originally as part of dominance interactions, it seems clear that the common human meaning of shame—the sense of oneself as bad, unworthy, deserving of contempt—can parallel, amplify, or contradict the individual's evaluation of the self as good or bad in interaction with caregivers.

In the usual course of events, juvenile monkeys and mature subordinates are quite likely to be challenged or to challenge others. They need to know—but especially they need to *show that they know* their place in order to avoid attacks (Keltner et al., 1997). At the same time, it is also advantageous for the winners of disputes to show acceptance of subordinates—both for the purpose of affective regulation and, in the long run, to reduce the level of hostilities in the group (although this latter function is not necessarily conscious).[3] Frans de Waal, the venerable primatologist from the Yerkes Primate Center, has emphasized the ubiquity of conciliation behaviors in primate species at the conclusion of these conflicts. It is the model, as he notes, for peace-making within human groups. Among primates, conciliation usually entails some kind of gentle physical contact, initiated either by the winner or the loser, depending upon the species, which signals "forgiveness", i.e., an invitation or a request to approach. The process of conciliation thus appears to be tantamount to "repair", which we usually discuss as regulating distress in the mother-child relationship. Figure 1.3 shows how this sequence of events might map onto a control systems model.

Figure 1.3 Proposed model for the shame system.

Let us consider now how shame is experienced in the course of early normative human development. It is easy to see how human maternal socialization techniques or simply the irritations of daily life almost inevitably result in the toddler or preschooler feeling he has lost the battle and experiencing some level of shame, since he is now old enough to perceive his parents' disapproval. Alicia Lieberman (1993) cites observational studies indicating that mothers and preschoolers have mild to moderate conflicts at the rate of about three per hour. In a large birth cohort study of over 30,000 children in eighteen medium to large U.S. cities, Mackenzie and colleagues (2011) found that about fifteen percent of children are spanked at twelve months, forty percent by eighteen months, and nearly fifty percent of children age twenty months or older. Clearly, the attachment relationship undergoes a transition in the preschool years and the quality of these battles and therefore of the relationship will be to some degree a product of their resolution. That is, the parents' response to the child's *attachment* signals will become less salient and their approach to power assertion will become more so. In our research with mothers of five year olds, Carol George and I examined the transcripts of mothers talking about their relationships with their children during our version of the Parent Development Interview, specifically looking for their descriptions of socialization confrontations and the quality of repair. Some of these battles were by no means exemplary—they involved considerable distress and the potential for humiliation on all sides. Yet, many mothers spontaneously described reparative actions at their conclusion. Here is an excerpt from the interview of one mother of a kindergarten-aged child recounting a conflict, edited a bit for clarity and brevity. In this vignette, in addition to the mother, there is also "C", a six-year-old girl, and her one-year-old sister, referred to here as "the baby".

> I was in the kitchen getting dinner ready and 'the baby' likes to climb in and out [under the TV table]. She's almost walking now just about a month ago she's climbing in and out of this thing that holds the shelf underneath the TV she's not in C's way because she's below the standing level but C is sitting there watching too, and C gives her a little nudge on the tush and I said 'C, don't do that' and I looked back again, and C was pushing harder! I don't think she was thinking about it …I don't know why she was doing it but I yelled at her and of course the baby fell over and hit her head. No big deal. But she cried and I told C 'Don't you know better? I've told you time and time again when the baby walks, she can only walk for herself and if you touch her it gets her balance out of whack, and she falls over and you can't do that!…. And I said it in rather an intense voice and C goes running into her room crying'.

The interviewer asks the mother how she usually handles a problem like this.

> M: (sigh) Usually, it's time out between me and C. I'll kind of finish what I am doing thinking through how I am going to repair the damage that I just did…. And, uh but uh just the main thing is to try to figure out what the best way of communicating with her is. You know to get the idea across. And so, I have blown up; until I figure those things out, I leave her there crying….And then I go back and I make sure that I don't go back unless I'm pretty certain that I can get a positive outcome. …And then I, you know, figure out what happened what my point is and how I am going to make it, and then I go back and soothe it over.

It is the phrase "soothe it over" that is the tip-off to repair. If this pattern were fairly consistent over time we would hope to see a reasonably well-socialized child emerge from this process. She is learning about her mother's expectations, and in this case, it seems that she is being guided toward a responsible and fairly empathic orientation toward her little sister. She ran to her room in tears, feeling, I imagine, misunderstood, hurt, and embarrassed or ashamed, since clearly she's heard her mother say these things before. We would not, however, expect her to be burdened with these feelings unduly because her mother helped to terminate or assuage C's sense of shame. This child was judged secure at the time of the interview.

How do these everyday battles go in the homes of insecure children? Briefly, mothers of avoidant and ambivalent children do not fully carry out repair. Their tendency is just to let matters drop. Later, mothers of avoidant children might restructure the situation so that, for example the baby and child tend not to get in one another's way so often; that is, the mothers look for distance and instrumental solutions to avoid the problem. Mothers of ambivalent children tend to be unclear or wavering in their expectations and their approach to repair would more likely be to bring the child ice cream, literally to *smooth over* rather than to address the problem directly.

There are no specific studies of how shame manifests or develops in secure and insecure children. We do have a hint though from Jude Cassidy's (1988) early study of self-concept as related to attachment in kindergarten children. Cassidy developed a puppet interview in which a puppet named Bix asked questions like: Bix, do you like (child?) Do you like the way (child) is, or would you like to make him better? and the children answered through the puppet as well. Children's coded answers revealed that secure children unlike insecure children were more likely to see good and bad qualities in themselves—suggesting self-acceptance—which is precisely what therapists trying to help shamed trauma survivors try to do more formally. In Cassidy's data, there was not a perfect correspondence between attachment and the other self-concept codes, but insecure-avoidant children were most likely to describe themselves as "perfect". Those of you who are familiar with findings from the adult attachment interview will see at once that the sense of oneself as "perfect" fits very well with the way Dismissing adults idealize their parents (Main et al., 1985). Quite likely many of us might immediately think about this person having a "narcissistic personality disorder" or "narcissistic features". Rather than think about pathology in this non-clinical sample, I suggest that within the framework of a shame control system, these data give us a hint about one of the basic defensive strategies available with regard to shame—and that is to see oneself as above reproach—to minimize or filter out shameful information about the self. Logically, we would expect there to be an opposite defensive strategy—that is, one that reflects a tendency to be over-focused on one's shortcomings, but the puppet interview and coding, at least, don't reveal this unambiguously.

This leads us to consider the insecure-disorganized classifications. This group covers the high-risk and high-stress end of the relationship continuum. As my study with Carol George shows, mothers of disorganized/controlling kindergarten children experienced chronic, unpredictable and/or intense fear and helplessness in the context of important attachment relationships. Sometimes, but not always, this comprised abusive relationships (Solomon & George, 2011).

Much of what we know about mother-child interaction in families with a child who shows a disorganized attachment pattern comes from the in-depth interviews that George and I conducted in the 1990s with non-clinical as well as divorced samples, comprising children from twelve to eighteen months or five to seven years (Solomon et al., 1999; Solomon & George, 1999). This means we know something of mothers' thoughts and feelings and have their detailed descriptions of interaction, but for the children themselves, we still have to rely mainly on inferences from their symbolic narratives of behavior. From the mother's perspective, shame about themselves as persons and caregivers is a common if not everyday occurrence. This is particularly true when we focus on what mothers describe about their efforts to control themselves and to control their children. Here are some excerpts:

Asked to describe herself as a mother, one mother of a controlling child (this is the kindergarten sequela or parallel to disorganization in infancy) was self-deprecatory, that is, ashamed of herself as a mother:

> Umm, I might be more strained as a parent, or, umm, I don't know…I'm a chaotic mother (laughing), you know, that's what I think, umm, as depicting things are……Um, yeah.. but I ha'.. you know, I do spank him, too. So, you know, I wish, umm.. umm.. I wish that I.. that there's times when I am very angry and I wish I wouldn't get.. I wish I wasn't as angry as I was you know, sometimes he just goes too far and.. and, umm, I.. you know, I wish I wasn't that angry.

Her child is ashamed of himself too—at least this is how she perceives it. At the end of a protracted battle about getting dressed, she says:

> Well, he felt, um.. I don't.. that he lost, I guess, you know. That he was, umm, I don't know. (Laughs.) That I, you know, that Mom, umm, was triumphant.. again, you know.

Here is how another mother described herself in interaction:

> We were in the bathroom.. he was complaining, he wanted company brushing his teeth. He was complaining about having to get up and.... and I mean.. 'You never.'. do something or other, he says to me 'you never... wait for me or you never let me or'... it was something like this so I was feeling a little berated and I'm.... trying.. I really try...

For theoretical reasons, as attachment researchers, Carol George and I have always focused on the fear and helplessness in these vignettes. Now I see the mothers' shame. It can be hard to quite put your finger on—if you don't listen carefully, you might focus on the anger and exasperation the mothers feel, the criticism they express toward the child. It is often even harder to see the shame behind the frightened behavior of the children. For example, what are we to make of the child, in the laboratory or the clinical playroom, who says nothing—who refuses to give us a glimpse into his inner world? Is the child covering for his own shame or, perhaps, his mother's?

Irresolvable shame

I would like to turn now to consider two circumstances that give rise to shame which, I believe, are among the most painful for the young child (as well as for adults) with potentially long-lasting, deleterious effects. The first of these we may refer to as *self-generated shame* that occurs in the absence, indeed, by virtue of the absence of the attachment figure. When the sting of shame erupts in early childhood, it is assuaged most readily by the attachment figure even when that figure is the source of the shaming experience. But it is an insidious quality of shame that it does not require a perpetrator, a "shamer". Very early on, it appears, young children can generate their own interpretation of events in which they are the villain. This seems to be a frequent consequence of separation from key attachment figures, particularly when the child cannot understand the reason for separation. Until or as long as there is no parent to make reparation, self-generated shame is irresolvable. Here is a passage from a previously unpublished manuscript by Bowlby (1939–1942), made available now by Robbie Duschinsky and Kate White (2020) and the Wellcome Collection—John Bowlby Archive, on the effects of evacuating children from their homes during the blitz. Bowlby is speaking of children during the period of middle childhood:

> [Children]… are largely at the mercy of public opinion especially the opinion of their parents or foster- parents. *To be in good odour is to be happy—to be in bad odour is to feel unwanted and unsafe.* Few children go through this period without days when they feel no one loves them or being haunted by fantastic fears of being turned out of hearth and home *for being naughty and disobedient. …… The child who feels unwanted, whether this is really so or only in his imagination, will find it very difficult not to interpret his being sent away as his parents' desire to be rid of him.*
>
> (Duschinsky & White, 2020, p. 118) (Italics added for emphasis by the author)

Wait, is this passage referring to fear—the underpinning of the attachment system—or is it referring to the child's experience of shame? Both interpretations, it seems to me, are manifestly true. To be "in bad odour", though just a turn of phrase, is to be smelly and disgusting. To be naughty and disobedient, is to be unwanted, essentially bad, unworthy of inclusion in the family, worthy only of banishment. Similar stories were reported in 2019 regarding children separated at the border in the United States. One little boy told reporters that his mommy left him alone because she didn't love him anymore. It is not surprising that such children, sent away from their parents without explanation, are frightened and distressed. But in the absence of information, children generate their own explanations, i.e., that they are unlovable, an explanation that plants the seeds of shame.

Parents don't have to disappear literally for children to generate shame. One five year old whose very depressed mother didn't come down for breakfast told her father, "Mommy doesn't want to take care of me anymore". Translation: I am not worthy of care; I don't deserve the trouble. Here we have, in essence, a case of inadvertent emotional neglect on the part of her mother. This interpretation of absolute rejection is, again, very shaming. (Luckily for this child her father was available.) You may know that the majority of children removed from their homes for maltreatment usually have not experienced physical or even verbal abuse, but physical neglect, therefore we might expect this kind of "self-shaming" to be prevalent among chronically neglected children. These are familiar anecdotes to child and adult clinicians. Given my attachment orientation, I have been used to hearing them through the lens of insecurity and fear—the loss of a secure base, an unloving, unreliable, or frightening mother. Now I hear the echoes of the child's shame at being neglected. In the language of a control systems model of shame, what stands out is that these are all situations in which termination of a shame state through physical or verbal repair, involving acceptance and comforting physical contact, are specifically absent and potentially unattainable.

When a system cannot be *terminated*, and so assuaged, it is correct, I believe, to say that it has entered or is approaching a state of dysregulation. By this I mean, following Bowlby's usage, that the available behavioral adaptations and psychological defenses, which can return the system to homeostasis, are no longer functioning properly (Solomon & George, 1999). Dysregulated homeostatic systems are characterized by adaptations that are either "all off", "all on", or in a state of unstable vacillations between the extremes. At the point of dysregulation of either the shame or the attachment system is where the generating conditions for pathology can be expected to lie. Note that a control systems definition of dysregulation can differ from what is usually implied, meaning, it seems "very upset" (Schore, 1994). (This difference in the use of the term "dysregulation" may be merely a matter of degree, however: after all, how long, how often, and how hard must a baby or child cry to be judged dysregulated? How often or how intensely shamed must a child feel in order for those experiences to overtake his or her adaptive capability?) As we have discussed, the answer to the questions above will likely be linked to the quality of repair available to the child. Earlier I mentioned Bowlby's important observation that shame about one's own thoughts and feelings is an important cause of segregated systems and dissociation. This is the "all off" aspect of dysregulated shame processes. Lewis (1987) highlights "humiliated fury" as a common outcome of shame. I surmise that this fury can be viewed as an "all on" consequence of shame, paralleling the child's rage during prolonged separation from attachment figures which has such a prominent place in Bowlby's thinking.

Shame, by its nature, wants to hide itself, making it especially easy to miss or misinterpret in the behavior of young children for whom fear and its defenses are such salient affects. This and the fact that shame develops chronologically later than the attachment system may explain, at least in part, why Bowlby did not make a place for it in his trilogy and why it figures so little in basic attachment theory. From the perspective of clinical work and research with young children, there is a great deal to learn. For example, we must be on the alert for the tell-tale signs—postures of shame, self-criticism, a preoccupation with eyes and being watched including, from my clinical experience, an aversion to the eyes of baby dolls.

On theoretical grounds, it is striking how similar the shame and attachment systems appear to be when viewed side by side within Bowlby's control systems framework. Fear is a common thread—fear emanating from external threats are the activators and the affective core of the attachment system; fear of rejection from conspecifics, including parents, is the essence of the shame system. Significantly, both attachment and shame are assuaged by acceptance and physical contact from primary attachment or powerful social figures. The neurophysiology of fear is also common to each, though undoubtedly current and future research will reveal distinctive features.

Finally, the analysis undertaken in this chapter brings us around to Helen Block Lewis' (1987) profound observation that shame should be understood "as a means by which people try to preserve their loving relationship to others". That is, shame may function as a "conditional attachment strategy" (Main, 1990) which permits the child to keep the parent "close" in actuality or psychologically, by taking the blame for misdeeds or imperfections rather than attributing them to the other. As with conditional strategies in general, the internalization of shame may have adaptive or non-adaptive consequences depending upon the particular parent-child relationship.

Notes

1   Another exception to this statement is a growing research literature focusing on adult attachment *styles* as related to shame, trauma, and clinical phenomena, which rests on the use of adult attachment questionnaire methodology developed by Bartholomew and Horowitz (1991) and Hazan and Shaver (1990). I have limited my search to what George and West (1999) described as "developmental attachment theory", that is, research based specifically on Bowlby's ethological attachment theory (Bowlby, 1969) and Ainsworth's (1979) research paradigm because the Ainsworth ABC and the D patterns and their underlying attachment dimensions do not map strongly onto adult styles (Waters et al., 2000).
2   Robbie Duschinksy, who is working with the entire Bowlby Archive housed in the Wellcome Collection, London, confirms the fact that "shame" is a rare entry.
3   In light of this discussion, readers may be interested in Shaver's (Shaver et al., 2010) use of Bowlby's control system approach to the analysis of the "Power" system. It will be clear that the model of the "Power" system should mirror that of shame.

References

Ainsworth, M. D. (1979). Mother-infant attachment. *American Psychologist, 134,* 932–937.

American Heritage Dictionary. (2020). 5th edition. Boston, MA: Houghton Mifflin Harcourt. https://www.ahdictionary.com/. American Heritage Dictionary, Fourth edition. Last accessed online on September 30, 2020.

Andrews, P. (1998). Evolution, social roles, and the differences in shame and guilt. In P. Gilbert & B. Andrews (Eds.), *Interpersonal Behavior, Psychopathology, and Culture* (pp. 99–125). Oxford: Oxford University Press.

Bartholomew, K., & Horowitz, L. M. (1991). Attachment styles among young adults: A test of a category model. *Journal of Personality and Social Psychology, 61,* 226–244.

Bowlby, J. (1939–1942). *Psychological Problems of Evacuation.* Wellcome Collection Archive, PP/BOW/C.5/4/1.

Bowlby, J. (1939–1942). *Psychological Problems of Evacuation.* Wellcome Collection Archive, PP/BOW/C.5/4/1. Ch. in R. Duschinsky, & K. White, (2020), (Eds.)

Trauma and Loss: Key Texts from the John Bowlby Archive (pp. 117–133). London: Routledge.

Bowlby, J. (1969; 1982). *Attachment and Loss, Vol. 1. Attachment.* 2nd edition. New York: Basic Books.

Bowlby, J. (1973). *Attachment and Loss, Vol. II. Separation: Anxiety and Anger.* New York: Basic Books.

Bowlby, J. (1980). *Attachment and Loss, Vol. III. Loss.* New York: Basic Books.

Bowlby, J. (1988). *A Secure Base.* London: Routledge.

Cassidy, J. (1988). Child-mother attachment and the self in six-year-olds. *Child Development, 59,* 121–134.

de Waal, F. (2000). Primates: A natural heritage of conflict resolution. *Science, 289,* 586–590.

De Young, P. (2015). *Understanding and Treating Chronic Shame: A Relational/Neurobiological Approach.* New York: Routledge.

Duschinsky, R., & White, K. (Eds.) (2020). *Trauma and Loss: Key Texts from the John Bowlby Archive.* London: Routledge.

Erikson, E. (1980). *Identity and the Life Cycle.* New York: Norton.

George, C., & West, M. (1999). Developmental vs. social personality models of adult attachment and mental ill health. *British Journal of Medical Psychology, 72,* 285–303.

Gilbert, P., & McGuire, M. T. (1998). Shame, social roles, and status: The Psychobiological continuum from monkey to human." In P. Gilbert and B. Andrews (Eds.), *Shame, interpersonal behavior, Psychopathology, and Culture* (pp. 99–123). New York: Oxford University Press.

Hazan, C., & Shaver, P. (1990). Love and work: An attachment—theoretical perspective. *Journal of Personality and Social Psychology, 59,* 270–280.

Keltner, D., & Harker, L. A. (1998). The forms and functions of the nonverbal signal of shame. In P. Andrews & B. Gilbert (Eds.), *Shame: Interpersonal Behaviour, Psychopathology* (pp. 78–98). New York: Oxford University Press.

Keltner, D., Young, R. C., & Buswell, B. (1997). Appeasement in human emotion, social practice and personality. *Aggressive Behaviour, 23,* 359–374.

Kohut, T. (1971). *The Analysis of the Self.* Chicago, IL: University of Chicago Press.

Lewis, H. B. (1987). *The Role of Shame in Symptom Formation.* Hillsdale, NJ: Lawrence Erlbaum.

Lewis, M., & Ramsey, D. (2002). Cortisol response to embarrassment and shame. *Child Development, 73,* 1034–1045.

Lewis, M., Sullivan, M., Stanger, C., & Weiss, M. (1989). Self development and self-conscious emotions. *Child Development, 60,* 146–156.

Lieberman, A. (1993). *The Emotional Life of the Toddler.* New York: Free Press.

Liotti, G. (2004). Trauma, dissociation, and disorganized attachment: Three strands of a single braid. *Psychotherapy: Theory, Research, Practice, and Training, 41,* 472–486.

MacKenzie, M., Nicklas, E., Brooks-Gunn, J., & Waldfogel, J. (2011). Who spanks infants and toddlers? Evidence from the fragile families and child well-being study. *Child Youth Service Review, 33,* 1364–1373.

Main, M. (1990). Cross-cultural studies of attachment organization: Recent studies, changing methodologies, and the concept of conditional strategies. *Human Development, 33,* 48–61.

Main, M., Kaplan, N., & Cassidy, J. (1985). Security in infancy, childhood, and adulthood: A move to the level of representation. In I. Bretherton & E. Waters (Eds.), *Growing Points in Attachment* (Serial No. 209 ed., Vol. 50). Monographs of the Society for Research in Child Development.

Porges, S. W. (2001). The polyvagus system: Phylogenetic substrates of a social nervous system. *International Journal of Psychophysiology, 42*, 123–146.

Shaver, P., Segev, M., & Mikculincer, M. (2010). A behavioural systems perspective on power and aggression. In M. M. Phillip & R. Shaver (Eds.), *Human Aggression and Violence* (pp. 71–87). Washington, DC: American Psychological Association.

Shore, A. (1994). *Affect Regulation and the Origin of the Self.* Mahwah, NJ: Erlbaum.

Solomon, J., & George, C. (1999). The place of disorganization in attachment theory: Linking classic observations with contemporary findings. In J. Solomon & C. George (Eds.), *Attachment Disorganization* (pp. 3–32). New York: Guilford Press.

Solomon, J., & George, C. (2011). Disorganization of maternal caregiving across two generations: The origins of caregiving helplessness. In J. Solomon & C. George (Eds.), *Disorganized Attachment and Caregiving* (pp. 25–51). New York: Guilford.

Waters, E., Hamilton, C. E., & Weinfield, N. S. (2000). The stability of attachment security from infancy to adolescence and early adulthood: General introduction. *Child Development, 71*, 678–683.

Chapter 2

Caring for the human spirit in pride and shame

A moral conscience seeking kindness from birth

Colwyn Trevarthen

Introduction: the dual self, guided by affections of sympathy

> When I endeavour to examine my own conduct, when I endeavour to pass sentence upon it, and either to approve or condemn it, it is evident that, in all such cases, I divide myself, as it were, into two persons; and that I, the examiner and judge, represent a different character from that other I, the person whose conduct is examined into and judged of. The first is the spectator, whose sentiments with regard to my own conduct I endeavour to enter into, by placing myself in his situation, and by considering how it would appear to me, when seen from that particular point of view. The second is the agent, the person whom I properly call myself, and of whose conduct, under the character of a spectator, I was endeavouring to form some opinion. The first is the judge; the second the person judged of. But that the judge should, in every respect, be the same with the person judged of, is as impossible, as that the cause should, in every respect, be the same with the effect.
>
> Adam Smith, 1759, *Theory of Moral Sentiments*, p. 182

This paragraph by Scotland's eighteenth-century philosopher of moral sentiments helps our understanding of how our social world, be it sentimental and affectionate in play and the "imitative arts" (Smith, 1777/1982), or practical and cooperative in work and industry (Smith, 1776), depends upon the in-born ability of a human being, with a human brain, to anticipate and support feelings of intersubjectivity, or "sympathetic relating" in kind company with other persons (Narvaez, 2014; Narvaez et al, 2016). Smith discovers in his conscience essential feelings of a duplex self-consciousness in relationships.

From two centuries of careful and unprejudiced observations, questioning the authority of philosophical or religious instruction in the form of lessons which an innocent child must learn, we now know that human life begins with intuitive desires to share playful invention in movement, every child wanting to find joy in affectionate companionship. A rich psychobiology of

DOI: 10.4324/9781003175612-3

how everyday actions are motivated in our social world is needed to explain this friendship (Trevarthen, 2019a).

In this chapter, I explore two radical principles of a good life that need recognition in psychology. First, we act for the future, with prospective motivation of self-conscious animation in our complex symphonies of body movement. And second, we act with sympathetic feelings of life together, with social affections that wish to build companionship and cooperation in a peaceful and creative community.

In his three-year voyage on the *Beagle*, as a young naturalist privileged to record his adventures in new worlds, Charles Darwin was excited to discover and describe intricate forms of life and societies of plants and animals in their different environments, including human races with their different rituals, arts and creative tools. His book *On the Origin of Species By Means of Natural Selection*, Darwin, (1859) demanded a new anthropology and human ethology. He challenged reductive philosophical descriptions of the nature of a human mind in a human body, composed to explain how it can learn to think out of the body, and then how to employ words and other symbols to take advice from authoritative texts.

After returning to England and becoming a father, Darwin wrote and illustrated another book, *The Expression of Emotion in Man and Animals* (1872), in which he described how a child is born with the spirit of human feelings in body movement, wanting to share joy with affectionate playmates, and acting weak and sad or angry when they feel left alone. In the introduction to the book he said:

> In order to acquire as good a foundation as possible, and to ascertain, independently of common opinion, how far particular movements of the features and gestures are really expressive of certain states of the mind, I have found the following means the most serviceable. In the first place, to observe infants; for they exhibit many emotions, as Sir Charles Bell remarks, 'with extraordinary force'; whereas, in after life, some of our expressions 'cease to have the pure and simple source from which they spring in infancy'.
>
> (Darwin, 1872, pp. 11–12)

Every newborn is expecting to join in a game of imaginative movement with curiosity and sense of fun. This hopeful impulse changes to expressions of feeling lost and betrayed when the baby is treated as an organic object needing only physical protection and nourishment, or when it is subject to total loss of responsive company, or to cruel abuse.

Not only did Darwin propose that the mechanism for expression of different emotional states was innate, but, more controversially, he supposed their perception to be direct: "An infant understands to a certain extent, and as I believe at a very early period, the meaning or feelings of those who tend him, by the expression of their features" (Darwin, 1877, pp. 293–294). He proposed that this development of sympathetic imitations evolved in the service of more effective modes of communication and cooperation, conferring great selective advantage on the human species. This is the psychobiological theory of the special "developmental niche" of the human child (Kurth & Narvaez, 2018).

A rich theory to explain expectations of pride and shame in the innate human spirit has had to battle with reductive scientific beliefs that we cannot be conscious of anything before we have learned conventional uses and symbols to specify what we know about the world outside us. In the past century the two most famous researchers, Jean Piaget (1936, 1952) seeking to explain early human learning for school, and Sigmund Freud (1923) attempting to give treatment for defensive emotional responses to hurtful life events, both declared that a newborn baby cannot imitate another person's expressions in movement. They were sure that the baby has only a reactive sensory-motor intelligence that cannot conceive that one's self or the self of another person is conscious, or has intentions of any kind. Now with accurate observation of imitation, there is proof of neonatal intentionality, and indeed that the baby's awareness is that reciprocal imitation is an entertaining game to play with signals of mutual engagement (Kugiumutzakis & Trevarthen, 2015; Nagy, 2011). Proof of neonatal imitation and observation of the joy in its sharing has required a new scientific understanding of how we come to life looking for evidence of our moving self in a community of other active selves, and how we share and compare experiences of this conception, sympathetically.

Throughout life we feel proud and invigorated when our actions are appreciated by a friend, and have a loss of spirit when unable to share adventures, real or imagined, with a sensitive companion, or with memories of ourselves as a trusted friend and teacher. Whatever the degree of familiarity or intimacy we discover in moments of encounter, even when our company and its cooperative endeavours are planned as projects to be guided by artificial rules or laws of action which we have been told to obey (Bruner, 2003), the feelings of advancing with joyful pride or of hiding and escape with sad shame come to life in a totally intuitive way. They are feelings that experience and display "aesthetic" appreciation of the grace and vigour of careful coordination in intentional body movements, and "moral" judgements of the graciousness appreciated from each other's gestures, all with a mind and imagination that is essentially double (Bråten, 1988, 1992, 1998, 2013).

The philosopher Martin Buber distinguished our awareness of persons from our awareness of physical objects as "I-Thou" and "I-It", respectively, and he asserted that a motivated relationship with another person must be the source of an awareness that can learn about an objective world of things that have no minds, and which can be shared as useful objects of knowledge or tools (Buber, 1923/1970). This is how, in all kinds of social relations, we sense our feelings and actions with that "spectator" and that "agent'" which Smith discovered passionately engaged with one another in his conscience.

The psychology of a single self is a fantasy of sceptical detachment or abstraction, an insensitive methodological story given exaggerated authority.

It does not allow open-minded curiosity concerning how we are aware of relationships in moving and with moods of conscience. Records in products of graphic art rather than in texts, over thousands of years, show that artists, prophets and philosophers, and children, have disputed about, or played with, acts of collaboration in appreciation of common sense, and explained mysteries and unexpected events as products of magic and divine invention. Now we can accept a new basis for explanation in terms of abilities of imagination in movement we are born with as human animals, with special anatomy and motives adapted to share knowledge, skills, and artefacts through centuries in the cultural habits of familiar communities (Dunbar, 2004).

The affectionate regulations of this sharing have evolved by elaboration of body parts, especially head and eyes, face and mouth, and agile hands, the movements of which can signal directions of interest, intentions to use specified objects, and the affective regulation of rewards and risks of their proper exercise. The anatomy and physiology of animal cleverness was explored by Charles Sherrington (1906), the discoverer of proprioception, the "self-sensing" of muscular forces inside the body, by afferent neurons in the spinal nerves. In a review of his life's work on how all the senses appreciate body movements, Sherrington (1955) paid rich tribute to the pioneer of physiological science as the life's use of the body's anatomy, the sixteenth century French doctor Jean Fernel, who was a skilled astronomer and physician to the court of Henry II and his wife Catherine de' Medici, and a famous doctor who gave sensitive care with outstanding results. Fernel introduced the concept of "physiology" as the body's brain-guided vitality, and this was developed by Sherrington into a modern science of the biology needed for identification of pathologies and their medical care. Importantly Sherrington gave rich appreciation of Fernel's science and his description of good medical practice. He explained his approach to care as follows:

> When I meet a patient I do not want to know his diagnosis. I want to share our interests, and, when I feel I know him and we are friends, I ask, what's wrong?

Sherrington, in agreement with Fernel, argues that the nature of humans is not in what they are, but in what they *imagine* they can be in the process of becoming a person in relationships. Every living organism, plant or animal, grows or moves with initiative and imagination, seeking with its evolved life-form a healthy and rewarding existence – a self-creating and self-protecting way of being, and of sharing life in community. This depends on processes that plan and evaluate actions in invented time of moving, making measured steps into the future with anticipation of rewards of well-being and avoidance of harm (Goodrich, 2010). And it depends on shared awareness of this animation.

This understanding of the nature and function of life awareness was given rigorous scientific confirmation in the 1920s by the work of a young Russian psychologist Nikolai Bernstein in the Central Institute of Labour,

Moscow. Using very precise cyclogrammatic measurements from films at forty frames per second, Bernstein showed that movements of an industrial worker using heavy tools, an athlete performing movements at high rates for competitive sport, and a child practicing artful styles of walking and running as a toddler all make their activities with almost perfect precision and no wasted energy, predicting the biomechanics of heavy bodies and their parts in action together (Bernstein, 1966, 1967, 1996). His theory of the *prospective control* of all movements disproved Ivan Pavlov's conditioned reflex theory of learning how to move in skilled purposeful ways, demonstrating that sensory-to-motor reflexes act only when a mistake has occurred and a rapid correction, of a predicted kind, has to be made.

Animal movement is coordinated and regulated by imaginative future sense. The spinning about, hopping, jumping, running, or slow walk of a playful teasing child are, as Bernstein recognized, "testing the degrees of freedom" of the control. This theory of *The Co-ordination and Regulation of Movements*, when available as a book in English in 1967, gave a boost to a new psychology of the creative, imaginative, and story-telling of consciousness in artful action of an individual, and in stories of communication between persons. It provides the scientific support needed to understand the syntax and prosody of spoken language, as well as the performances of drama, dance and music. Stephen Malloch and I incorporated Bernstein's work in our analysis of "communicative musicality" as the basis for all communication of experiences by moving (Malloch & Trevarthen, 2009).

The infant born as an imaginative person expecting life in affectionate company

Proof of the role of conscience or mutual awareness of responsibilities in our real shared lives has come from detailed descriptions in the last fifty years of the delicate social sensibilities of infants, even of foetuses in the last trimester of gestation – how they notice and respond to what other persons are doing as persons with the same sense of vitality, and how the development of the powers of self-expression are transformed through stages of development in body and brain from birth (Stern et al., 1999; Stern, 2000, 2010; Trevarthen, 2019b). This science, a developmental psychobiology inspired by Darwin's observations on the natural history of human emotions and their work in culture of societies, and aided by the development of video recording in the 1960s, motivated new philosophical, educational, and clinical sciences of human volition and sympathy of purposes in early life (Brazelton, 1973, 1979, 1984; Brazelton & Sparrow, 2006; Bruner, 1968, 1973; Lester & Sparrow, 2012; Trevarthen, 1979, 2001a, 2016). Children were discovered to come to life as sensitive "moral" creatures. That is as persons wanting to feel alive and noticed in kind company from the beginning (Trevarthen, 1989).

Indeed, a baby has been making careful actions of self-feeling and response inside their mother's body before birth (Trevarthen, 2001b). Foetuses test awareness of themselves by making gentle exercises with trunk and limbs, and they respond to the impulses of another person with expressions of emotion, as when they show attunement of their movements to the prosody of their mother's voice, or when they make face expressions of disgust when the mother smokes a cigarette (Reissland & Kisilevsky, 2015). Indeed when there are twins *in utero*, it is observed that they touch one another with gestures that are animated with cautious and gentle respect (Castiello et al., 2010; Trevarthen, 2016).

Adam Smith was following the advice of his teacher, the father of the Scottish Enlightenment, Frances Hutcheson, whose theory of "Innate Sympathy" as the motivating principle of all we achieve in our social lives, was intended to explain how collaborative conventions of our culture are acquired (Hutcheson, 1755/2013). Learning how to behave in a civilized community requires a creative sympathy for the motive principles and feelings of other human beings (Bråten, 2013). Rules and laws made up are products of impulses of the innate human spirit, tools for sharing animate purposes, and feelings. In the busy industrial times of his culture, Smith became famous for his illuminating study of how moral principles guide the creation and expansion of economic systems with their advances in tools and industry. He made clear that "The Wealth of Nations" needs consideration of shared needs and wishes of a responsible society (Smith, 1776). Selfish ambition of an individual or group for wealth and power is a destructive error.

Since the 1960s, advanced by invention of television to record and review fine behaviours of purposeful skill and interpersonal synchrony (Bruner, 1968), developmental psychology has found that we may gain better appreciation of the creative impulses of kindness and generosity in society by observing the manifestations of pride and shame of infants. They are observed to have feelings as persons who detect the feelings of other persons directly without imagining any form of symbolic description or explanation of particular actions or goals (Brazelton, 1979). They partake in dramatic story-making with innocent positions of respect and authority but sharing the same principles of affection and concern as adults (Bruner, 2003).

To illustrate the pride and shame of young infants in their responses to the attentions of other persons of different ages – parents, playmates, and other social acquaintances who may be recognized as friends or avoided as strangers – I have collected figures from my research or from colleagues who also work directly with infants under one year of age.

Figure 2.1 shows displays of pride in instinctive mastery of the human body for the admiration of others who are sharing conscience with the baby, and in one case offering physical aid that is closely attuned with the infant's effort to be in balance with forces of movement. Standing on two feet and displaying activity of interest and purpose with the hands while coupling gaze with a companion or group audience is clearly part of the intentions of these young people.

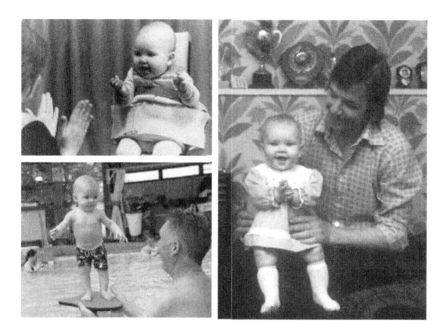

Figure 2.1 Sharing poise with pride, and learning the story of an action game.
Note: On the *lower left* Gunnar, a four-month-old boy, is standing on a rubber board held for him by a champion swimmer in Finland, Snorri Magnusson, who runs classes of mothers with their infants in comfortable thermal pools in all seasons in their far north country. The little boy stands with pride and perfect balance supported by an "understanding" Snorri, who uses his skill of motor coordination to balance Gunnar and to permit him to reveal a beautiful coordination and regulation of whole body movement. No physician expects four month olds to "know" how to stand confidently, but they do it with Snorri's conscience.

At the *top left*, Emma at six months, in my lab at Harvard in 1967, responds to her mother's lesson in "Clap Handies".

On the *right* Emma, seated on her father's knee at home responds with a proud display and big smile when the photographer, her mother, says "Clap Handies". Her father is proud too.

Social psychologists recognise the strength of our motivation to belong, not just in special relationships of love and trust, but in groups that celebrate ways of acting together in communities or tribes, for sharing art, sport, or productive industry.

Gunnar standing for Snorri is part of a large social occasion. He is having fun in the class in the big thermal pool with a crowd of children and their mothers. He has been invited by Snorri to float under water. He swims easily accepting the challenge, and surfaces to share the fun. It is certainly a festive crowd, and all the babies are aware of that. The important event in the photo is the balance of the weight of a very young boy erect on his feet when far too young to stand on his own and walk. Snorri is a skilled and helpful partner of what they both appreciate as human collaborative vitality, and its drama (Figure 2.1).

Figure 2.2 Self-consciousness in company, and sad displays of shame.
Note: *Top left*, a three month old girl looks away with a "coy" smile when her mother holds her up to meet her own image. She feels the look of her reflected interest is "embarrassing". "In this simple test, "coy" smiles beginning at two to three months in infancy, consisting of smiling with simultaneous gaze and head aversion and curving arm movements.... These smiles were elicited in contexts of social attention.... They occurred in interaction with familiar adults, with strangers and with the self in a mirror" (Reddy, 2000, p. 186).

Top right, escaping mis-understanding with a kind and careful stranger who wants to talk, Emma at six months hides her face.

Below, four boys aged about ten months show distress and a wish to be cared for when left by their mothers with a stranger. Even a nice stranger is hard to bear. Such responses, which begin to be common after six months, are called "fear of strangers". They show a shame of feeling meaningless, or inability to respond with the unknown person's interest (Figure 2.2).

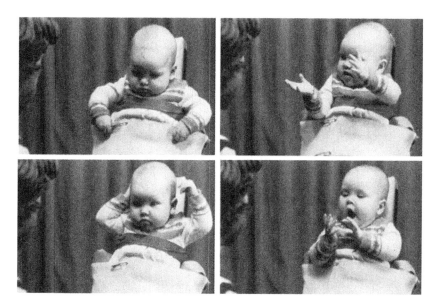

Figure 2.3 Testing friendship cautiously with a stranger.

Note: When approached by a Stranger, brave little Emma is worried and *Ashamed*. The kind man, who knows infants well, does not seem to "get it" when she shows her clapping in an attempt to be friends. So she withdraws with lack of confidence. Then she yawns and claps to herself.

In 1980, Lynne Murray, making her PhD study at the University of Edinburgh on *The Sensitivities and Expressive Capacities of Young Infants in Communication with Others*, developed a test of how young infants react when their mother is unresponsive.

Lynne made a Double Television system by which a baby and mother could communicate, as if on Skype (Murray, 1998; Murray & Trevarthen, 1985). In Figure 2.4, Shona, who is eight weeks old, sees in front of her a TV image of her mother who immediately responds, and they have a happy chat as if they were close together facing one another in the same room. Then the mother's display of joy and affection is replayed as a recording, which has no means of response. Immediately Shona is puzzled, and then she withdraws unhappily. She feels alone and shamed when her mother is a replay and not responding in real, shared, time.

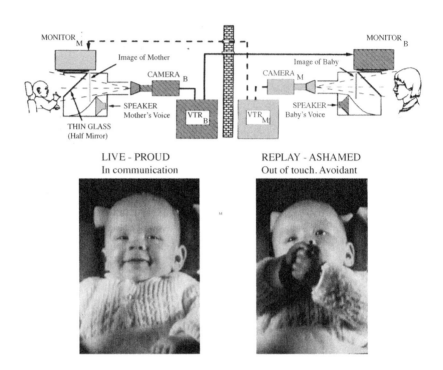

Figure 2.4 Seeking confident friendship that responds immediately.

Note: Years later, as a Professor of Psychology in the University of Reading, Lynne became a leader of studies of early communication (Murray, 2014; Murray & Andrews, 2000), and the effects of the emotional distress of mothers with post-natal depression on the emotional development of their babies (Murray & Cooper, 1997; Murray et al., 1993, 1996, 1999). Her work, in agreement with the work of Ed Tronick and Brazelton on the regulation of creative communication in a mother's affectionate engagement with a young infant (Brazelton et al., 1975; Tronick, 1989; Tronick et al., 1980; Tronick & Field, 1986), led to the development of therapies for mothers, and for babies, which carefully encourage pleasure in intimate and immediately sympathetic conversations (Hughes, 2006, 2017a, 2017b; Tronick, 2005).

Psychopathology of early childhood, and the importance of affectionate care

Appreciation by psychologists of the need and of happy and sensitive communication of feelings in human relationships for well-being in development from early weeks after birth was inspired by the observations of doctors and psychologists interested in the emotional processes in intimate relations, and who witnessed the sad consequences of a loss or disorder of maternal care in early months.

Attention to the development of emotions and the effects of early stress and trauma on future emotional health and self-confidence was inspired in the late nineteenth century by the work of Sigmund Freud. As a medical practitioner interested in the neuroscience of psychological disorders, he observed the distress of his patients, and drew the attention of his colleagues to the stories he heard from those suffering with depression or anger in their relations with family and people they work with in society, focusing on psychic wounds many recalled from a neglectful or abusive childhood. In his twenties, Freud had studied philosophy with a young German philosopher, psychologist, and priest Franz Brentano, who identified intentions as the core function of the mind responsible for the creation and guidance of perceptual awareness (Brentano, 1874; Delafield-Butt & Gangopadhyay, 2013). Influenced in the nineteenth century by the German philosopher Hagel, who, anticipating the discovery by Nikolai Bernstein of consciousness as prospective control of actions of the body, insisted that intentional action and perceptual awareness are inseparable from natural vitality.

Freud responded to the recollections of emotionally disturbed patients and their efforts to survive with more security, and he developed intimate therapy sessions aimed to elicit deep verbal exploration of the emotional complexes they had retained. The therapist, out of sight, talked with the patient who was lying on a couch. The method aimed to discipline or modulate powerful "drives" of sexual excitement, or a desire to escape fear and sadness by a "death drive", and to stabilize efforts of self-protection for a sense of well-being. The exploration of the patient's feelings and urges with the responses of the analyst in each session of therapy was recorded as a written narrative.

In the twentieth century, especially in the United Kingdom, psychiatrists qualified in this psychoanalytic practice included men and women offering therapy for troubled children, which required more attention to spontaneous playful experimentation with joy, and with imagination able to deal with risks of misfortune. There were many revisions of the theory, and experiments were made to try less disciplined, more considerate acceptance of enjoyable transformations of feelings and their description, (Daniel & Trevarthen. 2017). Thus evolved new "dyadic", "relational", or "conversational" models of care for fearful, shameful, and dissociated pathologies of mind (Baylin & Hughes, 2016; Hughes, 2017; Meares, 2005, 2016, 2012a, 2012b).

This development, qualifying and extending Freud's method of therapy, was inspired by work attending to the care and emotional support of young children by their mothers, and especially by the work of John Bowlby on the consequences in adolescence and later life of loss of this care in early years (Bowlby, 1958, 1969). Bowlby was beginning his training as a medical doctor when he became interested in the psychology of shame and distress, and the consequences of early childhood experiences of loneliness and lack of affectionate care. His own infancy was troubled by separation with his siblings from their mother's care. They were looked after by a nursemaid with little time to know and play with their mother, who believed young children needed discipline to control expressions of distress. He remembered his sadness as a four-year-old when the kind nursemaid left.

Part way through his medical course Bowlby sought training in developmental psychology and pre-clinical sciences. He took a brief post as a teacher at a school where he became aware of the relationship between teenage delinquency and early childhood separation from the mother. This inspired the development of his Attachment Theory to explain the child's need for affectionate maternal care, which he described after his studies in psychology, training in psychiatry and qualification as a psychoanalyst (Bowlby, 1958, 1979; Bowlby & Parkes, 1970).

Care for shame, with the development of less analytic, more responsive relational therapy, motivated by acceptance of the growth of natural sympathy at all ages

Peter Hobson describes the processes of development that guide growth of intelligent thinking and reasoning in his book *The Cradle of Thought* (Hobson, 2002). He is a Professor of Developmental Psychopathology who has studied children with autism, and those deprived of secure and affectionately supported company in refugee camps (Hobson, 1993). He argues that human thought is the product of an integrated system of knowledge sharing between young children and adult companions. This is comparable with the parent-infant system which is adapted to support early development of the skills of well-being of an infant, which doctor Louis Sander described from his work as a child psychiatrist and psychoanalyst (Sander, 2008; Trevarthen, 2019b). Education of the young by caregivers and companions in play shows that the expression of emotions benefits from sharing emotional understanding with an older, more experienced companion (Reissland, 2012). The intuitive powers of a human mind and body require sharing with pride, and support for correcting a sense of failure experienced as shame.

Pioneers of effective medical and educational care of infants and toddlers, in their attempts to provide effective care for developmental disorders in babies before they have acquired mastery of story-telling in speech, have learned to welcome the most feeble child as a potential collaborator in mastery of a happier, proud, companionship with sensitive efforts of a therapist to reduce the loneliness of shame. Therapies with this more positive approach are gaining attention as a consequence of Bowlby's work, seeking to collaborate with the hopes for kindness in the child, even one that has been badly frightened, have proved to be more successful.

This has been recorded well by Dan Hughes, one of the leaders in the change.

> Many, many years ago, I reflected on my frequent inability to help children who had been abused and neglected. … My initial goals were to help them to be less terrified by the traumatic events of their past. … I developed other goals, which focused on helping them to reduce the deep sense of shame they felt and which underpinned their conviction that they deserved the maltreatment that they had received.
>
> (Hughes, 2017a, p. 82)

Hughes was led to practise a more playful method of Dyadic Developmental Psychotherapy, which draws on hope for a better, happier life, extending the application of Attachment Theory (Hughes, 2017b).

> The impact of intrafamilial, relational trauma on the development of children is severe and pervasive, affecting all aspects of the child's functioning. The psychological treatment of children who have experienced such trauma may well have the greatest impact in facilitating their development when it adopts a relational approach incorporating central features of attachment theory while also including their caregivers when they are able to provide safety…. During the joint sessions, the therapist, utilising an intersubjective stance, actively facilitates a dialogue between therapist, child, and caregiver that incorporates the goals mentioned above and, within an open-and-engaged conversational tone, helps the child to develop a coherent autobiographical narrative that is not fragmented by terror and shame.
>
> (Hughes, 2017b, p. 595)

Hughes' DDP takes a positive approach to children assuming they all have hopeful motives. "It is intended to develop the capacity of abused and neglected children to experience comfort and joy with their caregivers", with a treatment based on principles of attachment and intersubjectivity. The therapist employs PACE – playfulness, acceptance, curiosity, empathy –to share with the child and caregivers.

In late infancy, from nine months after birth, and in the second year when the standing and walking toddler is exploring a wider world with new opportunities for the hands to seize objects to play with or eat, first words are being imitated. The active young person is inspired to speak about the curious and playful experience of his or her innate "human sense". Then, the desire to imitate acts of consciousness in exchanges with intimate older companions and teachers becomes guided for sharing special meanings and projects of the flourishing "common sense" of a particular culture (Donaldson, 1992). The young person's imagination becomes elaborated for complex adventures in fantastic arts and powerful industrial projects that build and value habits and habitats affecting every part of life with others (Bruner, 2003; Rogoff, 1990, 2003). Basic motor intentions, formed by the mind of an individual in the "present moment" within a direct, anticipatory awareness of the world actually present (Stern, 2004), later become abstract elements remembered in the life story of that person. Experiences of living are held as memories of "how" to move and communicate that can be reflected upon and re-evaluated (Stern, 2010; Trevarthen & Delafield-Butt, 2019). Margaret Donaldson (1992) traced this transition through stages of increasingly general and abstract consciousness, from the infantile "point mode'" to a line mode, and then to more abstract modes in imaginary times and places, or "nowhere, no place".

Each advance in use of skills of moving of "the self as agent" changes what can be done and learned in companionship with an affectionate and playful friend (Trevarthen & Aitken, 2003). These are the "touchpoints" of Dr. Berry Brazelton's programme for effective therapy for children in distress, or suffering from a developmental disorder that affects security of relationships.

> Touchpoints are periods, during the first years of life during which children's spurts in development result in disruption in the family system. (Throughout life, there are, no doubt, similar developmental crises of disorganization and reorganization that involve not solely the individual but those he or she is intimately connected with as well.) The succession of touchpoints in a child's development is like a map that can be identified and anticipated by both parents and providers. Thirteen touchpoints have been noted in the first three years, beginning in pregnancy. They are centered on caregiving themes that matter to parents (e.g. feeding, discipline), rather than traditional milestones. The child's negotiation of these touchpoints can be seen as a source of satisfaction and encouragement for the family system. Foreknowledge of these touchpoints and strategies for dealing with them can help reduce negative interactions that might otherwise throw the child's development off course and result in problems in the areas of sleep, feeding, toilet training, among others.
>
> (Brazelton & Sparrow, 2006)

The touchpoints plan has proved effective in guiding support and improvement of children and families living in poor conditions with limited social resources, by arranging community projects for the children to share their vital creativity in group celebrations and projects (Sparrow, 2018).

Learning and teaching for sustaining kindness of knowledge in a strong society

A child psychology that recognizes the creative powers of very young persons in collaborative experience inspires relational therapies, and it has also long found rewarding application in the practice of schooling for education. Understanding of how new habits of awareness and activity are created in mutual efforts of young learners and experienced teachers has been used to "reform" educational practice for centuries (Quick, 1894/2003). The reformers, from Comenius in the seventeenth century, have recognised the importance of "love for the teacher", one who responds to the child's genius.

> My aim is to show, although this is not generally attended to, that the roots of all sciences and arts in every instance arise as early as in the tender age, and that on these foundations it is neither impossible nor difficult for the whole superstructure to be laid; provided always that we act reasonably as with a reasonable creature.
>
> John Amos Comenius (1592–1671), *The School of Infancy*, in R. Quick, 1894, pp. 144–145

This goes into the moral principles of teaching and learning beyond the efforts of a bright young child to know the world as coherent and rewarding in the private time and place of one person's egotistic consciousness, such as that examined by Jean Piaget in his theory of intelligent learning by the child as an inquisitive experimenter with actions in a physical and social world (Piaget, 1926, 1958). A different theory of knowledge as an act of discovery in shared awareness of the affordances has found support through the centuries since the Industrial Revolution began to transform skills of production and communication in the eighteenth century.

When he was in his twenties, Jerome Bruner who was to become a famous educational psychologist and pioneer of a richer cognitive psychology of infancy, declared with Cecile Goodman that feelings of value and need shape perceptions (Bruner & Goodman, 1947). In masterworks (Bruner, 1966, 1973, 1983, 1986, 1990, 1996, 2003), he insisted that education is an imaginative collaboration between the motives of a learner and the willing understanding of a teacher or advisor eager to share accepted cultural knowledge and its conventions of sharing in language. He supported Margaret Donaldson in her critical assessment of Piaget's theory, based on what she and her students discovered young children contributed by sharing ideas with companions, beyond what they could learn by sensory-motor practice of their own actions (Donaldson, 1978).

Truly cooperative education requires the work of teachers, or members of governing organisations, who aim to be, or to support, "educational reformers". They work to change practices that have become too rigidly guided by curriculum requirements designed by adults to teach children techniques of reasoning in mathematics, use of grammar and semantics to share experience fluently in text, and standards of social behaviour that obey standard laws of fairness and punish acts identified as deceit or violence.

At the end of the nineteenth century, Robert Herbert Quick published a history of educational reformers, concluding with these wise words describing a natural psychology of teaching and learning:

> The New Education treats the human being not so much a learner as a doer and creator. The educator no longer fixes his eyes on the object—the knowledge, but on the subject—the being to be educated. The success of the education is not determined by what the educated *know*, but by what they *do* and what they *are*. They are well educated when they love what is good, and have had all their faculties of mind and body properly developed to do it…. The New Education then is 'passive, following', and must be based on the study of human nature. When we have ascertained what are the faculties to be developed we must consider further how to foster the self-activity that will develop them.
>
> (Quick, 1894/2003, p. 525)

This psychology accords well with the advice of psychotherapists who advocate relational dialogue and generosity of interpretation when planning and explaining their practice with a patient.

Welcoming the clever sociability and creativity of the young learner of human meanings

Animal ethologists, following Darwin, know that families and communities of animals communicate their interests and feelings by making expressive movements, creating sounds and rituals of display, which inspire and sustain cooperative habits, and they give the group a dynamic identity (Eibl-Eibesfeldt, 1970): birds when they sing or parade in flocks, cattle when they ramble together in search of food or fight for a higher rank, elephants when they migrate over a large territory, and wolves when they exchange howls in concert. They all adapt movements that are essential to their vitality, ways of moving about, breathing, eating, feeding comforting and protecting themselves and their social partners with special movements adapted to signal to their social group directions of interest and feelings or affections that value them.

In human communities these displays are greatly elaborated in traditions of works of visual art and music, and in acting for ceremonies or theatrical performances, comedies or tragedies, "playing" with expressions of pride and shame (Lock, 1980; Merker, 2009; Turner, 1982).

In the second half of the first year, as well as becoming interested in shared use of objects for play or as tools for important tasks, infants exhibit delight or mockery of displeasure in games with companions (Reddy, 2000, 2008). A happy child at this stage of development gives great joy to family and friends, contributing to a lively society and mastering its distinctive habits. They share in story-making with pride (Bruner, 2003), and this motivates their education. Anything unfriendly or cruel they do, or receive from others causes shame.

Conclusion: the healthy psychobiology of the human spirit in companionship, an autobiography, with tribute to my teachers

I recall my life as a story of relationships, of seeking to discover and enjoy life with, or for, other persons: first, the generous nurture and playful sharing of nature and making works of art with my parents and sister; then with my wife and children in a family; and a rich memory of habits learned in a familiar community and an endlessly rewarding, and challenging, environment of nature and of conscientious human industry. For example, my father, a lawyer helping inventors gain recognition for their work, made greenstone ornaments, and a wooden loom to help his wife create fabrics with weaving for which she prepared and dyed delicate materials to make useful articles.

Then, I was taught the meaningful understanding at school of formal, curricular, cultural techniques, especially reading, writing and mathematics, and responsibilities of their practice in a European society with its history transported from the other side of the globe to my island world of New Zealand.

Every stage of this journey has required responses attentive to my conscience, or "shared knowing" as described by Adam Smith. I believe he is right to assume our aesthetic and moral feelings are a product of an inborn awareness of another, a moral companion who appreciates how we act and think about the purposes and values of our actions. I add to this the need for "story-telling" emphasised by one of my greatest teachers Jerome Bruner (2003). It explores and stretches the rules of conscience in rewarding, or punishing ways.

I was educated first by the encouragement of parents who shared my interest in exploration of a rich nature by the seashore and in the forests near Auckland. I learned to identify the plants and animals, making collections of their forms and productions, and chose classes of Botany and Zoology when I went to University. My Botany teacher was a world famous expert on the marine algae and their adaptations to different coastlines. He chose an academic post in New Zealand to extend his studies towards the Antarctic. I learned Zoology from a man only a couple of years older than me who came from a rich education in humanities, animal behaviour, and anatomical adaptations for special ways of life. He too became a scientist of marine life – a teuthologist specialising in research on the cleverness of octopus, cuttlefish, and squids.

With incredible good-fortune I was led by other inspiring teachers, first into brain science which revealed the central role of motives for coordinated movements that orient a whole "self" to select ways to go in the world and things to seek for or escape from, to observation of the cleverness of infants in the two years before their walking about and speaking. My PhD in Caltech with Roger Sperry, on the visuo-motor awareness of monkeys with the links between their left and right cerebral cortices divided, led to Jacques Paillard in France, also a leader in research on the brain for motor skills. My wife Lee went with me to Marseille and our first son was born there in 1973. By wonderful coincidence, Jerome Bruner from Harvard visited Paillard and noted my use of high-speed movies, forty frames per second, to observe the very rapid hand movements of baboons. He was beginning a revolutionary project to find the roots of practical intelligence and language in infancy, which led him to abandon the cognitive psychology of his Center in Harvard, including the theory of innate grammar proposed by Noam Chomsky. As an educational psychologist, he conceived a different more socially responsible and emotional origin for learning how to share and develop meaning in speech and writing.

Work with Martin Richards in Bruner's group in the 1960s enabled me to appreciate the rich impulses of young infants to communicate thoughts and feelings about their actions with the support of their indulgent mothers. Later work at Edinburgh University, as described above, revealed the power of the baby's pride and shame to give sharable value to inventions of movement in shared play.

References

Arnold, J. C. (2014). *Their Name Is Today: Reclaiming Childhood in a Hostile World.* Robertsbridge: Plough Publishing House.

Baylin, J., & Hughes, D. A. (2016). *The Neurobiology of Attachment-Focused Therapy: Enhancing Connection & Trust in the Treatment of Children & Adolescents.* New York: Norton.

Bernstein, N. A. (1966). *The Active Search for Information: From Reflexes to the Model of the Future.* (Published by Josif M. Feigenberg and Onno G. Meijer, *Motor Control*, 1999, 3, 225–236 © Champaign, IL: Human Kinetics Publishers, Inc. The original paper appeared in the popular weekly *NedeZja* (The Week), 1966,

Vol. 20, pp. 8–9, shortly after Bernstein's death. It was translated by Ines M. Rubin and edited for clarity.)

Bernstein, N. A. (1967). *The Coordination and Regulation of Movements*. New York: Pergamon.

Bernstein, N. A. (1996). On dexterity and its development. In M. L. Latash & M. T. Turvey (Eds.), *Dexterity and Its Development* (pp. 3–244). Mahwah, NJ: Erlbaum. (Original manuscript written in 1945–46 and published 1991).

Booth, P., & Jernberg, A. M. (2010). *Theraplay: Helping Parents and Children Build Better Relationships through Attachment-Based Play*. Bridgewater, NJ: Wiley.

Bowlby, J. (1958). The nature of the child's tie to his mother. *International Journal of Psychoanalysis, 39*, 1–23.

Bowlby, J. (1969). *Attachment and Loss. Volume 1, Attachment*. London: Hogarth Press.

Bowlby, J. (1979). Self reliance and some conditions that promote it. In J. Bowlby (Ed.), *The Making and Breaking of Affectional Bonds* (pp. 103–125). London: Tavistock.

Bowlby, J. (1988). Developmental psychiatry comes of age. *American Journal of Psychiatry, 145*, 1–10.

Bowlby, J., & Parkes, C. M. (1970). Separation and loss within the family. In E. J. Anthony and C. Koupernik (Eds.), *The Child and His Family*, Vol. 1, New York: Wiley. (also in J. Bowlby, *The Making and Breaking of Affectional Bonds* (pp. 81–102). London: Tavistock, 1979).

Bråten, S. (1988). Between dialogical mind and monological reason: Postulating the virtual other. In M. Campanella (Ed.), *Between Rationality and Cognition* (pp. 205–235). Turin: Albert Meynier.

Bråten, S. (1992). The virtual other in infants' minds and social feelings. In A. H. Wold (Ed.), *The Dialogical Alternative (Festschrift for Ragnar Rommetveit)* (pp. 77–97). Oslo/Oxford: Scandinavian University Press/Oxford University Press.

Bråten, S. (1998). *Intersubjective Communication and Emotion in Early Ontogeny*. Cambridge: Cambridge University Press.

Bråten, S. (2013). *Roots and Collapse of Empathy: Human Nature at its Best and at Its Worst*. Amsterdam/Philadelphia, PA: John Benjamins Publishing Company.

Brazelton, T. B. (1973). *Neonatal Behavioural Assessment Scale* (Clinics in Developmental Medicine, 50. Spastics International Medical Publications) London: Heinemann.

Brazelton, T. B. (1979). Evidence of communication during neonatal behavioural assessment. In M. Bullowa (Ed.), *Before Speech: The Beginning of Human Communication* (pp. 79–88). London: Cambridge University Press.

Brazelton, T. B. (1984). *To Listen to a Child: Understanding Normal Problems of Growing Up*. Cambridge, MA: Perseus.

Brazelton, T. B. (1993). *Touchpoints: Your Child's Emotional and Behavioral Development*. New York: Viking.

Brazelton, T. B., & Nugent, J. K. (1995). *The Neonatal Behavioural Assessment Scale* (3rd edition). London: MacKeith Press.

Brazelton, T. B., & Sparrow, J. D. (2006). *Touchpoints 0–3: Your Child's Emotional and Behavioral Development* (2nd edition). Cambridge, MA: Da Capo Press.

Brazelton, T. B., Tronick, E. Adamson, L., Als, H., & Wise, S. (1975). Early mother-infant reciprocity. In M. Hofer (Ed.), *Parent-Infant Interaction* (pp. 137–154). Amsterdam: Elsevier.

Bretherton, I. (1992). The origins of attachment theory. *Developmental Psychotherapy, 28*, 759–775.

Bruner, J. S. (1966). *Toward a Theory of Instruction.* Cambridge, MA: Belknap Press of Harvard University Press.

Bruner, J. S. (1968). *Processes of Cognitive Growth: Infancy.* (Heinz Werner Lectures, 1968) Worcester, MA: Clark University Press with Barri Publishers.

Bruner, J. S. (1973). *Beyond the Information Given: Studies in the Psychology of Knowing.* New York: Norton.

Bruner, J. S. (1983). *Child's Talk. Learning to Use Language.* New York: Norton.

Bruner, J. S. (1986). *Actual Minds, Possible Worlds.* Cambridge, MA: Harvard University Press.

Bruner, J. S. (1990). *Acts of Meaning.* Cambridge, MA: Harvard University Press.

Bruner, J. S. (1996). *The Culture of Education.* Cambridge, MA: Harvard University Press.

Bruner, J. S. (2003). *Making Stories: Law, Literature, Life.* Cambridge, MA: Harvard University Press.

Bruner, J. S., & Goodman, C. C. (1947). Value and need as organizing factors in perception. *Journal of Abnormal and Social Psychology, 42*, 33–44.

Castiello, U., Becchio, C., Zoia, S., Nelini, C., Sartori, L., Blason, L., D'Ottavio, G., Bulgheroni, M., & Gallese, G. (2010). Wired to be social: The ontogeny of human interaction. *PLoS ONE*, 5(10). e13199. https://doi.org/10.1371/journal.pone.0013199.

Daniel, S., & Trevarthen, C. (Eds.). (2017). *Rhythms of Relating in Children's Therapies: Connecting Creatively with Vulnerable Children.* London: Jessica Kingsley.

Darwin, C. (1859). *On the Origin of Species by Means of Natural Selection.* London: John Murray.

Darwin, C. (1872). *The Expression of Emotion in Man and Animals.* London: Methuen.

Darwin, C. (1877). A biographical sketch of an infant. *Mind, 2*, 285–294.

Dunbar, R. (2004). *The Human Story: A New History of Mankind's Evolution.* London: Faber.

Eibl-Eibesfeldt, I. (1970). *Ethology: The Biology of Behavior.* New York: Holt, Rinehart and Winston.

Epstein, M. (1995). *Thoughts without a Thinker: Psychotherapy from a Buddhist Perspective.* New York: Basic Books.

Freud, S. (1923). *Das Ich und das Es (The Ego and the Id).* Vienna: Internationaler Psycho-Analytischer Verlag/ New York: Norton.

Goodrich, B. G. (2010). We do, therefore we think: time, motility, and consciousness. *Reviews in the Neurosciences, 21*, 331–361.

Hendry, A., & Hasler, J. (Eds.). (2017). *Creative Therapies for Complex Trauma: Helping Children and Families in Foster Care, Kinship Care or Adoption.* London: Jessica Kingsley.

Hobson, P. (2002). *The Cradle of Thought: Exploring the Origins of Thinking.* London: Macmillan.

Hobson, R. P. (1993). *Autism and the Development of Mind.* Hillsdale, NJ: Lawrence Erlbaum.

Hughes, D. (2006). *Building the Bonds of Attachment: Awakening Love in Deeply Traumatized Children* (2nd edition). Lanham, MA: Rowman & Littlefield.

Hughes, D. (2017a). Finding our way to reciprocity: Working with children who find it difficult to trust. In S. Daniel & C. Trevarthen (Eds.), *Rhythms of Relating in*

Children's Therapies: Connecting Creatively with Vulnerable Children (pp. 82–99). London: Jessica Kingsley.

Hughes, D. (2017b). Dyadic Developmental Psychotherapy (DDP): An attachment-focused family treatment for developmental trauma. *Australian and New Zealand Journal of Family Therapy*. Special Issue: *Relational Trauma and Family Therapy*, 38, 595–605.

Hutcheson, F. (1755/2013). *A System of Moral Philosophy 2 Volume Set: A System of Moral Philosophy: In Three Books: Volume 1* (Cambridge Library Collection – Philosophy) Reprint Edition, 2013. New York: Cambridge University Press.

Jernberg, A. M., & Booth, P. B. (2001). *Theraplay: Helping Parents and Children Build Better Relationships through Attachment-Based Play* (2nd edition). San Francisco, CA: Jossey-Bass.

Kennedy, H., Landor, M., & Todd, L. (Eds.). (2011). *Video Interaction Guidance: A Relationship-Based Intervention to Promote Attunement, Empathy and Wellbeing*. London: Jessica Kingsley.

Kugiumutzakis, G., & Trevarthen, C. (2015). Neonatal Imitation. In J. D. Wright (Ed.), *International Encyclopedia of the Social & Behavioral Sciences* (2nd edition, Vol 16, pp. 481–488). Oxford: Elsevier.

Kurth, A. M., & Narvaez, D. (2018). The evolved developmental niche and children's developing morality. In C. Trevarthen, J. Delafield-Butt, & A. Dunlop, (Eds.), *The Child's Curriculum: Sharing the Natural Talents of Young Children, for a Richer Education* (pp. 104–125). Oxford: Oxford University Press.

Lester, B., & Sparrow, J. D. (Eds.). (2012). *Nurturing Young Children and Their Families: Building on the Legacy of T. B. Brazelton*. Oxford: Wiley-Blackwell.

Lock, A. (1980). *The Guided Reinvention of Language*. London: Academic Press.

Macmurray, J. (1959). *The Self as Agent* (Volume I of *The Form of the Personal*). London: Faber & Faber.

Macmurray, J. (1961). *Persons in Relation* (Volume II of *The Form of the Personal*). London: Faber & Faber. (Paperback, 1970; New edition, with introduction by F. G. Fitzpatrick, Humanities Press International, 1991; reissued by Faber and Faber, 1995).

Malloch, S., & Trevarthen, C. (Eds.). (2009). *Communicative Musicality: Exploring the Basis of Human Companionship*. Oxford: Oxford University Press.

Maratos, O. (1982). Trends in development of imitation in early infancy. In T. G. Bever (Ed.), *Regressions in Mental Development: Basic Phenomena and Theories* (pp. 81–101). Hillsdale, NJ: Erlbaum.

Maturana, H. R. (1978). Biology of language: The epistemology of reality. In G. A. Miller & E. Lenneberg (Eds.), *Psychology and Biology of Language and Thought: Essays in Honor of Eric Lenneberg* (pp. 27–63). New York: Academic Press.

Maturana, H. R., & Varela, F. J. (1980). *Autopoesis and Cognition*. Dordrecht: D. Reidel.

Meares, R. (2005). *The Metaphor of Play: Origin and Breakdown of Personal Being*. London: Routledge.

Meares, R. (2012a). *Borderline Personality Disorder and the Conversational Model: A Clinician's Manual*. New York: Norton.

Meares, R. (2012b). *A Dissociation Model of Borderline Personality Disorder*. New York: Norton.

Meares, R. (2016). *The Poet's Voice in the Making of Mind*. London: Routledge.

Merker, B. (2009). Ritual foundations of human uniqueness. In S. Malloch & C. Trevarthen (Eds.), *Communicative Musicality: Exploring the Basis of Human Companionship* (pp. 45–60). Oxford: Oxford University Press.

Murray, L. (1998). Contributions of experimental and clinical perturbations of
mother-infant communication to the understanding of infant intersubjectivity.
In S. Bråten (Ed.), *Intersubjective Communication and Emotion in Early Ontogeny*
(pp. 127–143). Cambridge: Cambridge University Press.

Murray, L. (2014). *The Psychology of Babies: How Relationships Support Development from Birth to Two.* London: Robinson.

Murray, L., & Andrews, L. (2000). *The Social Baby: Understanding Babies' Communication from Birth.* Richmond, Surrey: CP Publishing.

Murray, L., & Cooper, P. J. (Eds.) (1997). *Postpartum Depression and Child Development.* New York: Guilford Press.

Murray, L., & Trevarthen, C. (1985). Emotional regulation of interactions between
two-month-olds and their mothers. In T. M. Field & N. A. Fox (Eds.), *Social Perception in Infants* (pp. 177–197). Norwood, NJ: Ablex.

Murray, L., Kempton, C., Woolgar, M., & Hooper, R. (1993). Depressed mothers'
speech to their infants and its relation to infant gender and cognitive development. *Journal of Child Psychology and Psychiatry, 34*(7), 1083–1101.

Murray, L., Stanley, C., Hooper, R., King, F., & Fiori-Cowley, A. (1996). The role
of infant factors in postnatal depression and mother-infant interactions. *Developmental Medicine and Child Neurology, 38*(2), 109–119.

Murray, L., Woolgar, M., Briers, S., & Hipwell, A. (1999). Children's social representations in dolls' house play and theory of mind tasks, and their relation to
family adversity and child disturbance. *Social Development, 8*(2): 179–200.

Nagy, E. (2011). The newborn infant: A missing stage in developmental psychology.
Infant and Child Development, 20, 3–19.

Narvaez, D. (2014). *Neurobiology and the Development of Human Morality.* New
York: Norton.

Narvaez, D., Braungart-Rieker, J. M., Miller-Graff, L. E., Gettler, L. T., & Hast-
ings, P. D. (Eds.). (2016). *Contexts for Young Child Flourishing: Evolution, Family,
and Society.* New York: Oxford University Press.

Pavlicevic, M. (1997). *Music Therapy in Context: Music Meaning and Relationship.*
London: Jessica Kingsley.

Piaget, J. (1926). *The Language and Thought of the Child.* London: Routledge &
Kegan Paul.

Piaget, J. (1936). *La Naissance de l'Intelligence chez l'Enfant.* 1952. *The Origins of
Intelligence in Children.* New York: International Universities Press.

Piaget, J. (1952). *The Origins of Intelligence in Children.* New York: International
Universities Press.

Piaget, J. (1958). *The Child's Construction of Reality.* London: Routledge & Kegan
Paul.

Porges, S. W. (2011). *The Polyvagal Theory: Neurophysiological Foundations of
Emotions, Attachment, Communication, and Self-regulation.* New York: Norton.

Quick, R. H. (1894/2003). *Essays on Educational Reformers.* London: Longmans,
Green & Co. (1909 edition republished as paperback in 2003 by the University
Press in Honolulu, Hawaii).

Reddy, V. (2000). Coyness in early infancy. *Developmental Science*, *3*, 186–192.

Reddy, V. (2008). *How Infants Know Minds.* Cambridge, MA: Harvard University Press.

Reissland, N. (2012). *The Development of Emotional Intelligence: A Case Study.* London: Routledge.

Reissland, N., & Kisilevsky, B. (2015). (Eds.) *Fetal Development: Research on Brain and Behavior, Environmental Influences, and Emerging Technologies.* London: Springer Verlag.

Rogoff, B. (1990). *Apprenticeship in Thinking: Cognitive Development in Social Context.* New York: Oxford University Press.

Rogoff, B. (2003). *The Cultural Nature of Human Development.* Oxford: Oxford University Press.

Sander, L. W. (2008). *Living Systems, Evolving Consciousness, and the Emerging Person: A Selection of Papers from the Life Work of Louis Sander.* Edited by G. Amadei & I. Bianchi. Abingdon: Taylor & Francis.

Schore, A. N. (2003). *Affect Regulation and the Repair of the Self.* New York: Norton.

Sherrington, C. S. (1906). *The Integrative Action of the Nervous System.* New Haven, CT: Yale University Press.

Sherrington, C. S. (1955). *Man on His Nature.* The Wisdom of the Body, pp. 103–104. The Gifford Lectures, 1937–1938. Harmondsworth: Penguin Books.

Siegel, D. J. (2012). *The Developing Mind.* New York: Guilford.

Smith, A. (1759). *Theory of Moral Sentiments.* Edinburgh (Modern Edition: D. D. Raphael and A.L. Macfie, General Editors, Glasgow Edition. Oxford: Clarendon, 1976. Reprint, Indianapolis: Liberty Fund, 1984).

Smith, A. (1776). *An Inquiry into the Nature and Causes of the Wealth of Nations.* Edinburgh (Modern Edition: R. H. Campbell and A. S. Skinner, General Editors; W. B. Todd, Textual Editor; Glasgow Edition, 2 volumes. Oxford: Clarendon, 1976).

Smith, A. (1777/1982). Of the Nature of that Imitation which takes place in what are called the Imitative Arts. In W. P. D. Wightman & J. C. Bryce (Eds.) with Dugald Stewart's account of Adam Smith (ed. I. S. Ross), D. D. Raphael and A. S. Skinner (Eds.), *Essays on Philosophical Subjects* (pp. 176–213). Indianapolis, IN: Liberty Fund, 1982.

Sparrow, J. (2018). Communities raising children together: Collaborative consultation with a place- based initiative in Harlem. In C. Trevarthen, J. Delafield-Butt, & A. Dunlop, (Eds.), *The Child's Curriculum: Sharing the Natural Talents of Young Children, for a Richer Education* (pp. 256–276). Oxford: Oxford University Press.

Spitz, R. A. (1945). Hospitalism -- An inquiry into the genesis of psychiatric conditions in early childhood. *Psychoanalytic Study of the Child*, *1*, 53–74.

Spitz, R. A. (1957). *No and Yes: On the Genesis of Human Communication.* New York: International Universities Press.

Stern, D. N. (2000). *The Interpersonal World of the Infant: A View from Psychoanalysis and Development Psychology.* New York: Basic Books.

Stern, D. N. (2004). *The Present Moment: In Psychotherapy and Everyday Life.* New York: Norton.

Stern, D. N. (2010). *Forms of Vitality: Exploring Dynamic Experience in Psychology, the Arts, Psychotherapy and Development.* Oxford: Oxford University Press.

Stern, D. N., Bruschweiler-Stern, N., Harrison, A. M., Lyons-Ruth, K., Morgan, A. C., Nahum, J. P., Sander, L., & Tronick, E. Z. (1999). The process of therapeutic change involving implicit knowledge: Some implications of developmental observations for adult psychotherapy. *Infant Mental Health Journal, 19*, 300–308.

Trevarthen, C. (1979). Communication and cooperation in early infancy. A description of primary intersubjectivity. In M. Bullowa (Ed.), *Before Speech: The Beginning of Human Communication* (pp. 321–347). London: Cambridge University Press.

Trevarthen, C. (1989). Motives for culture in young children their natural development through communication. In W. Koch (Ed.), *The Nature of Culture* (pp. 80–119). Bochum: Brockmeyer.

Trevarthen, C. (2016). From the intrinsic motive pulse of infant actions, to the life time of cultural meanings. In B. Mölder, V. Arstila, & P. Øhrstrom (Eds.), *Philosophy and Psychology of Time* (pp. 225–265). Springer Studies in Brain and Mind, Vol. 9. Dordrecht: Springer International.

Trevarthen, C. (2017a). The affectionate intersubjective intelligence of the infant, and its innate motives for relational mental health. *International Journal of Cognitive Analytic Therapy and Relational Mental Health, 1*, 11–53.

Trevarthen, C. (2017b). Foreword, In A. Hendry & J. Hasler (Eds.), *Creative Therapies for Complex Trauma: Helping Children and Families in Foster Care, Kinship Care or Adoption* (pp. 7–11). London: Jessica Kingsley.

Trevarthen, C. (2019a). The psychobiology of the human spirit. In G. Apter, E. Devouche, & M. Gratier (Eds.), *Early Interaction and Developmental Psychopathology, Volume 1: Infancy* (pp. 1–18). Cham: Springer Nature Switzerland AG.

Trevarthen, C. (2019b). Sander's life work, on mother-infant vitality and the Emerging Person. *Psychoanalytic Inquiry, 39*, 22–35.

Trevarthen, C., & Aitken, K. J. (2003). Regulation of brain development and age-related changes in infants' motives: The developmental function of 'regressive' periods. In M. Heimann (Ed.), *Regression Periods in Human Infancy* (pp. 107–184). Mahwah, NJ: Erlbaum.

Trevarthen, C., Delafield-Butt, J., & Dunlop, A. (Eds.) (2018). *The Child's Curriculum: Sharing the Natural Talents of Young Children, for a Richer Education.* Oxford: Oxford University Press.

Trevarthen, C., & Hubley, P. (1978). Secondary intersubjectivity: Confidence, confiding and acts of meaning in the first year. In A. Lock (Ed.), *Action, Gesture and Symbol: The Emergence of Language* (pp. 183–229). New York: Academic Press.

Trevarthen, C., & Malloch, S. (2017). Grace in moving and joy in sharing: The intrinsic beauty of communicative musicality from birth. In S. Bunn (Ed.), *Anthropology and Beauty: From Aesthetics to Creativity* (pp. 115–130). London: Routledge.

Tronick, E. Z. (1989) Emotions and emotional communication in infants. *American Psychologist, 44*(2), 112–126.

Tronick, E. Z. (2005). Why is connection with others so critical? The formation of dyadic states of consciousness: coherence governed selection and the co-creation of meaning out of messy meaning making. In J. Nadel and D. Muir (Eds.), *Emotional Development* (pp. 293–315). Oxford University Press.

Tronick, E. Z., Als, H., & Brazelton T. B. (1980). Monadic phases: A structural description analysis of infant-mother face-to-face interaction. *Merrill-Palmer Quarterly, 26*, 3–24.

Tronick, E. Z., & Field, T. (Eds.). (1986). *Maternal Depression and Infant Disturbance. New Directions for Child Development*, No. 34. San Francisco: Jossey Bass.

Turner, V. (1982). *From Ritual to Theatre: The Human Seriousness of Play.* New York: Performing Arts Journal Publications.

Winnicott, D. W. (1958). *Playing and Reality.* London: Tavistock.

Winnicott, D. W. (1964). *The Child, the Family and the Outside World.* London: Penguin Books.

Chapter 3

Primary shame

Needing you and the economy of affects

Orit Badouk Epstein

Our attachment needs

> The child's healthy desire to communicate her subjective experience to a needed other is infused with shame because the needed other cannot or will not acknowledge the child's experience as something legitimately 'thinkable'.
>
> Philip Bromberg (2011, p. 43)

The other day, as I was queuing to pay at the till at my local supermarket, I overheard a parent behind me saying to his son (who was roughly aged five): "Today you were a good boy!" The boy's eyes lit up with pride, the parent then continued: "unlike the cry baby you usually are, right?!" The apparent helplessness visible on the boy's face left him looking confused, his muted gaze slid down as if to seek refuge in the concrete floor of the shop. The boy then nervously fidgeted with the button on his shirt until it tore off. It seemed to me that this was his only means of expressing some form of protest against the crushing humiliation voiced by his father. What else could he do? After all, no child would wish for an unwanted parent.

It is with this kind of exhaustive exteriority which, John Bowlby insisted, hinders the development of our sense of security and true autonomy in the world. In one of Bowlby's earlier unpublished essays from 1929, *Essay on Experimental Education*, the young Bowlby argued for the need to bring a scientific approach to psychological questions and the requirement to recognise children's specific needs from a developmental perspective. He stated that:

> This essay has for its purpose the recommendation of experiment in education and evaluation…and the results of their practice tested in a scientific spirit and that forcing children only to satisfy adult tendencies is to overlook the fact that if these childish impulses remain unsatisfied they are very likely to interfere with the development and satisfaction of adult ones.
>
> (Bowlby, 1929, p. 8)

DOI: 10.4324/9781003175612-4

Although Bowlby wrote very little about shame as an individuated affect, his monumental acknowledgement of children's feelings of anxiety when separated from their caregivers has confronted us with what our society has taught us to defend against the most. I would summarise this fundamental need when the child says something like: "I still need you, please don't leave me!"

For centuries, parents were encouraged to believe that premature independence made their children function better as adults. What seems to have happened at some point in the history of humanity, is that we became ashamed of our own attachment needs. Children were discouraged from expressing their feelings of dependency on their attachment figures and instead early separations, controlled feeding, leaving infants to cry themselves to sleep, corporal punishment, early potty training, and early schooling became the normative modes for raising a child and were considered to be harmless. The style of pedagogy that emphasised independence in the nineteenth and twentieth centuries taught parents to expect their offspring not to cry, making demands like: "don't be such a baby," "stop crying or I'll give you a reason to cry!", "pull yourself together!" Such attitudes often seemed to engage in conspiracies of fear, silencing the child while rushing her to grow up prematurely since it was believed that these methods led to the formation of an independent individual and a robust society. In his book, *The Origins of Love and Hate,* the Scottish psychiatrist, Ian Suttie (in whom Bowlby found much inspiration) critiqued Freud's drive theory and death instinct while expanding his ideas on Western civilisation's dread of mollycoddling and encouraging its children to quickly outgrow their childishness. "Hate" he writes, "I regard not as a primal independent instinct but as a development or intensification of separation-anxiety which in turn is roused by a threat against love" (Suttie, 1988 (1935), p. 31). "This philosophy of life is idealised in Stoicism, which avowedly seeks a defence from suffering by eschewing desires that expose us to privation and rebuff" (Suttie, 1988 (1935), p. 90). In Bowlby's way of thinking, this is nonetheless a form of loss.

"Loss", according to Bowlby,

> gives rise to grief and mourning, a field for a long time of central concern to psychoanalysts but, once again, one about which there has been no agreement. It happens, however that these problems, to the understanding of which Darwin himself made important contributions which, when rediscovered and applied, have proved of the greatest clinical value.
>
> (Bowlby, 1980, p. 111)

Following on from Darwin's initial theory about the biology of survival, Bowlby's work showed us that humans will always seek proximity to protect against a fear of annihilation and as a means of survival.

Since the goal of attachment behaviour is to maintain an affectional bond, any situation that seems to be endangering the bond elicits action designed to preserve it; and the greater the danger of loss appears to be, the more intense and varied are the actions elicited to prevent it. In such circumstances, all the most powerful forms of attachment behaviour become activated – clinging, crying and angry coercion.

(Bowlby, 1980, p. 26)

Furthermore,

For Bowlby, the need to survive physically as well psychologically, is the key to understanding the organisation of mental life: We survive by forming relationship and adapting to the mind of others. Relationships are the remedy for fear – of loss, of annihilation, of psychic emptiness – and offer us the deepest expression of our humanity.

(Slade, 2013, p. 41)

Primary shame

In response to his own personal pain of separation and loss during his own childhood, the young John Bowlby began writing about the impact of separation and loss on individuals and children in particular during the Second World War. As primates, humans are hard wired biologically to become attached, thus, according to Bowlby (1973), separation from an attachment figure provokes anxiety and anger in the young child. Whenever the attachment to a caregiver is disrupted or impaired, the first affect the infant will feel is fear, and in many cases exacerbated by the caregiver's insensitive response, this will be followed by shame. Why? Following on from the extensive empirical research studies conducted on infant/parent interactions we now know with greater confidence that it is the quality of the caregiver's response which determines how the child will feel and behave later in life. These sequences of everyday interactions with caregivers accumulate over time and shape the child's expectations in their attachment relationships. Bowlby referred to this process as the child building a set of Internal Working Models (IWM). From this standpoint, it is the misattuned responses from the caregiver towards the child which will start off as fear but then will set off shame and will pave the way for other defences to take their turn. This is what I consider to be "Primary Shame." It is this repetitive and accumulative absence of empathic responsiveness from an attachment figure – be it minimisation: "don't be silly, you'll be fine" or lack of recognition: "I have to go because I have a lot to do" or retaliation: "Stop crying or I'll give you a reason to cry" which interferes with healthy dependency and further activates the attachment system. These are micro-moments of accumulative grief which never seem to go away, quite the opposite; they will continue to generate a sense of insecurity and shame in the growing child and be present during adulthood.

In the opening chapter of this book, Judith Solomon eloquently calls this early sense of wrongness created in the child "Irresolvable Shame." She argues as follows:

> Very early on it appears young children can generate their own interpretations of events in which they are the villain. This seem to be a frequent consequence of separation from key attachment figures, particularly when the child cannot understand the reason for separation.
>
> (Solomon, 2021, p. 15)

In Chapter 5, Uli Schultz-Vernath also discusses this and calls it "Primal Shame" (Schultz-Vernath, 2021, p. 97).

The shame dynamics we see in all insecure attachment relationships are often associated with the child being told that their attachment needs and feelings are not acceptable and that something is fundamentally wrong with them. Michael Balint (1968) described it as the "basic fault" and one which we carry within us throughout life: "The patient says that he feels there is a fault, within him, a fault that must be put right" (Balint, 1968, p. 21).

Bowlby postulated that our primary motivation as humans is relationship seeking (not pleasure seeking as Freud stated), developing within a specific social framework which in one way or another then governs how we manifest our original experience of the loss of relationships. According to Bowlby, the social impact goes even further, the greater one's sense of loss experienced within society, the less flexibility of mind there will be and can result in the mobilisation of anger as a defence against that loss. With the traumatising events in recent human history such as the high child mortality rate in many parts of the world, Spanish flu, two World Wars, the Holocaust, Hiroshima, and other human atrocities, it's hard not to read how these traumatic disruptions have influenced our relationships. While men were called to the battlefield, millions of individuals were forced to lean more towards self-reliance and become less emotionally dependent. With such patriarchal thinking and war accommodating minds, in Bowlby's words (1988), we have learned to disconnect from what we are "not supposed to know" and suppress what we are "not supposed to feel" (Bowlby, 1988, p. 99).

Following on from Bowlby's observations, it was the researcher Mary Ainsworth et al. (1978) who came up with a set of astute empirical observations about infants' interactions with their mothers, all of which cleverly mapped out the three adaptive strategies against separation and loss. These became known as attachment patterns: Secure, Avoidant, and Ambivalent, and become apparent when the infant has to resort to these strategies as a defence against their basic fear of abandonment.

In the absence of a caregiver, the child with a secure attachment pattern will nonetheless react with distress but on reunion will easily be comforted since the nature of the relationship in general is one of empathic responsiveness and collaboration, knowing that:

1. Upon separation the caregiver will eventually be back.
2. The caregiver will provide comfort and safety in times of distress.
3. The caregiver will not ridicule and shame the child when they try to differentiate and individuate.

The child with an avoidant attachment pattern will under react because:

1. Upon separation they will show indifference towards their caregiver's departure; nevertheless the fear of separation will be remembered and somatised in their body.
2. The caregiver will not be soothing and comforting.
3. The caregiver will reject, ridicule, and shame the child's need for seeking comfort.

The child with an ambivalent attachment pattern will overreact because:

1. Upon separation the caregiver's inconsistent availability will only elicit more anxiety.
2. The caregiver's tantalising responsiveness will be a source of confusion and anger.
3. The caregiver will oscillate between being affectionate and available (often because of their own needs) and being unavailable, rejecting, and shaming.

Later, Main and Solomon (1986) identified a fourth group of children who showed the disorganised attachment pattern. These children often came from more abusive environments. Dependency for this group meant a collapse of strategies because the caregiver could not be trusted to provide a sense of safety nor sensitivity, in fact were often the source of the child's fear. This would result in not only dissociation but also controlling and aggressive behaviour as a defence against the shame of feeling helpless.

Looking at these attachment patterns through a fresh lens, it has become clearer that Ainsworth's empirical research based on Bowlby's core ideas, has in essence, provided us with a helpful map of understanding how, within the context of secure attachment, insecure children have learned to defend against the fear and shame of needing their attachment figures:

• Avoidant pattern: Behind the averted gaze, the child with an avoidant attachment pattern has learned to hide their emotions of neediness, as if to say: "I need you but I have learned not to show it to you, because if I do, you'll not be available for me, so I better rely on myself and not risk your shaming rejection. What else can I do?"

- Ambivalent pattern: Behind the continuous wailing and protesting, the needs of the child with an ambivalent attachment pattern are met but with aggravating inconsistency to which they feel the despair and the agony of confusion, as if saying: "It's so comforting when you are around but why can't you stay? I feel ashamed for needing you so much, I am too much, I'm too needy. This angers me, just waiting and hoping for a moment of resumed connection."

- Disorganised pattern: Behind the dissociated dread, the needs of a child with a disorganised attachment pattern are always entwined with an added layer of fear unpredictably inflicted by the "scaregiver" (Badouk Epstein, 2015, 2017, 2019). Under conditions of repetitive frightening experiences such as emotional, physical, and sexual abuse, a child will fail to show healthy attachment behaviour, therefore, hiding behind dissociative barriers is the only way they can survive this paradoxical conjunction, as if to say: "To need you means to be both afraid of you and confused by you. It hurts, but since feeling anything is shaming, I'll have to dissociate these frightening experiences from my consciousness and instead learn to control my environment."

Later in life these adaptive strategies can give the illusion not only of independence (particularly with the avoidant attachment pattern) but also of false intimacy (in particular with the preoccupied attachment pattern). Here are some anecdotes from the therapy room:

- Clients with an avoidant attachment pattern: Whenever I used to open the door to Tara, she would have her head buried in her handbag as if searching for something or would be opening letters, anything but meet my eyes or greet me. Completely unaware of her own behaviour, we later found the link between her dissociated yet apparent impolite behaviour and the fact that she grew up in a home with a very sick and bed ridden mother who prior to her illness was never emotionally available and later could not greet her children. Tara was never sure if, upon her return from school, her mother would still be alive. A "now moment" between us occurred when, after six months, Tara rang the doorbell, but this time as I opened the door, our eyes met, we looked directly at each other with a tender dignity. Another client, a mother who is working very hard on repairing her relationship with her now adult children, sobbed while describing her fear of showing any emotional vulnerability in case they rejected her. Furthermore, during therapy, it became apparent how difficult it was for her to tolerate her children's negative affects since, to her mind, these were a reflection on her own "bad mothering."

- Clients with a preoccupied attachment pattern: Joanna was a highly anxious individual who had difficulty finding any kind of relational pleasure or express any form of playfulness. As a child Joanna remembered frequently hiding behind her mother's apron when she needed her, but her mother would push her away, experiencing Joanna as suffocating her. At other times her mother would plead for her daughter's company and affection and get angry when Joanna rejected her. Riddled by guilt and shame for being "too much," the enmeshed relationship Joanna experienced with her mother felt both crippling and confusing and also generated a sense of resentfulness for being stuck in a double bind. In therapy, Joanna would regularly question the value of therapy and make me feel somehow unappreciated. A turning point in therapy was when I told Joanna that we must honour her inquisitive mind, that "why? child" whose many protests against her parents were never heard. This kind of deshaming acknowledgement had an immediate effect on Joanna that enabled our relationship to stabilise and move on.
- Clients with a disorganised attachment pattern: the imprinted fear often masks shame affects with an added layer of intensity and force. Alex got furious with me whenever I showed the slightest tenderness towards him. He would find it hard to be present in the session and would often say: "Please stop talking about my little self, I find it patronizing and self-pitying." Later we recovered early memories of him being regularly beaten and locked in a dark room whenever he expressed any form of attachment need towards his parents and nanny. Moreover, it appeared he was an "accident," an unwanted baby. In the poem *The Sovereignty and the Goodness of God, Together with the Faithfulness of His Promises Displayed*, the poet Liz Waldner wrote:

> In the beginning, then,
> it was willed that I won't be.
> This shamed me, however good
> An act I learned to put on.
>   (Waldner, 2009)

After reading these lines to Alex, tears filled our eyes and his intense anger then decreased dramatically.

Parental shame is equally prevalent in our society and deserves equal inclusion and sensitivity. In understanding the child's needs, Bowlby's attachment theory was not about parent blaming and shaming rather he stated: "If a community values its children it must cherish their parents" (Bowlby, 1953, p. 84). The intergenerational transmission of trauma is nonetheless a major contribution to the shameful way we relate to our children. Seeing the parent's shame reflected in the child's shame deserves more attention and research and will help us provide empathic tools of how best to approach a struggling parent without them feeling criticised and shamed. However, since every parent was once a child, the scope of this chapter is to understand primal shame in relation to the child's response to the separation and misattunement they receive from a caregiver.

Dependency and the economy of affects

The socio-economic conditions previous centuries have imposed upon us has inevitably impacted on our emotional development, in particular on our biological dependency. In his last interview in February 1990, when asked about dependency, Bowlby replied:

> Once you call attachment 'dependence' you at once put an adverse evaluation on it, because in the ordinary course of events people say that you oughtn't to be dependent you should be independent. And so, some anxious person who is desperately eager for assistance is looked down upon as being a rather poor, weak thing.
>
> (Bowlby, 1990, transcribed by Oskis, 2015, pp. 141–142)

In this context the word dependency, in its pejorative sense, has become a shaming noun, and a sign of inherent weakness, ensuring that society at large remains dismissive about our basic attachment needs. This down-regulation and affect avoidance has contributed to the ossified world we have had to adapt to, where many of us have experienced shame whenever needing the proximity of our attachment figures. The way in which our affects have been economised means that they have become deeply embedded in social institutions such as crèches for infants as young as six months, boarding schools, the army, sports academies, psychiatric hospitals, and other organisations which are all designed to promote premature independence. They routinely use controlling strategies, medication, and symptomatic treatment as short-term solutions to what has become a long-term problem.

We have grown accustomed to a shaming culture when our separation anxieties tend to fuel the intensity of other forms of affect dysregulation and an increase in what would be considered as numbing behaviours such as using drugs, drinking alcohol, eating, shopping, watching pornography, excessive interactions on social media, and other forms of addiction.

With the help of the digital revolution, it has only been in the past two decades or so that society at large has begun to wake up to the realisation of our unmet needs. Parents are now better equipped to attune to their children; however, it is through the illumination provided by this new understanding that we can better notice the darkness that still surrounds us and see how the minimisation of these needs is still influencing government policies and therapeutic interventions.

Recently, I came across an idea that has been circulating in some webinars and conferences, which claims that the term "caregiver" is a bad one, since it implies a mono-directional way of relating while perceiving the relationship between infant and parent to be bidirectional. For example, if the baby is looking back at the parent, they both feel good but if the baby looks away this can make the parent feel bad. Such messages do indeed foster the parent's own shame, nevertheless it is confusing and even misleading to the public. In their book *The Circle of Security*, Powell et al. (2014) describe the child's need for a safe haven, where essentially the infant is a care-seeker dependent on the caregiver's ability to recognise, protect, comfort, take delight, and organise the child's feelings. So, if we were to go back to Ainsworth's Strange Situation Procedure (SSP), we know that an infant who doesn't look back at her caregiver, has to resort to an adaptive strategy, namely the avoidant attachment pattern. I often wonder whether it is shame which prevents the infant from looking directly at their parent's unreliable gaze. Parent child relationships are not equal but asymmetrical. With the help of Alan Schore (1994) and neuroscience we have learned that it usually takes between two to three years for an infant brain to grow, the infant then develops an intimate positive affective relationship with their parents and has confidence in the relationship. We can only become truly independent if we are first truly dependent or what Winnicott (1960) considered as the move from:

- "Absolute Dependence – In this state the infant has no means of knowing about the maternal care which is largely a matter of prophylaxis. He cannot gain control over what is well and what is badly done but is only in a position to gain profit or to suffer disturbance."
- to "Relative Dependence – Here the infant can become aware of the need for the details of maternal care and can, to a growing extent, relate them to personal impulse, and then later, in psycho-analytic treatment, can reproduce them in the transference."
- and "Towards Independence – The infant develops means for doing without actual care. This is accomplished through the accumulation of memories of care, the projection of personal needs and the introjection of care details, with the development of confidence in the environment. Here must be added the element of intellectual understanding with its tremendous implications" (Winnicott, 1960, p. 590).

As with Bowlby who wrote: "All of us, from the cradle to the grave are happiest when life is organised as a series of excursions, long or short, from the secure base provided by our attachment figures" (Bowlby, 1988, p. 62). Winnicott, too, saw dependency as a personal and societal journey, while the movement from dependence to independence is never complete. My only slight dissatisfaction with Winnicott's brilliant recognition of the infant's dependency, is his categorisation of the phases of dependency. Like many of his contemporaries, Winnicott too seemed to economise on the child's basic needs for proximity and rush us through the phases of developmental growth. We know that it is only when the child is around 3 or 4 years of age that they learn to accumulate memories of positive care, which I have named as the "Reservoir of Love" (Badouk Epstein, 2019). This is when the child begins to see their mind and the mind of others as separate. This is what Fonagy and Bateman (2008) call the mentalisation process which is a feature of securely attached children.

Fairbairn (1952) also considered dependency as the process of psychological maturation which relies on the movement from infantile to mature dependence. This implies the recognition of a state of separateness of the child from its object as they move towards a progressively more adult mode of mature dependence. This movement represents the growth of the self as a whole. Alan Schore (1994) termed this as part of his theory of affect regulation with the infant's move from a state of dysregulation to self-regulation.

The insecurity many of our clients present us with, tells us how they have never outgrown these early absences of "absolute dependency" as can be seen in people with a disorganised attachment pattern and the absences of "relative dependency" as seen in all other insecure attachment patterns:

- For the client with an avoidant attachment pattern, whose attention is routinely directed away from an expected source of stress, admitting a need for the "other" is the challenge, since it can feel shaming and even humiliating to be rejected. During therapy this may manifest in small gestures such as when the therapist goes on vacation. As one client once told me: "You deserve a break; you are reading too much into it." Such dismissals are there to protect the client from the shame that they actually matter to the "other." When the client eventually told me: "This is how I feel, and I need some help," it felt like an important breakthrough in therapy.
- The client with a preoccupied attachment pattern will try to master a degree of control over separation, and move against the attachment figure, sometimes generating a conflict in the session before a break (such as a holiday), as if protesting: "I will leave you before you leave me, so in this way, I won't feel the shame of needing you." The consistent empathic offerings during therapy helps these clients to move fairly quickly to a place of better reflective functioning and an understanding that their efforts to control their surroundings, was their way of not resolving the pain of confusion and separation from the tantalising parent.

- For the client with a disorganised attachment pattern, the dread and shame of early abandonment and maltreatment evokes fearful/frightening behaviour and contradictory relational moves. This is often communicated literally, for example, a client might threaten suicide or ending the therapy one week before the therapist's break, saying that they do not intend to resume the therapy since therapy is a total waste of time and money, but then resuming therapy as if nothing had happened. This is an indication that dissociated self-states are operating to protect the self against the pain of annihilation.

For example, Mary a client with a history of emotional, physical, and sexual abuse expressed intense dependency during the first year of therapy which was allied to intense separation anxiety and suicidal ideation, in particular around certain anniversaries and just before my breaks. Maintaining healthy boundaries during the phase of "absolute dependency" meant being consistent with empathic responsiveness, always validating her young parts and her attachment cries rather than seeing her as being "disruptive, manipulative or sabotaging" the therapy. The mourning process meant that the focal point of our work needed to gradually shift in focus from the therapeutic relationship to her early relationships and the unresolved grief she endured all her life. During my breaks, these acts of attunement were also aided by connecting with her child part, giving her a transitional object or offering an organised time for a text message that felt manageable. These gestures of empathy were consistent and gradually helped Mary feel more regulated and her trust in the relationship with me grew. After two years of working intensively, Mary's suicidal ideation lessened to a large degree and so did her absolute dependency on me.

As professionals working in mental health, admitting that even as adults we still need the comfort and support of an attachment figure is still considered something about which we should feel ashamed. We see this in the manufacturing of various low budget and short-term methods and techniques for mental health interventions. In some countries the current trend is to manualise attachment theory and repackage it for short-term therapy which will promote everything except what Bowlby originally intended – our need for a reparative long-term attachment relationship.

The different denunciations of our attachment needs may also arise in particular around the needs of the therapist herself and the therapist's own avoidant strategies, sometimes leading to perceiving the client's "neediness" as "narcissistic" or "borderline." Such misattunments can have a devastating effect on the client, continuously being left feeling flawed and alone. In some situations, the therapist's own fear of the client's dependency on the therapist leads them to perceiving the client as "too much." This protects the therapist herself against her own shame arising from perhaps feeling inadequate and limited in her capacity to help. In fostering the client's dependency as integral to the therapeutic process and providing healthy boundaries we need the essential support of supervision. Once we recognise shame affects, we feel the invitation of compassion calling to us. Therefore, acknowledging the client's attachment needs as legitimate while owning the limitations of what can be offered by the therapy relationship, is all part of the mourning process and is already an advance towards relational honesty and away from the culture of client blaming.

Tenderness: the opposite response to shaming

I would like to return to Ian Suttie's book and the chapter on "The 'taboo' on tenderness," (Suttie, 1935). Suttie critiqued Freud for confusing tenderness with sexuality and also how as the result of a puritanical upbringing, people in the West had developed an intolerance of tenderness and by doing so, caused great emotional pain to their children. He wrote:

> What we call tender feelings and affection is based not on sexual desire but upon the pre-oedipal emotional and fondling relationship with the mother and upon the instinctual need for companionship which is characteristic of all animals which pass through a phase of nurtured infancy. ... The measure of this pain can perhaps be found in conscious memories of solecism and blunders, which are attended by an acute sense of shame years after they are committed.
>
> (Suttie, 1935/1988, p. 86)

Moreover,

> The repression of affection seems therefore to be a process likely to be cumulative from one generation to another. The mother who was herself love-starved and who in consequence, is intolerant of tenderness, will be impatient of her own children's dependency, regressiveness and claim for love.
>
> (Suttie, 1935/1988, p. 89)

In a world of harsh socio-economic conditions, one would rightly assert that the sort of sensitivity required to attend to the infant's needs is too idealistic a proposition, and mostly belongs to the privileged middle classes, where children don't have to bid for attention at the cost of their parents' financial struggles. However, it is the caregivers' genuine and tender response which is of paramount importance to the child's mental wellbeing. By the same token, as part of the transference matrix and reflective functioning, in my attempt to combat shame and seeing it primarily as a relational failure, my mode of surveillance is firstly to be mindful of the tension created between my shame prone feeling and thoughts, and the formation of more generous and considerate thoughts towards my clients. This is indeed a tall order and one which will present itself in a non-linear manner throughout the therapeutic endeavour. Still, the therapist's tender response and the validation of the client's unmet needs is what is, first and foremost, essential to the processes of gaining trust and "earned security" whilst at the same time acknowledging the limitations of therapy.

Conclusion

It is the shame of not knowing and the shame of not feeling which tends to be so palpably painful for our clients to recognise. Rather than continuing to deny our attachment needs, we need to be kind and compassionate about our defences because they were created to protect and sustain our survival under conditions of fear and indifference.

We are never going to move forward if we dissociate from our primary shame, therefore, if we pause for a second and see the old structure of therapy partly as a product of a traumatised and rigid world we have inherited, perhaps it's time we should consider revisiting the ground rules handed down to us by the traumatised giants of our profession from the previous generations schooled in self-reliance. While we slowly mourn the shame of the loss of affects as seen with the clients with an avoidant attachment pattern, the shame of the loss of consistency as seen with the clients with preoccupied patterns and the shame of loss of safety as seen with the clients with disorganised patterns, we may need to emphasise that in the process towards earned security there is nothing to be ashamed of in recognising dependency as a primary human need.

References

Ainsworth, M. D. S., Blehar, M. C., Waters, E., & Wall, S. (1978). *Patterns of Attachment*. Hillsdale, NJ: Erlbaum.

Badouk Epstein, O. (2015). Cross the bridge to redefine the pain. *Attachment: New Directions in Relational Psychoanalysis and Psychotherapy, 9*, 290–294.

Badouk Epstein, O. (2017). The occupied body. *Attachment: New Directions in Psychotherapy and Relational Psychoanalysis, 11*, 257–272.

Badouk Epstein, O. (2019). The most tender place in my heart is for strangers: Sexual addiction, the fear system and dissociation through an attachment lens. *Attachment: New Directions in Psychotherapy and Relational Psychoanalysis, 13*, 43–60.

Balint, M. (1968). *The Basic Fault; Therapeutic Aspects of Regression*. Evanston, IL: Northwestern University Press.

Bowlby, J. (1929). *Essay on Experimental Education*. Wellcome Collection, (PP/BOW/A.1/19).

Bowlby, J. (1953). *Child Care and the Growth of Love*. London: Penguin.

Bowlby, J. (1973). *Attachment and Loss, Vol. 2, Separation, Anxiety and Anger.* London: Pimilco.

Bowlby, J. (1980). *Attachment and Loss, Vol. 3, Loss, Sadness and Depression.* London: Pimlico.

Bowlby, J. (1988). *A Secure Base: Clinical Applications of Attachment Theory.* London: Routledge.

Bowlby, J. (1990). An interview by Virginia Hunter, February 14, 1990. Transcribed by Andrea Oskis. *Attachment: New Directions in Psychotherapy and Relational Psychoanalysis, 9*, 138–157.

Bromberg, P. (2011). *The Shadow of the Tsunami and Growth of the Relational Mind.* New York: Routledge.

Fairbairn, W. R. D. (1952). *Psychological Studies of the Personality.* London: Routledge.

Fonagy, P., & Bateman, A. (2008). The development of borderline personality disorder – A mentalizing model. *Journal of Personality Disorders, 22*, 4–21.

Main, M., & Solomon, J. (1986). Discovery of a new, insecure-disorganised/disoriented attachment pattern. In T. B. Brazelton & M. W. Yogman (Eds.), *Affective Development in Infancy*, (pp. 95–124). Norwood, NJ: Ablex.

Oskis, A. (2015). John Bowlby: An interview by Virginia Hunter. Transcribed by Andrea Oskis. *Attachment: New Directions in Psychotherapy and Relational Psychoanalysis, 9*, 138–157.

Powell, B., Cooper, G., Hoffman K., & Marvin, B. (2014). *The Circle of Security Intervention.* New York: Guilford Press.

Schore, A. N. (1994). *Affect Regulation and The Origins of the Self: The Neurobiology of Emotional Development.* New York: Norton.

Schultz-Venrath, U. (2021). Mentalising shame, shamelessness and fermdscham (Shame by Proxy) in Groups. In O. Badouk Epstein (Ed.), *Shame Matters: Attachment and Relational Perspectives for Psychotherapists*, (pp. 90–113). London: Routledge.

Slade, A. (2013). The place of fear in attachment theory and psychoanalysis. In J. Yellin & O. Badouk Epstein (Eds.), *Terror within and without: Attachment and Disintegration: Clinical Work on the Edge*, (pp. 39–57). London: Routledge.

Solomon, J. (2021). Shame as a behavioural system: Its links to attachment, defence, and dysregulation. In O. Badouk Epstein (Ed.), *Shame Matters: Attachment and Relational Perspectives for Psychotherapists*, (pp. 6–20). London: Routledge.

Suttie, I. D. (1935/1988). *The Origins of Love and Hate.* London: Free Association Books.

Waldner, L. (2009). The Sovereignty and the Goodness of God, together with the Faithfulness of His Promises Displayed. *The New Yorker*, January 5, 2009.

Winnicott, D. W. (1960). The theory of the parent-infant relationship. *International Journal of Psycho-Analysis, 41*, 585–595.

Chapter 4

Attackments

Subjugation, shame, and the attachment to painful affects and objects

Richard Chefetz

An early paper by John Bowlby, Forty-Four Juvenile Thieves (Bowlby, 1944), was an exploration of work carried out at the London Child Guidance Clinic from 1936 to 1939. It was stunning to take in the level of intensity and the scrupulous attention to exquisitely detailed observation that this work revealed. Of particular importance, to me, was Bowlby's clear commitment to discerning the actual details of the real experiences of the children entrusted to his care and for research purposes, effectively engaging these thieves with dignity. Especially relevant to the exploration of attackment are his words from this paper regarding emotional trauma in the first decade of a child's life:

> The fact therefore that observations such as those reported here are not found if old case records of similar patients are perused is neither here nor there. My experience has shown me again and again that if these factors are not looked for they are not found, and that as in any other branch of science trained and experienced observers are essential.
>
> (Bowlby, 1944, p. 19)

Observation is not always easy. In fact, it is an art form in and of itself. Even then, being a good observer can be a challenge, especially if the one being observed isn't fully interested in the opportunity.

In the practice of psychotherapy, there is no "fast-food," no short-cut to relatedness, no hyper-link to the creation of intimacy with people who may only have experienced a relationship as a source of pain. Deep human relatedness is the "slow-food" of a well-lived life. Who knew? Intimacy is created by all sorts of engagements.

Consider scenes where the intensity of attacks on a psychotherapy may sometimes be matched only by the tenaciousness with which that same person forcefully grips the fabric of the therapy relationship and holds on. These contradictory behaviors go beyond predictions generated by a frightened or frightening parent in a disorganized attachment relationship and associated controlling behaviors (Lyons-Ruth, 2003). "Attackment"

DOI: 10.4324/9781003175612-5

describes the quality of relating that simultaneously or sequentially feels desperate for connection while remaining intolerant of being met or known and urgently needing to keep others at a distance. Attackment patterns represent activation of an additional and parallel mental system aside from attachment, a competitive or ranking motivational system that organizes relational structures of raw domination and submission in the context of sadistic abuse (Gilbert, 1989). Proximity seeking to achieve felt safety when there is fear without solution is activated in concert with efforts to maintain distance or neutralize threat (Slade, 2014). Resolution of fear may be temporized through its isolation in dissociative self-states and by obeying and enacting the admonished sadistic "pecking" order. These tried and true enduring constellations of self-states are persistent in the wake of traumatic experience in part because dissociative process often destroys the experience of the passage of time and leaves the switch to emergency procedures in an always-on position. The extinction of post-traumatic reaction is undermined. The footprint of traumatic experience is embossed on a vulnerable mind. As the self disorganizes and becomes incoherent there is loss of agency, physical and mental sovereignty, and the feeling of being real in a real world takes flight and disappears in clouds of shame facilitated by depersonalization and derealization accompanying the collapse of agency in the experience of abject terror, not simply fear. The sense of self may feel lost, if it ever was even sensed in the first place.

Shame does matter. It matters a lot. Intense shame is at the core of attackments. Ridicule, humiliation, and other forms of intentional shaming not only cast a shadow on human development, they may also fracture the still soft growing stalk of a child who is emerging into a toxic world. There simply may be no words to describe the carnage done to the structures and functions of a human mind in the wake of sadistic abuse and the objectification of a child. We know that early secure base experiences may leave only sensorimotor traces (Waters & Waters, 2006). This is also the case after sadistic abuse when the only traces of memory may be in bodily movement, facial expression, the jolt of an adrenalin surge, and similar sensory experience (Ogden et al., 2006). Discussion about these experiences may hardly be possible. They may emerge in a disjointed fashion. Such a scene is visible in all its horror in an email from a woman with dissociative identity disorder (DID), fifty-five-year-old Scylla, as in Scylla and Charybdis. That's how she thought of herself. She wrote to me in her fourteenth year of psychotherapy after negotiating with herself that a younger part of her could write and get my reaction to the writing rather than be in my presence when disclosing shame-laden information for the first time. Small wonder:

> i remember walking in the side door into the kitchen having come from the neighbor's house. my short and top were covered in blood and dirt, it was if they had used me to mop up a blood-filled floor. my mother

was sitting in the private room off the back of the kitchen, my sister was sitting with her and she called my name. when i went into the room sis vomited, my mother yelled at me to go take a bath. i was less than 4 yo. i went in to the bathroom and turned on the water. i really didn't know what was hot or cold and i took off my clothes and threw them in the trash. i climbed in to the tub, the water was icy cold and i tried to get it warmer because the coldness stung the open cuts on my body with a numbing sensation. i was trying to wash the blood off w/o getting it bleeding again. my mother came in the room[.] she was angry with me, ''m not sure why. she turned the water on way hot and kept holding my head and body under the water for what seemed like an eternity. when she would let me up i would be gagging for air and kept trying to get out of the scalding water. this was not the first time my mother had done this and i think she wanted me to die. i was a disgrace. after several attempts of holding me under the water she called me a bad name and left the room. there were no towels in the bathroom and so i tried to dry myself off with toilet paper, it didn't work very well. my body was swollen and aching and i was scared. i went to my room and put on clothes and went out the front door to my friend nickys [sic] house. we played army and i got to use his jeep. i came home again many hours later and my mother said nothing about what had gone on earlier in the day. i still don't understand what i did wrong. i only did what i was told and i didn't talk because they told me not to. it all feels like some sort of dream to me and scares me.

Scylla had been sexually assaulted by her father from the age of two onwards, but perhaps even before. The incestuous relationship lasted over fifty years, and these kinds of relationships are not as unusual as we might imagine (Middleton, 2013), and it only ended when a stroke made him too feeble to force her to comply with his wishes. Her mother had, by Scylla's description, regularly beaten her when she would return bloodied from the basement of a neighbor's home where her father directed movies of her being abused. An older sister had also been abused and betrayed her by introducing her to the world of pornography. If beating her with a wire hanger didn't satisfy her mother, then scalding hot bathwater was next, and there were times where her mother's rage generated a scene of trying to drown Scylla in the bath, or the toilet. Scylla was gang raped at the age of six by a group of young teenagers and hospitalized. She was abused by teachers at her high school whom she had seduced. During hospitalizations she would seduce male patients and elope with them into local hotels, sometimes during the hospitalization, and sometimes after her discharge. While she could be seductive it's also true she described in painful detail how she was abused by a previous psychiatrist through his use of drugs and hypnosis. I came to understand why I might have threatened her just to have shown some interest in her or even for her to be in the same room with me. In fact, the other two patients in my practice who have demonstrated an attackment mode of relating with me were betrayed by their former therapists, and they have been just as lethally suicidal and self-destructive as Scylla, alternating with periods of intense work, a sense of intimacy, and profound insight. Betrayal by a therapist has tremendous gravity, much as does betrayal by a parent (Freyd, 1996).

Trying to understand what generates this kind of clinical rhythm has been daunting. The music of the treatment needs to be heard, understood, and put to work. Listening to the score has been painful; and knowing that in its off-key moments I have been contributing to its writing, however small or large, has also been fraught with my own shame and knowledge of sometimes failing to correct my behavior in a timely way before once again I was drawn into enacting in the attackment. Understanding this constellation of experience has become more than an intellectual exercise; it has been essential to my own stabilization and the maintenance of my dignity as a clinician and human being. There are several lines of thinking that seem to intersect when sorting out attackment operations: the shame spectrum of emotion, the attachment system and coincident errors in communication, the competitive (ranking) system as informed by controlling behaviors in childhood, dissociative processes, countertransference responses, and a multiple self-state model of mind.

Shame experience

In Sylvan Tomkins' nosology of affective experience, shame is regarded as an affect modifier that mediates affect by appearing when positive affects are undermined (Tomkins & McCarter, 1995). This has always felt to me to be an oddly unemotional view of shame. The shame that conjures a private sense of diminished self-esteem (I am unworthy) can be such a toxic experience it is hard to see why thinking of shame as an affect modifier might be useful in healing shame-generated wounds. Shame conjures negative assessments of a person's intrinsic value. Shame's cousin, guilt, is more about being taken to task for an action; in guilt the essence of a person's value remains intact. There are mixed states of shame and guilt that can be complex and seem to defy assessing the proportion of one or the other. I have argued that the opposite of shame is dignity, and the opposite of guilt is pride (Chefetz, 2017). Historically, pride has often been considered the opposite of shame (Benau, 2018), and in that usage has had much more connotative weight about valuing one's achievements (Nathanson, 1992), what a person has accomplished, rather than considerations of self-worth. Scylla used to admonish me: "Stop treating me like I'm a person, I am so much less than you are. Stop it!" This is about shame over even existing (Wille, 2014) and as such it is not the opposite of pride, as in pride in existence. The quality of it is off. It's worth considering what might generate this discrepancy.

Acute shame may serve the positive function of creating movement toward repair and restoration of a relationship (Scheff & Retzinger, 2001). Chronic shame is the game-changer for me and has the explanatory power to help with shame over existing. It is a very different personal experience than acute shame where redemption of the shamed self is within reach. The chronically shamed person is like a bird plucked clean of its feathers while alive: naked and unrecognizable, completely vulnerable, devalued, unable to flee, and unable to hide. Averting one's eyes and bowing one's head at least stops receipt of the anticipated penetrating gaze of disgust and contempt, but this smirking observation is still imagined, vividly. In chronic shame, the opportunity for restoration and repair of relatedness to self or other has passed and a person becomes ensconced in an ongoing state of shame. Redemption feels impossible (DeYoung, 2015) when a state of shame comes home to permanently roost. If there is enough active dissociative process, then repetitive states of shame may organize into self-states and become even more complex repositories of isolated affect (Chefetz, 2003; Kluft, 1999). These self-states are often associated with emotional constellations of welded shame-rage (Chefetz, 2015; Lewis, 1987). The understandable rage response of the abused child is crushed and humiliated as the child is overwhelmed by the perpetrator's power, a total eclipse of self-esteem and agency. Shame and rage become densely woven together. Eliciting one often provokes the other. The target of assassination is often the already wounded self, held as pathetic. This is sadly typical of people with severe complex post-traumatic and dissociative disorders. These shame-laden self-states may anchor a person's overarching sense of self and act as a constant undermining influence in diminishing any positive emotion, experience, or regard from others. Shame becomes an omnipotent organizer of the sense of self (Chefetz, 2000). The psychodynamics of shame-related experience are often exceedingly complex and impervious to the winds of change.

Shame is a core emotion of some complexity and can imbue a state of mind. But I now see that my proposed opposite of shame, dignity, is more of a personal quality than a feeling that can form part of an emotional aspect of a state of mind. Dignity is also not something a person is likely to declare they feel in the same way somebody might say "I feel ashamed." While I will continue to talk with my patients about assaults on their dignity and safeguarding their dignity from their self-generated attacks or the attacks of others, I'm no longer satisfied with dignity as an affectively alive opposite of shame. What feeling IS the opposite of shame? If we can't articulate this, then do we really understand shame, or can we fully understand attackment?

We often talk about shame without qualifying the specificity with which we might alternatively speak of embarrassment, humiliation, or mortification. Moreover, the shame spectrum has its aggressive pecking-order aspects in relational terms that become immediately visible in considering contempt and disgust, as well as Tomkins' less well-known primary affect dis-smell, the identification of something that "stinks," or someone who is "a stinker." Tomkins' work can also guide us in searching further for an opposite to shame. We need more and better language to talk about shame, an experience that can leave us mute. Shame is the affect modifier that appears as the intensity of positive affects suddenly decrease. Is there an affect modifier that appears as the intensity of positive affects increase? Is that feeling obviously also the opposite of a feeling of shame, either acute or chronic?

Before continuing the important search for an opposite to shame, one other aspect of shame experience ought to be noted: shame is always relational (DeYoung, 2015; Trumbull, 2003), an evaluative emotion judging self from elsewhere, even when the evaluation is about me judging myself. While shame may occur in an individual, without apparent attack from another, the brutality of the internal attacks of one aspect of self on another aspect meets with no protective barrier of protest at being treated poorly, an "inside job." These are often the most intractable in psychotherapy. Chronic shame is certainly of this ilk. Just like Freud's prescient mechanism of taking a part of the ego as an object in melancholia (Freud, 1917), such use of an aspect of self is the case in shame. However, we now have the relative luxury of an appreciation of the organization of mind as one of multiple self-states to sometimes account for repetitive self-negation, self-disgust, and self-hatred. These psychodynamics (Chefetz, 2019) are often the presenting complaint in dissociative identity disorder.

The shaming of love

In looking for the opposite of shame in the form an affect modifier that appears with increasing positive emotion, love is a complex and intense emotion that ought to be considered. Love is powerful enough that its capacity to positively skew perception of the emotional and other qualities of a person may lead to the age-old conclusion that love is blind. Love can also imbue a state. What kind of love is this that appears as positive emotions intensify?

But wait, isn't love a bit unwieldy to be considered in a serious discussion of the work of a psychotherapy? Isn't it the subject of the poets and the other arts rather than being part of a scientific psychology? Wouldn't we all be at risk of being accused of tree-hugging and other somewhat fringe ideas if love were held as having clinical value, a real place in a psychotherapy? Isn't it folly to think we can love our patients into health? Certainly, that's true. But nevertheless, is it possible for somebody to even begin to heal from chronic shame in a psychotherapy if love can't show its face? Must the appearance of love in psychotherapy be shunned, banished, eyes averted, cast down, and then be cast out? Is it not with the greatest of caution and qualification that a clinician might declare they felt a kind of love for their patient? Wouldn't the wise clinician just talk about the feeling of being "fond" of a patient? Wouldn't it be easy for a patient to disastrously misinterpret a clinician talking about loving them as a romantic intrusion and invitation? Who would be so naïve as to say to their patient: "I love you."

Freud appreciated that love and hate were not all that different; both preoccupy the owner of the feeling, both entangle, and both hold two people in an intense relationship, painful or not. He reasoned that the opposite of love was indifference (Freud, 1915). Sharing my excitement about the potentials I saw in love as a positive affect modifier that increased emotional intensity, my psychoanalyst wife, Kathryn, was quick to point out that indifference was shaming (personal communication, Kathryn J. Chefetz, LICSW, July 25, 2018). We were both then immediately captured by the resonance of shame as part of all the insecure infant attachment models (Chefetz, 2017), and how a loving relationship can form the basis for felt safety in a secure attachment. Kathryn also qualified the opposite of feeling ashamed as feeling beloved. This love is neither of the erotic variety, eros, nor of the brotherly kind, philos. It is firmly rooted in the love that is given because it is needed, required, a love called agape. This is a love that is felt when one heart gently holds another and validates dignity, valuing the essence of all living things while acknowledging our vulnerability (Hicks & Tutu, 2011). There is little discussion about the role of agape in a psychotherapeutic relationship. I am not talking about some kind of "clinical love" as a construct. I'm talking about love that becomes part of and grows inside a relationship between two people who relate intensely.

The Jungian analyst, Kenneth Lambert, can take credit for having the only paper on agape in all of PEP-Web's holdings (Lambert, 1973). He describes the dictionary definition of agape as "…'love, generosity, kindly concern, devotedness' or…the verb agapao which is 'to love, value, esteem, feel or manifest generous concern for, be faithful towards, to delight in, to set store upon'." There is something other than the erotic or brotherly attitude in agape and agapao that speaks to the opposite of shaming: value, esteem, faithful, to delight in, etc. Dignity is visible in this language. To shame is to degrade. To love is to uphold and value in the sense of agapao. To feel beloved is to know the dignity of a confirmed and enduring positive and growth promoting relationship, to be cherished. Chronic shame is often about feeling unlovable. It is painful to be caught in the internal meat-grinder of fear without solution. Seeking proximity for safety while simultaneously making an effort to resolve fear with contemptuous distancing can create confusion in the seeker of safety as well as the one who is sought while being pushed away. It could also generate the pull push dynamics we sometimes see in patients who have experienced inconsistent and unpredictable caregiving, as experienced by many survivors of trauma and abuse. These dynamics of "don't leave me, stay away from me" are often encountered in patients who have been labelled as "borderline." This is also typically found in people who have "dissociative identity disorder," as Adriano Schimmenti (personal communication, September 10, 2018) reminded me. Attachment system dynamics meld with ranking system demands. Both systems try and reduce fear. Controlling behaviors may maintain attachment (Lyons-Ruth, 2008), but with a price. Activation of competitive-ranking systems deactivates attachment (Liotti, 2011).

In attackment-based relationships, shame in constellation with fear is supplanted by a toxic brew of shame mixed with terror. This is a more intense and physiologically destabilizing level of arousal. Importantly, terror in the child is celebrated by the sadistic perpetrator who humiliates the child for their emotional collapse and derides their worthlessness with emphatic disgust. Once referred to as a "sitting duck" (Kluft, 1990), the child with amnesia for their abuse, a not uncommon occurrence, is subject to repeat what their personal recollection of history cannot tell them until it's too late. In those moments of personal recognition at having fallen once again into a trap there is a cementing in place of feelings of incompetence, loss of agency, and a collapse of the self that is somewhere beyond mortification. This is the stuff out of which attackments seem to emerge. The desperation to avoid such a collapse or terror is ample motivation to create distance, as necessary, and at all costs, regardless of coincident active attachment needs for proximity. Attackment grows out of a double-bind.

Feeling beloved is certainly at the opposite side of the world from feeling ashamed. Love heals. Shame wounds. Love is a complex emotion and so is shame. Assaults on dignity destroy love and conjure shame. Sadistic abuse makes a mockery of the notion of dignity or feeling beloved. Attackment, in a word, conjures misery in a prison of failed, painful relatedness. Nobody can get in, and nobody can get out. There may only be a visitor's area, a meeting place negotiated with see-through walls. Emotion can't get across the barrier. Intimacy is forbidden by the internal guards. Attackment dynamics create impossible binds on behavior. This is made worse when dissociative processes and a multiple self-state organization of mind are adaptively present. The possibilities for maintaining interpersonal affective awareness is undermined through sequestration of felt-knowing in different states.

Infant attachment and terror

Arietta Slade made clear that the evolutionary and adaptive proximity seeking of an infant was activated by fear, and that the non-matching responses of parents became represented in the child's patterns of insecure attachment (Slade, 2014). For the parent who alternates between frightened and frightening (or unresponsive) behaviors, the parents' disorganization leaves the child with an insoluble dilemma in not being able to approach the supposed caregiver, leading to incoherence, disorientation, and dysregulation. What kind of internal working model does sadistic abuse leave in its wake? Activation of dissociative processes provides an escape from fear when there is no escape (Putnam, 1992).

Slade cites Porges regarding the psychological collapse represented by immobilizing and unspeakable fear that mimics death (as if in the paw of the lion) (Porges & Furman, 2011) and is concordant with "...resistant (fight), avoidant (flight), or disorganized/disoriented (freezing) patterns..." (p. 257) in attachment research. While this feels like an oversimplification to me, the notion of immobilization and conjuring of both sympathetic activation and parasympathetic deactivation, simultaneously, from the tugs and pulls of differently endowed self-states is the stuff out of which confusion in relatedness is present on a physiological level, too. Attackment patterns, in my view, are less about the lion's paw and more about being "in the belly of the whale," swallowed up whole, taken over, in terror and then beyond it, fully depersonalized, numb, being in a wholly new world, an unfamiliar place of captivity (Herman, 1992). This is the place from which the child floats up to the ceiling after the rape and looks down upon the poor kid being savaged on the mattress below, a dissociative not-me experience. Identity alteration creates the "glad that's not happening to me experience," while depersonalization rescues the survivor from the lion, but traps them in the bloody guts of a world that is invisible to others. It leaves them confused and unable to discern what's going on from their newly disembodied and disoriented place. Emotional deadness may hide terror and pain, and these may be made even more difficult to reach with the isolation of multiple self-states in DID. Shame-rage may only be activated with renewed threat leading to sudden confused and violent responses. To put it another way, Alice in Wonderland has gone down the rabbit hole and there's no visible means of return. One patient responded with self-directed violence after a therapy session where we touched just for a moment on a scene of abuse which I had no idea we were actually discussing. Their sentiment was that they got violent when terrified and the only thing they felt they could do was to destroy things until they were exhausted, and then the terror somehow passed.

I agree with Slade's preference to interpret her patient's behaviors as in the service of seeking safety. The password in working with people who experience dissociative states is adaptive self-protection. Acting to protect self is enlivening and speaks to an ongoing sense of dignity, even in extremis. I prefer not to use the word "defense," however historically apt it might be. Words are important.

Punitive controlling behaviors and errors in communication

Controlling behaviors in attachment disorganization tended to emerge around the age of six in the study of disorganized attachment (Liotti, 2011; Lyons-Ruth, 2003). In the service of trying to understand the roots of attackment patterns, attachment disorganization is poised to occupy a central role. The attachment system fails to find a solution to the child's fear when the parenting figure's frightening behaviors over-activate adrenalin release in the child and prompt the dilemma of fright-fight-flight that runs counter to movement toward an attachment figure. Liotti speaks to this problem from the perspective of controlling behaviors when he proposes:

> The activation of the caregiving system (Solomon & George, 1996) in the service of a defensive inhibition of the attachment system yields controlling caregiving strategies in the child. The activation of the dominance-submission inborn strategies in a competitive or ranking system: (Gilbert, 1989, 2005) lies at the base of controlling punitive strategies.
>
> (Liotti, 2011, p. 237)

Both caregiving and ranking systems inhibit the attachment system. In sadistic abuse the punitive controlling strategy enlarges and intensifies when years are spent "in the belly of the whale" and parental behaviors are not simply inconsistent and fear-provoking but are intentionally destructive of selfhood and the independence of the body and mind of the child.

The insidious nature of these processes is brought further into the light as Lyons-Ruth noticed that maltreatment by parents is associated with attachment disorganization but only at the level of fifteen percent of the sample she examined. On top of that, insensitive parenting is poorly correlated with attachment disorganization. So, what could predict the trajectory of infants toward attachment disorganization if neither maltreatment nor insensitivity, two trusted landmarks of attachment insecurity, were not responsible for attachment disorganization? Her team advanced two hypotheses. First, did parents display competing or contradictory strategies? Second, was overall parental behavior experienced as unresponsive to the child's attachment bids? Described by the overarching term of "errors in communication," I discussed this template with one of my long-term patients whose negativity and attacks on the meaning of the psychotherapy relationship to which she was simultaneously deeply committed was robust. She almost came out of her chair with an enthusiastic endorsement of the reality of these experiences with her very dissociative mother. My patient could endorse all five patterns of these disrupted parental communication styles:

> ...a.) parental withdrawing responses, b.) negative intrusive responses, c.) role-confused responses, d.) disoriented responses, and, e.) a set of responses termed affective communication errors, which included both simultaneous conflicting affective cues to the infant and failures to respond to clear affective signals from the infant.
>
> (Lyons-Ruth, 2003, p. 108)

What might an adult psychotherapy correlate be of such a behavior by a clinician? How would you rate the experience for an already destabilized patient to have their therapist slowly bring them back to sessions they were refusing to attend, only to find that their therapist had double-booked the hour? Even though the other patient readily agreed to return at a different time, my already destabilized patient could not tolerate being in the office, and summarily left. (They did attend their next appointment.) Are there any older clinicians who have had the experience of their less than optimal hearing misleading them about what their patient said and so making an off-key remark, then even mistaking the words of the patient's protest as they mumbled their indignation and the clinician mistakenly doubling-down on their error? There's not much need for an imagination about these things when there is already easy access to these kinds of errors in communication. But who reports these kinds of things when describing their work? And, if a clinician is actively destabilized by the verbal assaults of the patient that are clearly meant to hurt, then who has not replied out of anger to such an attack with less than a gracious reply?

An attackment scene

Let's pick up with Scylla, the woman we met earlier, when she was in her seventh year of twice weekly psychoanalytic psychotherapy (I've written about her elsewhere (Chefetz, 2015)). She sat across from me and taunted me by alternately convincing me of her dangerousness and of being actively at risk of suicide, after which she deftly undermined what she had said by assuring me of her safety. I had never got used to this kind of communication. Talk about errors in communication. I was getting an earful. This had been going on, more and less, since the beginning of our work together. Recently, it had become a regular occurrence. I was exhausted by these crises. Seven years of crises like these was a long time. She expertly made the case for dying at her own hands. She had nearly succeeded in doing that three times before I had begun working with her, once leading to a week in the ICU recovering from an overdose that ought to have destroyed her liver, but somehow didn't. I had discovered she was capable of persuading clinicians to prescribe large amounts of benzodiazepines. I learned this early in our relationship. She was taking nearly 40 mg of clonazepam a day. I was dumbfounded that anybody could possibly walk or even be awake while taking that dose, but she did. Her howls of protest when I restricted her drug use went on for weeks, but there was simultaneously a tacit recognition that she knew I cared about her as I openly noted I would tolerate her protests if it meant keeping her safe.

Now, during in-between moments of her taunting me about her safety over nearly a half-hour, I found myself picking up the telephone next to my chair to call the police, and then putting it down, several times. I had become convinced that she used hospitalization to get her out of my office when we were making what I believed was progress. I didn't want to fall for that. Any progress was experienced by her as a threat. Giving her a break from our therapeutic work would do her no real good. On the other hand, if I was wrong about her safety outside the hospital she might be dead. I had met her husband, and, under various circumstances, the rest of her family, including her parents. Along with the loss I anticipated about losing a patient in whom I'd invested a lot of effort and had become fond of in her better moments, there was the painful thought of having to face her family if she died. She was a patient well-known to the staff of the hospital where she was often an inpatient, a hospital where I had trained, and I would be facing the responses of the staff, too, if she died. My personal shame scenarios were painful as I fantasized about her possible suicide.

She was somebody who used pills, razors, and cigarette burns to provoke internal order and shut down her mind, as necessary. She provoked dissociative experience when she couldn't just switch states and change the emotional music. The scars on her forearms created a washboard like surface. She had once cut herself so badly that I was prompted to put my old blood pressure cuff into service to quickly staunch the flow of blood from her arm. She'd cut herself before coming in to my office. Soon after she returned from the hospitalization provoked by that cutting she frightened herself by making a bloody scene of her bath and bedroom. In our ensuing conversation I told her that if she cut again it would mean there was obviously some way in which I'd failed to understand her. If I was somehow unable to figure out how to do that, then the psychotherapy relationship wasn't working. I'd have to refer her to somebody else. She would remind me of my statement when she lamented how much she wanted to cut herself but knew she couldn't risk losing me.

As she continued her "in-my-face" pendulating suicide predictions and retractions, I was struggling to make sense of what was happening while she, undeterred, continued to try and provoke me. Finally, in one last effort on her part to drive home her potential lethality, she both taunted me about killing herself and then withdrew the threat, again: "Nothing would make me feel better than to go home and slice myself open so that when he found me it would be much too late…But you don't really think I would do something like that, do you?" She delivered the last piece with a sarcastic grin as I picked up the telephone receiver, and slammed it down, and as what was left of my self-control broke I resorted to what in more relaxed times I called the use of "technical language." I said: "Dammit, get out. Fuck you, just get out! I'm not doing this anymore. Get out! Now!" I was sitting in my chair shaking with rage and embarrassment, having just cursed and yelled at her and then forcefully silenced myself in horror at the boundary I had crossed over in my verbal lashing out. Then, the most remarkable thing happened. She changed her expression completely, and with her arms outstretched toward me as if she were trying to quieten an upset child, she gently told me:

It's okay. I'm sorry, but I had to know what you would do if you lost it. You're always so damned calm. I can never really tell what you're thinking or feeling. I needed to know. Can you understand why? I just needed to know how you'd behave.

I had been played, and quite well at that. It was not my best moment, but I at least responded on cue and apparently had passed the test. The vehemence of my reaction is a clear memory, nearly fifteen years ago, and we are now approaching the last phase and the ending of her therapy. One might honestly wonder how we'd both got through it all.

Attackment and countertransference

Objective countertransference to attackment patterns of relating might seem like the general rule, but my personal experience is that subjective countertransference (Gorkin, 1987) reactivity is much more to the point and nearly always involves impasses via enactment. The danger of intimacy is palpable. Who has not heard of a clinician who dreads the coming appointment with a particular patient? I have thought that my willingness to work with people who had been severely traumatized was a fluke constructed of relentless serendipity: doing a second residency after ten years in practice as a family physician and becoming a psychiatrist put me on an inpatient service where my first three patients had DID. My fourth had schizophrenia. My fifth and sixth patients had DID. I thought this was a rarity. Had I fallen through my own rabbit hole? Apparently.

My view of the inside of the belly of a whale showed me the wonders of destructive human behavior that few people discussed or even seemed to know about. It was, after all, a killer of social conversation with the uninitiated. People went blank or made excuses to go elsewhere. My close friends were more to the point: "I really can't listen to this. I don't know how you do what you're doing." I'm talking about my psychiatrist friends, not my tennis partners. One senior psychoanalyst, an actual tennis partner, said to me it looked as if I'd had a hard day. I told him a bit about the acuity in my practice that day. He said he appreciated that I saw people who were suicidal: "Nobody else will. I admire you for it. I'm glad you are doing it. Somebody needs to do it." I think that was a compliment, but I'm not sure, exactly.

Why am I doing this work? How do I react to it, and particularly, what is my role in attackment processes with my patients? I'm going to try and spell out some of the things I've learned about me in this process, and I'm doing this in the hope that the uninitiated, or less initiated, will benefit.

The countertransference themes with which I've worked and which I'm willing to openly note are these: a fear of humiliation, a fear of rage in others and in me, a willingness to suffer in the service of another person healing, and a determination to honor the honest request of somebody to help them. I will work hard to sustain the therapy relationship even if somebody fight's like hell to get out of their commitment at the same time they fear I'll abandon them and warn me to never ever consider backing out. As one person said, "That happened to me once before, and I don't think I could survive that again."

My fear of humiliation has become accessible to me more recently as I now appreciate the dynamics of my own childhood in which both my parents participated. From my mother's struggles with her own anxieties came my earliest experiences with being shamed. She was oblivious to her contempt, and still is, not out of malice, but because the earnestness and desperateness to reduce her own anxieties by doing the right thing, as she sees it, over-rules any other person's thoughts, feelings, or mindfulness. To have one's mind summarily dismissed takes in the drift. From my father was his loving over-correction of signs of anger or rage in me that were familiar to him in his own childhood, and for which he was severely punished. Like Peter Fonagy's notion of the alien self, I had learned to over-rate my own anger and rage as dangerous and destructive, not because it was any more potent than anybody else's anger or rage, but because if it existed, then I believe my father reasoned I'd suffer like he did. So, he worked pretty hard to banish it from me. At the same time these things are true, both my parents loved me deeply in ways that were also satisfying and reassuring. Still, the discordance between their conflicting and contrasting behaviors left me struggling in ways that my patients have deftly exhumed, sometimes without my cooperation. I suspect errors in communication may appear from within a parental dyad. Sometimes I duplicated in myself the very behaviors in which they engaged and then tried to erase in me. These understandings have taken a long time and are deeply complex. It's been worth the work, I believe, for me, for my family, and for my patients.

This is not a confession. This is by way of saying that my severely abused patients have taught me about these previously unknowable aspects of who I am and who I have been. I've been willing to listen and learn, and they've been gracious in not sending me a bill for their work. Some of my early psychotherapy relationships foundered and did not recover. In those days, I wasn't even aware of the countertransference potentials on these levels. Self-advertised as a nice person, the normal discourse of my own personal psychotherapy did not even vaguely approach the intensity of these feelings. I think that's pretty much the norm. Given my work in consultation for other clinicians with difficult and complex psychotherapy clients I have come to understand that. It also gives me pause to regard their struggles with the utmost respect and compassion. Restoring or just maintaining the dignity of people for whom I consult on a professional level is very important. The same goes for my patients. We are all patients, really. We're just at different points on the trajectory of healing.

I'm identifying personal issues with shame, humiliation, anger, rage, contempt, disgust, and related core affective issues as having a central place in the genesis of attackment relationships. Even if it turns out I might hug an occasional special tree, I'm still thinking about feeling ashamed, feeling beloved, and the ways out of attackment relating. It might very well be that each clinician has to locate the lovable-ness in them and in their patient in order for their work together to mature and ripen. It's also true that we can't require that our patients locate the lovable-ness in their therapist or we destroy their emotional freedom (Searles, 1967). We have to tolerate being hated, having intense anger come at us at high velocity, and we have to have a place within us where we keep in view, most of the time, the beloved imprisoned person in our patient who is too frightened to emerge or be known. We have to tolerate another chorus of "I'm shit and deserve to die." We have to listen to the music that's alive in our patients even as they grab another free ride on the road to hell. Sometimes we must act to protect them at the same time that they object most strenuously.

Most of all, I believe we need to know what being brought to our knees is like, to know what despair, terror, hopelessness, and the like are about in our bellies, the whale guts of it. We must dare to tolerate holding hope, respect, dignity, and compassion alongside the worst life has to dish out, up front and personal. I can't always do this, but I think that sometimes I approximate it. It sometimes seems to be good enough. Time will tell if it is, or not.

Just before a recent vacation started, Scylla wrote to me and we had a brief exchange. She's come a long way since attackment days:

> i am having terrible anxiety knowing that you are starting your time off at the end of the week. its not that i think its not right, it just scares the hell out of me because you are the only person in the world i trust. i just feel so sad.

> I'm glad you trust me, Scylla. Do you think there might be some other people out there you might grow to trust? How could that happen? It's OK to be scared. It will pass. It's OK to be sad. That will pass, too. The challenge is to engage in living and have all your feelings. What do you think?

> i know i am suppose [sic] to live my life and have trust in the people that i know love me and would never hurt me, but sometimes they do because they just can't understand what is in my mind and not just assume something without knowing. i always miss you when you're gone and i know i will this time also. its so hard sometimes to keep pushing forward. i am so depressed and i think i will probably cry all day. its just a process i have to go through.

References

Benau, K. (2018). Pride in the psychotherapy of relational trauma: Conceptualization and treatment considerations. *European Journal of Trauma & Dissociation*, *2*, 131–146.

Bowlby, J. (1944). Forty-four juvenile thieves: Their characters and home-life. *International Journal of Psychoanalysis*, *25*, 19–53.

Chefetz, R. A. (2000). Disorder in the therapist's view of the self: Working with the person with dissociative identity disorder. *Psychoanalytic Inquiry*, *20*, 305–329.

Chefetz, R. A. (2003). Healing haunted hearts – toward a model for integrating sub-jectivity: commentary on papers by Philip Bromberg and Gerald Stechler. *Psy-choanalytic Dialogues, 13*, 727–742.

Chefetz, R. A. (2015). *Intensive Psychotherapy for Persistent Dissociative Processes: The Fear of Feeling Real*. New York: Norton.

Chefetz, R. A. (2017). Dignity is the opposite of shame, and pride is the opposite of guilt. *Attachment: New Directions in Psychotherapy and Relational Psychoanaly-sis, 11*, 119–133.

Chefetz, R. A. (2019). Dissociative processes bias the psychodynamics underlying the subjective experience of self and the organization of mind. In D. Kealy & J. S. Ogrodniczuk (Eds.), *Contemporary Psychodynamic Psychotherapy*, (pp. 295–305). New York: Academic Press.

DeYoung, P. A. (2015). *Understanding and Treating Chronic Shame: A Relational/ Neurobiological Approach*. London: Routledge.

Freud, S. (1915). *Instincts and Their Vicissitudes. S. E.*, 14: 111–140. London: Hogarth Press.

Freud, S. (1917). *Mourning and Melancholia. S. E.*, 14: 239–258. London: Hogarth Press.

Freyd, J. J. (1996). *Betrayal Trauma Theory: The Logic of Forgetting Abuse*. Cambridge, MA: Harvard.

Gilbert, P. (1989). *Human Nature and Suffering*. Mahwah, NJ: Lawrence Erlbaum.

Gilbert, P. (2005). Social mentalities: A biopsychosocial and evolutionary ap-proach to social relationships. In M. W. Baldwin (Ed.), *Interpersonal Cognition*, (pp. 299–333). New York: Guilford Press.

Gorkin, M. (1987). *The Uses of Countertransference*. Northvale, NJ: Jason Aronson.

Herman, J. L. (1992). *Trauma and Recovery*. New York: Basic Books.

Hicks, D., & Tutu, D. (2011). *Dignity: The Essential Role It Plays in Resolving Conflict*. New Haven, CT: Yale University Press.

Kluft, R. P. (1990). Incest and subsequent revictimization: The case of the therapist-patient sexual exploitation, with a description of the sitting duck syn-drome. In R. P. Kluft (Ed.), *Incest-Related Syndromes of Adult Psychopathology*, (pp. 263–287). Washington, DC: American Psychiatric Press.

Kluft, R. P. (1999). An overview of the psychotherapy of dissociative identity disor-der. *American Journal of Psychotherapy, 53*, 289–319.

Lambert, K. (1973). Agape as a therapeutic factor in analysis. *Journal of Analytical Psychology, 18*, 25–46.

Lewis, H. B. (1987). *The Role of Shame in Symptom Formation*. Hillsdale, NJ: Lawrence Earlbaum.

Liotti, G. (2011). Attachment disorganization and the controlling strategies: An illustration of the contributions of attachment theory to developmental psycho-pathology and to psychotherapy integration. *Journal of Psychotherapy Integra-tion, 21*, 232.

Lyons-Ruth, K. (2003). The two-person construction of defenses: Disorganized at-tachment strategies, unintegrated mental states, and hostile/helpless relational processes. *Journal of Infant, Child, and Adolescent Psychotherapy, 2*, 105.

Lyons-Ruth, K. (2008). Contributions of the mother-infant relationship to disso-ciative, borderline, and conduct symptoms in young adulthood. *Infant Mental Health Journal, 29*, 203–218.

Middleton, W. (2013). Parent–child incest that extends into adulthood: A survey of international press reports, 2007–2011. *Journal of Trauma & Dissociation, 14,* 184–197.

Nathanson, D. L. (1992). *Shame and Pride: Affect, Sex, and the Birth of the Self.* New York: Norton.

Ogden, P., Minton, K., & Pain, C. (2006). *Trauma and the Body: A Sensorimotor Approach to Psychotherapy.* New York: Norton.

Porges, S. W., & Furman, S. A. (2011). The early development of the autonomic nervous system provides a neural platform for social behavior: A polyvagal perspective. *Infant and Child Development, 20,* 106–118.

Putnam, F. (1992). Discussion: Are alter personalities fragments or figments. *Psychoanalytic Inquiry, 12,* 95–111.

Scheff, T. J., & Retzinger, S. M. (2001). *Emotions and Violence: Shame and Rage in Destructive Conflicts.* Lincoln, Nebraska: iUniverse.

Searles, H. (1967). The dedicated physician. In R. W. Gibson (Ed.), *Crosscurrents in Psychiatry and Psychoanalysis,* (pp. 128–143). Philadelphia, PA: Lippincott.

Slade, A. (2014). Imagining fear: Attachment, threat, and psychic experience. *Psychoanalytic Dialogues, 24,* 253–266.

Solomon, J., & George, C. (1996). Defining the caregiving system: Toward a theory of caregiving. *Infant Mental Health Journal, 17,* 183–197.

Tomkins, S. S., & McCarter, R. (1995). What and where are the primary affects? Some evidence for a theory. In E. V. Demos (Ed.), *Exploring Affect: The Selected Writings of Silvan S. Tomkins,* (pp. 217–262). New York: Cambridge University Press.

Trumbull, D. (2003). Shame: An acute stress response to interpersonal traumatization. *Psychiatry, 66,* 53–64.

Waters, H. S., & Waters, E. (2006). The attachment working models concept: Among other things, we build script-like representations of secure base experiences. *Attachment & Human Development, 8,* 185–197.

Wille, R. (2014). The shame of existing: An extreme form of shame. *The International Journal of Psychoanalysis, 95,* 695–717.

Chapter 5

Shame and black identity wounding

The legacy of internalised oppression

Aileen Alleyne

I would like to start with the quote used in the synopsis of my talk at the conference *Shame Matters*:

> In the words of a black client: 'Shame told me there was something fundamentally wrong with me and those who looked like me. Society said so and I accepted that I was inferior; I was the Other; I was a mistake. Life then became a task to do rather than a journey to enjoy. I had bought into the lie'.

In this poignant quote, we can clearly identify the tenets of *black identity shame* and *identity wounding*, which will be the focus of my chapter through the lens of the black experience. I will be using black to describe anyone with known African heritage or who can be discriminated against because of the colour of their skin.

But first, a word about the emotion shame itself.

Shame makes us feel essentially flawed, and in that sense it IS a damn good thing, because none of us is perfect. I have not met a supreme being! Have you? So, being flawed is what makes us human. This human quality of being imperfect and feeling incomplete means that we all – to an extent – carry shame. Psychotherapy in one form or another, enables us to strive towards a sense of wholeness … completeness, even though we will never get there. The journey is a lifelong pursuit. One good aspect of shame is that it allows us to have a conscience; that sense of guilt, of right and wrong, when we transgress personal and societal standards, values, and boundaries. It keeps us civilised and respectful towards each other. So, it is good to have some shame.

But, to return to the afore-mentioned quote: when society tells you (unconsciously, and more consciously these days), that your God-given features are less than inferior, and wrong, then these racial and cultural signifiers become the genesis for toxic shame and deep identity wounding.

Identity shame in the black context is an intersectional issue. The concept of *intersectionality* was coined in 1989 by American legal scholar, Kimberlé

DOI: 10.4324/9781003175612-6

Crenshaw (1996). The concept is not an abstract notion, but a description of the way multiple oppressions are experienced. For those who may not be too familiar with the concept, consider intersectionality as analogous to traffic at a crossroad. The traffic is coming and going in all four directions. Discrimination, like traffic at a crossroad, may flow in one direction or it may flow in another. If an accident happens at the crossroad, it can be caused by cars travelling from any number of directions and, sometimes, from all of them. Similarly, if a black person is hurt in this accident situation, namely racially offended or discriminated against at the crossroad, their wounding could result from sex and gender discrimination, race discrimination, ethnicity discrimination or class discrimination, religious or faith discrimination. But it is not always easy to prove the extent of the accident (personal wounding). What is clear, however, is that the skid marks and injuries simply indicate that an accident has occurred, but how it was caused is not so easily identifiable. This is what makes identity wounding in the context of race so difficult to address. Crenshaw argues that Black people are discriminated against in ways that often do not fit neatly within the legal categories of either "racism" or "sexism" or "classism". And for these complex unheeded reasons, black identity wounding and shame go forever unnoticed.

The experience of shame and black identity wounding as discussed thus far must be understood against the backdrop of *intergenerational trauma and transgenerational trauma*. However, I must point out that black people do not monopolise this identity trauma. The grandchildren of Holocaust survivors were overrepresented by 300 percent among the referrals to child psychiatry clinics in comparison with their representation in the general population. Combat veterans, hostages, prisoners of war, and modern-day migrants from war torn countries and genocidal dictatorships, who are both survivors and witnesses of atrocities and traumatic events, transfer secondary trauma to subsequent generations with devastating mental health consequences. But, to me, it feels like when it comes to the black Diaspora, the clear manifestations of this Complex Trauma are overlooked. The word "trauma" with respect to Trans- and Intergenerational Trauma, describes long lasting experiences and situations that are psychologically and emotionally injurious to people, rendering them powerless, wanting, and struggling for their fully individuated status in society. Intergenerational trauma should, in my opinion, be recognised in a separate category of a Type 3 Complex Trauma, because of its very specific nature. The American Psychiatric Association and the World Health Organization provide distinct trauma-based diagnoses in the fifth edition of the Diagnostic and Statistical Manual (DSM-5), and the forthcoming 11th version of the International Classification of Diseases (ICD-11), respectively. DSM-5 conceptualises post-traumatic stress disorder (PTSD) as a single, broad diagnosis, whereas ICD-11 proposes two "sibling-disorders" of PTSD and Complex PTSD (CPTSD). Although various forms of complex trauma are listed, none sufficiently explicates the prolonged history of subjugation of many indigenous peoples of the world by white foreign invaders, who invaded with impunity and the appropriated the wealth of those nations for their own purposes and benefits. For Caribbean and black African peoples, British Colonisation and its 400 years of British rule that bolstered the British Empire, has created one of the most complex – even disorganised – attachments between these races.

One text that has stimulated my thinking regarding considerations for a new and revisionary DSM-V – or possible addition to a DSM-V1, is the paper by Lenore Terr (1991), *Childhood traumas: An outline and overview*. In her scholarly work on trauma, Terr highlights crossovers of Type I (single incident traumas) and Type II (interpersonal and relationship, e.g. betrayals) psychological trauma. The complexity of trauma elucidated in this research has led me to think of further crossing overs into the unrecognised dimensions of historical trauma that should warrant fuller and formal recognition for this proposed new *Type III Complex Trauma category.*

Cycle of Events (Alleyne, 1993, 2006) – the roots and cycle of black identity shame

As illustrated in Figure 5.1, Cycle of Events, Intergenerational Trauma and Transgenerational Trauma occur when untreated trauma experienced by the survivors is passed on to second and subsequent generations. In other words, what is overwhelming and unnameable is transferred to those to whom we are closest. How does this happen? Transmission of historical trauma gets passed on in the following ways:

- through parenting practices;
- by family scripts that shape our thinking and behaviours;
- from our internalised beliefs and value systems;
- from the impact on our mental health as we face societal and personal challenges in everyday life.

Epigenetic studies hint at the parents' own experiences of trauma possibly changing the child's stress hormone profiles. This makes transgenerational trauma an excellent area for further evidencing of historical trauma impacting on the cellular structure and gene makeup of subsequent generations in damaging ways.

The legacy of this cultural malady with its roots in racism and racial oppression is pernicious and destructive. The human tragedy of slavery inevitably reminds us of terrible atrocities that were carried out on a wide spread industrial scale, by mainly so-called enlightened people with high civil values for their own people. But, when it came to the African, these values had neither place nor relevance. Until the nineteenth century, African slavery

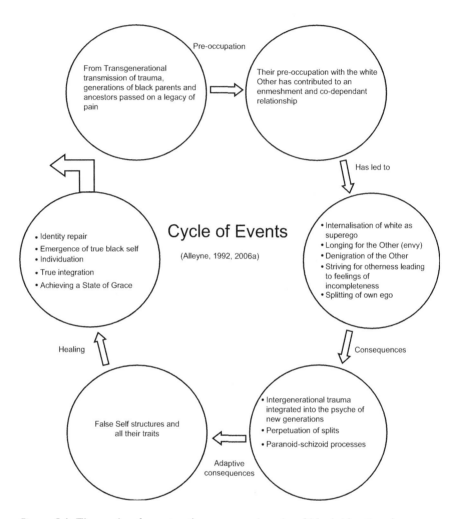

Figure 5.1 The cycle of events: the roots and cycle of black identity shame.

was considered an acceptable economic system in Britain and many other countries in Europe. It was condoned by politicians and businessmen, and even scientists and churches justified the legitimacy of this practice, which we now recognise as morally reprehensible.

I believe it is the discomfort that comes from such incongruously different attitudes towards this race of people that makes the trauma so painful for black people. I recall a client asking in total bewilderment as she spoke about her very painful experiences of blatant racism in her workplace. *Why is it we black people always get placed at the bottom of everything – why does the colour of our skin evoke such negative and ugly reactions?* The legacy of

pain and hurt and anger about our past is never too far away from consciousness. For some of us, this legacy makes for an attachment with such a past
an avoidant and detached one, because to remember, is to keep alive what is
unbearable. For others, this painful history is constantly alive, thus creating
an enmeshment – an over-attachment with the past – that can cause historical wounds to be continually re-opened in the present. Historical wounds
compound our wounds in the present, and I think it is this constant re-
opening and the re-tracing of these traumatic historical imprints that make
black identity wounding an ongoing process of intergenerational trauma.

This silent impact of racism is still an unheeded phenomenon. And it does
not help when it is said that

> "slavery is something that happened such a long time ago", ... "we can't
> keep looking backwards, we must look forward", or ... "I don't want to
> be made to feel guilty for something I didn't do…so please don't burden
> me with your feelings".

Pretentious curiosity is no better either, because its flakiness is always so
palpably felt by the receiver as disingenuous and fake.

All these responses may feel valid to the responder, but I do believe that
the lack of attention and detachment from the impact of black historical
trauma, demean the dreadful issue in a way that for example, the holocaust
is not demeaned. The holocaust – everyone knows – is not just an issue for
Jews. It is something that defines everyone's humanity: you cannot properly
be a human being without knowing something about the holocaust –
probably the most awesome crime ever committed in world history. The fact
is, this is also true of African slavery, but we relate to this racial abomina-
tion so very differently. Even though it is everyone's shame and everyone's
loss, this second terrible crime is allowed to be forgotten, in a way which I
believe, creates an added trauma and ever-present identity shame alive for
black people to endure on their own. It makes me wonder why these three
poignant words – "*Lest we forget*" have no commemorative value nor place
for black lives.

The world's forgetfulness, its neglect of something so huge, increases the
anguish and in turn, keeps something of the old shame wound alive within
the wronged. Being forgotten creates a sense of not being valued – and leads
to a kind of damaging, stubborn indwelling on the old wound so as not to
have it forgotten. I believe it is this turning inwards, this bind with the past,
that keeps black people so entangled in the cycle of the transgenerational
transmission of trauma and the resultant black identity shame.

I am suggesting therefore, that the trauma of carrying alone something
so monumentally significant makes it difficult to let go of the past, a phenomenon which Bowlby saw as unresolved grief, a grief which overlays these
conflicts with another between the effort to recapture the meaningful world

before the loss. Yet how can black people recapture and mourn something that is still ongoing and unresolved? I believe this trauma interferes consciously and unconsciously with our self-structure, and ultimately contributes to difficulties in present day relating. This is the legacy of pain that we need to let go, to achieve our full individuation and collective healing process.

Several notable writers have addressed the black experience in relation to the white Other. Frantz Fanon (1986) has pointed to the dynamic of "when the Negro makes contact with the white world, a certain sensitizing action takes place. If his psychic structure is weak, one observes a collapse of the ego" (p. 154). In this quote, he is addressing self-esteem and shame-based issues for black people. Fletchman Smith (2000, 2011), Lipsky (1987), and Joy DeGruy-Leary (2005) have all talked about a "post-traumatic [slave] syndrome", which they describe in their own way, as pathology arising from the damage of holding on to ancestral baggage. Their theory suggests that centuries of the painful history of slavery followed by systemic racism and oppression have resulted in multigenerational adaptive behaviours, some of which have been positive and reflective of resilience, and others that are detrimental and destructive.

Madan Sarup (1996) has addressed in his works, the fact that identity is not an inherent construction but, arises from the interactions with others and the processes therein. His inclusion of history, psychological and sociological factors, labelling, our actions and their consequences, retroactive interpretations of events, he suggests, all shape the complex nature of both our "public identity" and "private identity". He also makes the point that any study of identity must be localised in *space* and *time*. It is my contention that the *time* (400 years) of slavery and colonisation has left in its wake, a space of untreated trauma, one manifestation of which is identity shame for black people.

I will highlight a few shame-based scripts that are passed down the generations. These are lifted verbatim from the recorded narratives of my research respondents. You may ponder on whether they are helpful or unhelpful to self-enhancement.

Cultural 'scripts' – entitlement or impediment?

Verbatim responses taken from doctoral research (Alleyne, 2006a).

Some of the more protective scripts are usually attributed to a general lack of trust – what William Grier and Price Cobbs (1969) refer to as "healthy paranoia". Grier and Cobbs were keen to make a distinction between clinical paranoid disorders and a healthy state of paranoia, the latter, considered to be adaptive behaviour developed from being mistrustful of Whites. This distinction has been supported by others in the field who remind health practitioners of the need to be flexible with Western criteria and values when

---

Scripts highlighting black archetypal experiences

1. "People will always see your colour first and personality second"
2. "We have to work twice as hard to be noticed"
3. "No matter how much we succeed; people will always try to beat you down"
4. "We can't afford to wash our dirty linen in public – that's like giving white people ammunition – we must stick together"

Scripts highlighting a defensive (protective) mindset and value system

1. "I am not interested in theory – I go by my instincts"
2. "What's the point in trying – you'll only get no for an answer"
3. "Promotion is not for me – it forces you to conform to the system – I don't want to lose who I am as a black person"
4. "I don't do deference where white people are concerned"
5. "I can never trust white people – I have a healthy disrespect where they are concerned"
6. "You can't afford to show vulnerability – people will walk all over you"
7. "When things get too much, I just walk away"
8. "You take me as you see me – what you see is what you get – like it or lump it"
9. "This is who I am – I say what's on my mind – ain't changing for no one"
10. "I don't trust anyone but myself"

---

determining what constitutes normality, abnormality, and mental disorders in specific cultural groups.

In my presentation at the John Bowlby Memorial Conference, I showed a short clip from the film *Dark Girls* that highlighted the theme of the talk – shame and black identity wounding (*Dark Girls,* Duke, & Channsin Berry, directors, 2011). This film, which can be found on the Oprah Winfrey Network, is an excellent teaching tool that highlights the ongoing struggle black people, particularly black women, still have with issues such as, their hair texture and skin tone (colourism or shadism). *Dark Girls* is a fascinating and controversial film that goes underneath the surface to explore the prejudices dark-skinned women face in the world. It explores the roots of classism, racism, and the lack of self-esteem within a segment of cultures. Natural black tightly curly hair is still measured negatively against the standards of (white) Western beauty. Colourism/shadism, which has always been a political and commercial issue, continues to contribute to complex issues of not being good enough. Put quite simply in this Caribbean rhyme, ... *"If you're white, you are right; if you are brown, stick around; if you are black, get the hell back"*. The ever-present shame and dissatisfaction with these racial aspects of self, are classic examples of identity shame throughout the black (and Asian) Diasporas.

It would take a separate paper, maybe even a book, to take a necessary sideways glance at the expressions of white colonial and imperial shame. I have much to say on this topic, but, for this chapter, I would like to offer one salient conclusion arrived at through what I will term, the abundance of evidential cultural phenomena. Three major events have unveiled the workings of white shame in recent times. They are, namely, Brexit, Covid-19, and the Black Lives Matter movement. Three little words with enormous impact. The tremendous impact from all three events threatens to destabilise and denude our ontological security.

Brexit, in my view, has particularly questioned white English identity, as we see it struggle to separate from the perceived *imperialist* rule by the European Union (EU). Language harping back to British colonial rule was and continues to be spouted in exalted Churchillian fashion in the ongoing battles for the UK to get what it wants on its terms. Being put on the back foot at every twist and turn and not getting their own way, has revealed the UK's exposure to identity shame.

In British society, and more specifically in England, Covid-19 has been personalised as if it were a human enemy that needs to be beaten into submission. As the fatalities grew to just over 40,000 in July 2020, the English establishment adopted language such as, *it will not defeat us*, while exercising the World War 2 "blitz spirit" to defeat Covid-19, the mortal enemy. The intrinsic script of *we will not be beaten; we will not surrender; we will not cow tow to this microscopic virus*, appeared to show the shame covering individuals who had an investment in maintaining some superior omnipotence in the face of the pandemic. A further shame covering was hidden in language once again, which spoke of *all of us being in this together*, which conveniently allowed shame to dissipate into a faux unity and togetherness.

The most recent notable impact of white shame has and continues to reveal itself in the powerful reverberations of the Black Lives Matter Movement struggle. White shame – and white vulnerability – are both being fiercely resisted in ways that resemble the struggle to keep white-pride's knickers from falling around its ankles, that is, being denuded of its former glorious imperial and colonial identity. The analogy of "knickers" is not in the least gratuitous, when you consider the origins of shame to be linked to prematurely uncovering that which if exposed reveals what is private, secret, and hidden.

The abundance of these *evidential cultural phenomena* leads me to conclude that, *the antidote to white arrogance is humility (and accountability)*, and here, I do not imply that humility should mean that a whole race of people should deny its proud self and achievements. But I point to a transparent fact that a lily-white, unblemished sensibility cannot allow for the experience of freedom from white shame. Yes, it is a fact that shame exposes. Shame denudes. Shame gets us instinctively in touch with our primitiveness. But to re-work shame therapeutically is to engage in a process of negotiating something akin to Klein's (1933) depressive position, where grieving and mourning the loss of the ideal must take place. To be able to engage in this important developmental healing process, is to allow a conscience to be truly developed for a sense of right and wrong to be fully embraced, and thence towards individuation and proper atonement. To ignore this work is to remain continually engaged in fight or flight responses, where the possession of a kind of English verbal gymnastics and shame cover, allowing a cultivated stance of *false* pride and arrogance to remain steadfastly in place. However, in this unstable position, I see white vulnerability and white shame residing precariously in its psychic glass house, forever hypervigilant of how it is seen and what it must protect – at all costs.

We do not have to look too far to find another white oppressive regime, Germany, to make a comparison. However, Germany, in my view, is an exemplar of how the oppressor can begin to think about and manage national identity shame and fulfil obligations to atone and honour necessary reparation programmes to deal with its crimes against humanity. Many can take a leaf out of Germany's historic book in this regard.

How do we address the shame phenomenon in the consulting room?

Firstly, acknowledge the impact of what I call a *Type 111 Complex Trauma*. This trauma is Historical, Collective, or Intergenerational, and is characterised by psychological or emotional difficulties, which can affect diverse minority groups and generations. Adaptive coping patterns can be passed on intergenerationally and affect subsequent generations in negative and damaging ways. Examples might include:

• Racism
• Slavery
• Forcible removal from a family, community, or country
• Genocide
• War

Meeting the impact of such trauma in the consulting room, therefore requires a trauma approach in the clinical work. I suggest that we work therapeutically with both manifest and latent contents of the client's presenting crisis and pain. And we must remember that pain and distress may well be occurring at the intersection of gender, race, class, ethnicity, sexuality, and disability.

Secondly, we should bear in mind that we are dealing with cultural and historical enmeshment, and as with all other enmeshment issues (whether family, mother/daughter, black/white relations), the aim of the work, is to help your client separate out from the co-dependent unhealthy attachment and re-enactment patterns, and individuate. As part of the separating out process, enable your client to achieve a deeper sense of reflexivity, which is a way of being in the world that is not shaped *only* by our environment and society, but by our own norms and values, tastes, desires, and dreams. To be reflexive is to have a sense of one's history, which is in continual development for self-awareness, and thus ideally, a self-assurance leading to a degree of autonomy and liberation.

Thirdly, offer psycho-education of the workings of "*The Internal Oppressor*" (Alleyne, 2006a, b) to better create understanding of the effects of holding onto re-activated historical trauma, which keeps psychic wounds alive and impedes our moving on process. The internal oppressor is distinct from internalised oppression in that it is an aspect of the self – it is part of the ego structure that functions as an internal adversary. It is the enemy within. Shame exists in this place where we are hostage to our past. Perhaps, a distinction between internalised oppression and *The Internal Oppressor* is worth delineating at this juncture. I see internalised oppression as the process of a person or group absorbing, sometimes believing and accepting an inferior status, imposed by the oppressor who perpetuates negative images, messages, stereotypes, information, and myths about that person, group, or a race of peoples. Internalised oppression refers to a process. It is a verb – an action word that typically expresses the relationship between the oppressor and the oppressed. The process of consuming, absorbing, and being affected by negativity in the form of – racial prejudice, stereotypes, biases, preconceptions, foregone conclusions, people's predispositions, and structural racism – are the elements that make internalised oppression something that happens from the outside that perpetuates the ongoing and wounding process for black people.

To elaborate, my concept "*The Internal Oppressor*" (Alleyne, 2006a, b) is an internal phenomenon. It is a proper noun, describing an essential nature of the black person's self-structure. For this reason, I afford the concept capital letters for all three words. *The Internal Oppressor* is part of the self and functions like an internal adversary or inner enemy that is in a continual fight with the rest of the self....and the outside world. This conflictual dynamic creates anxiety and self-doubt in the self. *The Internal Oppressor*, I would argue, is one of the most important concepts that overarches the focus in psychotherapy and psychoanalysis when working with black clients presenting with shame-based identity issues. Focus in this area will be important to enable the client to address their negative internalisations that merge and twin with the self – a bit like the parasitic plant that attaches itself to the host, and whose prolific growth continues to infiltrate and keeps the host hostage in its presence. *The Internal Oppressor* is the internal saboteur. To stretch the parasite analogy further, one can say, *Internalised Oppression* is the process of being overtaken by the parasite which results in *The Internal Oppressor*, becoming merged with the invader, the very things that stunt its own fertility. Effective therapy facilitates the "outing" of this damaging process so it can be clearly seen and understood in all its complexities and manifestations within the person's real life struggles. Working with *The Internal Oppressor* offers ways to help the client to separate out from suffocating enmeshed states of being and emerge into a healthier more independent, more autonomous place of living.

At this juncture, it would be unfair not to acknowledge the fact that black people do not monopolise identity shame. White shame and white vulnerability in the context of black/white race dynamics are equally problematic, and may also benefit from utilising Alleyne's (2006) concept of working with *"The Internal Oppressor"*. In this context, white shame and white vulnerability should, I would suggest, be addressed psychoanalytically from the point of view of clinical narcissism – namely having a superiority complex that prevents the group from being realistic about its place in today's world. The concept of narcissism describes people with an unstable sense of identity, but who manage their vulnerability by clinging to notions of grandiosity and entitlement. They cannot consider others except as objects to be manipulated or enemies to be fought. Marked by a mixture of bravado and contempt, those who are perceived as weaker get short shrift. Narcissists cannot accept criticism and feel no genuine interest in others – let alone empathy. But they may engage in noticeable, over-compensatory, and benevolent acts of tolerating and accommodating the Other. Employing the concept of *"The Internal Oppressor"* *might* enable a deeper understanding of the "False Self" structure that fears letting go and relaxing the pathological fears of disintegration – losing face, being ordinary, lack of admiration from others, and not being important. It entails looking deep into one's soul and reckoning with the past and showing remorse. Deepening awareness of the psychic harm and emotional disadvantages caused by this narcissistic self-structure, is key to healing from white shame, for to ignore its existence is to leave the *shamer* hoist with his [or her] own petard.

Fourthly, enable the client to tune out expressions of black rage and pain and delight in their distinct hybrid vigour. We can do this by reframing negative scripts about black identity and strengthening a sense of self-worth. Build shame resilience through authentic pride for one's self and one's group. In this psychic state, we can achieve *a state of grace.*

I have chosen three quotes with which to end.

The Inner Enemy [my reference to The Internal Oppressor] is like a throwback, a vestigial tail we no longer need now that we have conquered the elements and are in fact no longer at the mercy of fire, thunder and wild animals.

George Bach (1988, p. 47)

Freedom is what you do with what's been done to you.

Jean-Paul Sartre (1943)

If you find the psychic wound in an individual or a people, there you also find their path to consciousness.

Carl Jung (1964, p. 166)

References

Akbar, N. (1979). African roots of black personality. In W. Smith, K. Burlew, M. Mosley, & W. Whitney (Eds.), *Reflections on Black Psychology* (pp. 136–144). Washington, DC: University Press of America.

Akbar, N. (1996). *Breaking the Chains of Psychological Slavery.* Tallahassee, FL: Mind Productions.

Alleyne, A. (1992). *Cycle of Events.* Unpublished MA dissertation, University of Hertfordshire and updated 2006 for Doctoral Thesis, Middlesex University.

Alleyne. A. (2006a). *A Psychotherapeutic Understanding of Black Identity in the Workplace Context.* Doctorate in Psychotherapy, Thesis, Middlesex University.

Alleyne, A. (2006b). The internal oppressor and black identity wounding. *Counselling and Psychotherapy Journal, 15*(10), 48–50.

Bach, G. R. (1988). *The Inner Enemy: How to Fight Fair with Yourself.* New York: Berkley Books.

Bowlby, J. (1969). *Attachment and Loss, Vol. 1: Attachment.* New York: Basic Books.

Bowlby, J. (1973). *Attachment and Loss, Vol. 2: Separation: Anxiety and Anger.* New York: Basic Books.

Crenshaw, K. (1996). *Critical Race Theory.* New York: The New Press.

DeGruy-Leary, J. (2005). *Post-Traumatic Slave Syndrome: America's Legacy of Enduring Injury & Healing.* Milwaukie, OR: Uptone Press.

Duke, B., & D. Channsin Berry. (2011). *Dark Girls.* Directors, B. Duke & D. Channsin Berry. RLJE Films. https://www.youtube.com/watch?v=Csa1YON62OI&t=120s. Last accessed on September 15, 2020.

Fanon, F. (1986). *Black Skin, White Masks.* London: Pluto Press.

Fletchman Smith, B. (2000). *Mental Slavery: Psychoanalytic Studies of Caribbean People.* London: Routledge.

Fletchman Smith, B. (2011). *Transcending the Legacies of Slavery: A Psychoanalytic View.* London: Routledge.

Grier, W., & Cobbs, P. (1969). *Black Rage.* New York: Bantam Books.

Jung, G. (1964). *Man and His Symbols.* New York: Anchor Doubleday.

Klein, M. (1933). The early development of conscience in the child. Change in nature of superego from vengeful to concerned with guilt and moral sense. In M. Klein (Ed.), *Love, Guilt and Reparation and Other Works 1921–1945 (The Writings of Melanie Klein, Volume 1)* (pp. 248–257). New York: Free Press.

Lipsky, S. (1987). *Internalised Racism.* Seattle, WA: Rational Island Publishers.

Sartre, J.-P. (1943). *Being and Nothingness* (Original title: *L'Être et le Néant*). Éditions Gallimard, Philosophical Library (London: Routledge edition, 1956).

Sarup, M. (1996). *Identity, Culture and the Postmodern World.* Edinburgh: Edinburgh University Press.

Terr, L. C. (1991). Childhood traumas: An outline and overview. *American Journal of Psychiatry, 148*(1), 10–20.

Winnicott, D. (1960). Ego distortions in terms of the true and false self. In D. W. Winnicott (Ed.), *The Maturational Process and the Facilitating Environment* (pp. 140–153). London: Hogarth Press.

Chapter 6

Mentalizing shame, shamelessness and Fremdscham (shame by proxy) in groups

Ulrich Schultz-Venrath

Introduction

There are numerous reasons why psychotherapies are not successful. A mostly overlooked reason is not seeing and therefore not addressing the shame experienced by our clients in our work together. In the last few years there have been a growing number of publications about shame in all its different aspects both in general and also within our field. With globalization and the shifting boundaries on many different levels of our lives the issue of shame, shamelessness and "Fremdscham" ("shame by proxy") have become of enormous importance. However, it is apparent that we as psychotherapists, though dealing with emotions, have not yet adequately responded to the impact of these important social factors. The neologism and German expressions "Fremdscham" or "fremdschämen" were first published in the German Dictionary, called "Der Duden" (2009). It describes the phenomenon of a feeling of being ashamed for someone else; this means, it is an empathic or vicarious embarrassment. Recognition of shame in its different facets is – by the way – part of what we are identifying as "mentalizing competences". Recently in the media, shame has become apparent in audiences watching music talent shows such as "Germany is Looking for the Superstar" or "Pop Stars" (both similar to the TV show "Britain's Got Talent") when the jury dismisses a performance by giving it a thumbs down gesture accompanied by derogatory remarks. These shows are favoured by young adults and represent a permanent frenzy of body-related humiliation. Here, "wannabe pop stars" appear, whose musical performances are occasionally questionable and thus can evoke the phenomenon of "Fremdscham", shame by proxy. It seems that in recent years these shows have gained attractiveness through the experience of "Fremdscham" in the group, possibly in connection with "Schadenfreude". However, Schadenfreude could be approximated to malicious joy in response to the failings of others (Krach et al., 2011). But shame by proxy also occurs in another realm, for example, among voters who realize that an elected president repeatedly presents fake news or false facts that are the result of a certain shamelessness.

DOI: 10.4324/9781003175612-7

What is shame?

Shame is the first feeling named in the Bible and is related to the moral emotions, like guilt and empathy (Mikulincer & Shaver, 2014). "In the beginning was shame" – in the first book of Moses in the Bible it reads as follows: "both Adam and his wife were naked, but they were not ashamed of each other" (Moses 3, 16). This is known to have changed quickly after the two tried the forbidden fruit from the tree of knowledge. But what is going on in their gaze, what do they see? The classical view is that they see each other, but obviously from different perspectives. However, the crucial point of shame is the discovery that the other can see me and I have no control over what can be seen nor has the other any control over my ability to see them. Intersubjectivity is the prerequisite for all shame, but without a particular self-consciousness or the ability of self-object and subject-subject differentiation, one could also question the myth that there is no shame. Again the classical view is as follows: This self-awareness was associated with the perception that Adam and Eve could be recognized and judged by each other as an "object". It is precisely here that the "object" terminology seems particularly problematic because seeing the other as an object means destroying or neglecting his or her embodied subjectivity. With the awareness of nudity, Adam and Eve became aware of their gender differences and thus their own fundamental incompleteness, the inscribed lack of gender (Hell, 2018; Küchenhoff, 2018). The philosopher Jean-Paul Sartre states: "I am ashamed of myself before the other" (Sartre, 2014 [1943], p. 518), a sentence, which locates shame as an intersubjective feeling first.

The famous British natural scientist Charles Darwin wrote in 1872 in *The Expression of the Emotions in Man and Animals* the following thoughts:

> Under a keen sense of shame there is a strong desire for concealment. We turn away the whole body, more especially the face, which we endeavour in some manner to hide. An ashamed person can hardly endure to meet the gaze of those present, so that he almost invariably casts down his eyes or looks askant. [...] Most persons whilst blushing intensely, have their mental powers confused.
>
> (Darwin, 1872, [1934], p. 156)

This early description of shame as a specific bodily expression, involves some relevant aspects of inhibition or loosing mentalization, especially if the gaze is avoided. In contrast to Darwin, it is interesting that psychoanalysts like Garfinkle (2012), understand shame as hidden resistance, and have lost the physical expression of this affect. "The word shame is derived from the Indo-European root skam or skem, meaning 'to hide'. Shame involves an internal experience of disgrace coupled with fear that perceived others will see how we have dishonoured ourselves" (Garfinkle, 2012, p. 45).

Mentalizing is a form of *imaginative* mental activity about others or one-self, namely, perceiving and interpreting human behaviour in terms of *intentional* mental states (Bateman & Fonagy, 2019). The ability to be ashamed is an important developmental and psychological achievement by higher order representations. These are characterized by defensive omissions and or distortions resulting in not having developed representations when experiences with early caregivers are characterized by neglect or abuse. It seems that the intentionality of shame is to hide oneself with the opposite, often hidden desire and hope to finally be seen. Shamelessness is therefore the opposite of this, it is the inability to mentalize the feelings of the other and therefore may frequently be related to violence and insult. "Recognition of the other person having a separate mind inhibits violence. It is the loss of mentalizing the other that allows a physical attack, because the other person then becomes no more than a body or threatening presence" (Bateman & Fonagy, 2019, p. 296).

Also in contrast to Darwin, shame doesn't belong to the seven "basic emotions", which were otherwise brilliantly studied by the Estonian neuroscientist Jaak Panksepp in his neuroevolutionary work on *Affective Neuroscience* (Panksepp & Biven, 2012), which forms one of the pillars of the theory of affects in the mentalization model. "Social emotions" such as shame, guilt and envy tend to be counted among the complex affects. Regardless of their complexity, emotions and affects are intentional (Dennett, 1987). Rage has the intention of destroying someone. Fear and panic have the intention of escaping from something. Disgust, which is also missing from his list has the intention of externalizing a toxic object.

Regardless of the discussion about whether affects are innate or inter-subjective or both, they are also culturally embedded and change over time. For example, in the Middle Ages, it was common for people to shamelessly defecate and urinate in public wherever they went. As time went on, there were even communal toilets. The change in experiencing shame correlated with the construction of individual toilets and washrooms, which defined new boundaries of the body and promoted at the same time modern civilization as Norbert Elias, a pioneer of a historically informed sociology of the body and his follower Peter Gleichmann wonderfully described (Elias, 1939a, 1939b; Gleichmann, 1979b, 1979c).

Just as an aside, even Freud's phase theory (oral, anal and genital) was significantly influenced by this. Around the turn of the century, the stench of Viennese faeces reached such a level that the sewage system was to provide relief not only in Vienna but in many major European cities. Whereas farmers used to collect these "legacies" as fertilizer and payed for them, city dwellers now had to pay for the sewage system. Incidentally, this influenced Freud to equate anality with money (Gleichmann, 1979a).

Norbert Elias, a very dear friend of S. H. Foulkes, and also a pioneer of group analysis, summed this up as follows: "....there are people in front of whom one is ashamed, and others in front of whom one is not. The feeling of shame is clearly a social function, moulded according to the social structure" (Elias, 1994, p. 113). Elias described in his work an increase in the modest control of physical needs, "reflecting changing structures of society, and simultaneously make for change in the psyche" (Dalal, 2002, p. 124). He also foresaw that, as a result of European states being formed, all kinds of shame would increase. The abolition of feudal ways of relating and the subsequent development of participatory democracies, was accompanied by a change from externally imposed foreign pressures to inner-psychological self-constraints.

It seems that in the course of time these inner-psychological limitations on the self have also been internalized by our psychotherapy community in the sense of it being blind to the socio-economic context of our work with people. As if in a vacuum, very little has been written about the body in relation to shame. Even in the mentalization model, the body was underrepresented in the three known, empirically derived pre-mentalistic modes. These are modes in which we are not able to mentalize – so we put the "body mode" (instead of "embodied mentalizing") before the others as one of the earliest, developmentally, pre-mentalistic modes (Figure 6.1). But it is these apparently small but crucial cultural differences, including the social unconscious, that give the "body" and the "subject" a different meaning in French, British and German psychodynamic theory and practice. It seems that French and German people relate a little bit more to the body, at least in theory.

But times have changed and it is hard to miss that we are living in times of increasing shame, embarrassment and shamelessness. The faces of shame and shamelessness have changed throughout the last century and the question is whether this has to do with our changed experiences of borders through globalization and the flood of information on the internet. As with all affects,

Prementalistic Mode	Description
Body	Pre- and postnatal the baby can not experience body and psyche separately until around the ninth month. He/she is **primarily concerned with his/her body and skin** sensations.
Teleological	Mental states such as needs and emotions are expressed in action. **Only actions** and their available consequences **count** - not words.
Equivalent	**Outer world = inner world.** Mental states are experienced as real, as happens in dreams, flashbacks and paranoid delusions.
Pretend	Mental states are disconnected from reality, retain a **sense of unreality** because they are not connected and anchored to reality

Figure 6.1 Prementalistic modes (modified, Bateman & Fonagy, 2019).

shame is associated with a strong physical reaction, which is most clearly made visible by blushing, sweating and an increased heart rate. These signals highlight the ambiguity of shame: on the one hand wanting to hide and on the other hand attracting attention by blushing (and other automatic body reactions). This has been demonstrated by Nummenmaa et al. (2014) through body topography of basic (upper) and non-basic (lower) emotions associated with words. The body maps show regions whose activation increased (warm colours) or decreased (cool colours) when feeling each emotion. On the one hand we know that shame causes the body to shrink, pride leads to an expansive physical movement, which is expressed in the phrase "with her head held high".

Shamelessness has rarely been studied scientifically – this correlates with the frequency of quotations in Psychoanalytic Electronic Publishing (PEP) from 1920 to 2018 where shame is mentioned 224 times and shamelessness only 113 times, despite shame and shamelessness being so closely intertwined. There was an interesting exhibition in the German Hygiene Museum of Dresden in 2017 entitled *Shame – 100 Reasons to Blush*. It was precisely in this city, where the xenophobic, racist and right-wing populist mob named PEGIDA – Patriotische Europäer gegen die Islamisierung des Abendlandes (Patriotic Europeans Against the Islamization of the West) – celebrated its resurrection, shamelessly using the exclamation: "We are the People". This was the iconic declaration made by the East-German people in their demonstrations for freedom before the fall of the Berlin Wall.

> Tatjana Festerling, one of the speakers of PEGIDA, said on the 9th of November 2015: 'We declare, here and now, the end of the guilt complex resulting from twelve years of Nazi leadership [...]. Leave us in peace with your cult of guilt regarding the past – we do not share the responsibility for that!'.
>
> (Brandes, 2018, pp. 422–423)

The rise of right-wing populists across Europe who scapegoat migrants and identify them as the most important or only political problem, is still not well understood. A speculative consideration could be that some kind of non-mentalized, deep shame as a result of unprocessed and unmourned losses (such as jobs, parents and partners) plays a special role in all these movements? Anna Freud's concept of "identification with the aggressor" suggests that the shame-prone person reacts to a potentially shame-provoking situation in such a way, that they proactively inflict on the others their own most feared injuries, derived from their own past experiences.

The handling of social shame coming from within society is still an unresolved challenge. Young people, especially, are exposed to such a pressure to conform which, in the name of the internet and social media, is almost monstrous. "Shitstorms" are reminiscent of what happened to people in the seventeenth or eighteenth century when they stood in the stocks and were pilloried, spat at by the public and pelted with excrement. Today, the faeces have become verbalized and visualized, without having lost their disgusting quality (Frevert, 2015). However, in some countries, public acts of shame are still a sanctioned practice, if small in number. With public actions and a high media expenditure the "Stop Acid Attacks" (SAA) movement was formed in India 2013 drawing attention to the crimes of spurned admirers who reach for the acid bottle to disfigure the faces of women. There are many examples which demonstrate that shame is an important tool for controlling social interaction, sometimes with fatal consequences. In a culture, dominated more and more by social media, its function as a means of social control is evident in the bullying and other humiliating strategies found on social media. A fifteen-year-old girl jumps off a bridge because she cannot stand the public humiliation instigated by her father. Angered by a selfie circulating at her school showing his daughter in a sports-bra and leggings, he cuts off her long hair and films her. As the video goes viral and becomes the talk of the school, she takes her own life (Frevert, 2017, p. 8).

Shame is "one of the earliest social emotions, which like anxiety, anticipates and warns, consciously and unconsciously, of the danger of immediate social rejection" (Friedman, 2017, p. 7). In all parts of Europe, we can observe that the destructive tendencies of scapegoating result from group members' hatred towards the scapegoat, which are today represented by migrants or indeed often whole nations who are despised. Friedman (2017) argues that these tendencies in groups

> … are often an effort to avoid becoming a scapegoat themselves, because groups believe in selection processes, which 'improve' the group's standards, as well as other motivations. The main aspect in scapegoating as an interpersonal process is the unconscious relationship between a rejecting group with the scapegoat, who is unable to separate from the wish to belong to the perpetrator's group. A further central aspect of the emotional processes evolving into the 'scapegoating position', is that violence-inhibiting emotions such as shame, guilt and empathy become progressive or have never existed.
>
> (Friedman, 2017, p. 2)

The non-mentalized, shame-driven scapegoating includes the further phenomenon that after rejecting or eliminating the scapegoat, groups are hoping for a more "efficient" group, which indeed is mostly an illusion.

Shame has many faces or consists of a "family of shame affects" (Haesler, 2008; Hell, 2018; Wurmser, 1990). These include humiliation, embarrassment, shyness, modesty, dishonour, denunciation, social anxiety, narcissistic violation or feeling of inferiority (Nathanson, 1994 [1992]). Probably less well known is the fact that phenomena such as negative therapeutic reaction (Alonso & Rutan, 1988a) or dissociation, masochism, victim-identity and "anti-group" phenomena (Nitsun, 2006a) also belong to the family of shame affects when shame is unbearable. These are mobilized either as a defence against shame like revenge and aggressive breakthroughs or as non-mentalized shame. In that sense, the enormous dimensions of shame range from the malignant feeling of extermination or exclusion of the group in the worst case to milder experiences of shame, for example slips of the tongue, all of which require different kinds of interventions. These different dimensions of shame are linked to the various developmental phases, in which shame-producing experiences occur. The most archaic one is the most malignant one and inhibits the social life of the individual. This corresponds to the existential shame a child feels when she or he is unwelcome, rejected or despised for their very existence (Hell, 2018; Thußbas, 2015; Wille, 2014; Wurmser, 1990). In that sense, the act of violence can also have the function of transforming extreme, unbearable forms of shame (such as existential shame) into moderate forms of shame. Both dimensions appear in groups as inhabiting the psychic equivalent mode, in which the individuals have a tendency to equate mental phenomena with objective phenomena and vice versa (Hadar, 2008, p. 168). But it is of particular importance that shame should be thought of as multidimensional, running from "...the most malignant shame to a necessary and healthy ability to feel the shame in order to be a part of society" (Hadar, 2008, p. 168) (Figure 6.2).

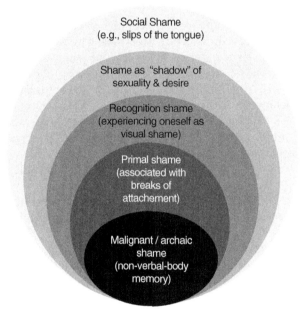

Figure 6.2 Dimensions of shame (modified, Hadar, 2008).

Primal shame, blending guilt, disgust and panic, is a form of shame that goes back to the belief that "something is wrong with me". In the mentalization model, this is now conceptualized as "epistemic mistrust" (Fonagy & Allison, 2014). This concept is based on studies, identifying the implications of attachment disorganization for the epistemic aspects of the mother-child relationship. Although insecure avoidant attachment seems generally associated with epistemic mistrust, children whose attachment relationships had been disorganized in infancy tended to mistrust particularly both information from their own experience and that arising from their attachment figure's or the stranger's views. The unresolvable question of "who can I trust?" corresponds simultaneously with the phenomenon of trusting simple truths or fake news on the other side. With these children and later these adults we encounter "shamelessness", since they do not locate themselves socially, the level of social shame is missing.

This horizontal and vertical diversity of the different faces of shame is a little bit confusing. The thing connecting it all together is the content of shame, which "is always associated with a subjectively felt lack of right to life, of competence, of protection, of demarcation, of the ability to fulfil foreign or individual claims. Every subjectively experienced deficit can trigger feelings of shame" (Küchenhoff, 2018, pp. 295–296).

However, it now seems necessary to distinguish more clearly between non-pathological and pathological manifestations of shame, and to focus on the pathological manifestations of shamelessness, which also can be non-pathological in the case of necessary shifts or the opening of boundaries.

History

Freud mentions shame forty-one times in his collected writings; it is mostly cited as a motive for defending against sexuality, and also as a protection from any experience that involves the fear of revealing repulsive secrets to an audience. This is not very surprising. He and his followers often combined shame with morality, disgust and authority and saw it as a reason for the suppression of sexuality, again as a function of defences. Shame was considered as one of the dams built in latency to channel the drives, especially to the coprophilic sexual excitements associated with the excrements of childhood. Without being specific here Freud made an indirect reference to his later famous quote, "the ego is above all [...] a bodily ego". The so-called "anal phase" plays a central role in the development of the self because shame and embarrassment of a developing child are closely connected with bodily experiences. Thus, it is not surprising that shame is likely to be observed when the externalization of excretory material makes it possible to distinguish between the Ego and the Non-Ego as Self and Object. Despite the role of shame as an "interface" and a social affect, shame was theoretically elaborated numerous times but only as an intrapsychic phenomenon.

Masturbation was also significant in this respect: "...guilt for the forbidden drives and shame for the weakness and inability to control them, the common denominator being the wish to hide one's failings from other people" (Lowenfeld, 1976, p. 63).

Nevertheless, in contrast to his fundamental concepts of anxiety or pain as affects (Kütemeyer & Schultz, 1989), Freud didn't present a specific theory of shame and even less of shamelessness, which he attributed only once to "sexual deviations" of a significant kind and to what he called "perversions". In the last years of his life, he considered shame as "an exquisitely feminine quality" and claimed in 1933 that shame "is far more conventional than one might think, ... attributed to the original intention of concealing the defect of the genitals" (Freud, 1933 [1932], p. 142). Against this background, Sigmund Freud and Josef Breuer developed the well-known concept of repression as the most comprehensive concept of defence, mobilized to defend against the fact that unpleasant affects, including shame, penetrate consciousness. However, the view of shame as a social or interpersonal affect, which has to do with the experience of being observed, is rarely mentioned in his letters to Wilhelm Fließ (Freud, 1985) and in his interpretations of dreams (Freud, 1900)" (Tiedemann, 2013 [2016], p. 13f.).

Within Freud's self-analysis there is an interesting section where, quoting his own childhood memory, Freud clarified how he coped with his own shame.

> I have been told the following scene from my childhood: I occasionally wet the bed at the age of two .... When I was reproached for this, I attempted to comfort my father with the promise that I would buy him a new, beautiful bed.
>
> (Freud, 1900, p. 221)

Although at this time infants used to be potty trained at the age of one, this scene sheds light on the fact that Freud must have felt less afraid of his own shame than the shame his parents might have felt for him (Tisseron, 2000). This example of "Fremdscham" (shame by proxy) does not quite fit with the current results of mentalization research where the ability to mentalize is first observed in children at around the age of four or five. Perhaps Freud was mistaken about his age and was more likely to be older than two. If Freud had not been mistaken, it would indicate that affect representations can apparently be created from the sensations of the body mode even earlier than contemporary research suggests.

A deeper understanding of shame did not develop in psychoanalysis until the emergence of relational and intersubjective approaches around thirty-five years ago. Although it is not yet clear whether shame is the first social affect, as some authors emphasize (Friedman, 2008; Tisseron, 2000) (all affects have a socially directed intentionality), the psychoanalytic community has

been forced, more and more, to recognize affects and emotions, and especially shame, as an intersubjective process. However, an understanding of
shame depends on our theoretical perspective, whether we prefer the classical psychoanalytic model, the self-psychology approach or object relations
theory, intersubjective or relational psychoanalysis, the group analytic or
more recently, the mentalization model, which actually seems to be the most
integrative model of all.

Shame and shamelessness in groups

Alonso and Rutan (1988a), the authors who first introduced the concept of
shame into group analytic theory, followed classical psychoanalytic theory
and were criticized for not being psychoanalytic enough (Roth, 1989). It is
ultimately due to the fact that group analysis has had a hard time asserting
its theoretical independence from psychoanalysis. There are some reasons to
consider Freud as shame prone and shame sensitive. He admitted his dislike
of being constantly looked at by his patients which later resulted in the typical analytic setting with the patient on the couch and the analyst sitting out
of sight behind the patient. So it is not surprising Freud wasn't amused by
the development of group analysis which had been experimentally founded
by Trigant Burrow in Baltimore 1924 and twenty years later by the German
emigrant Michael Foulkes in Exeter and in the Northfield Military Hospital
(Gatti Pertegato, 2014; Gatti Pertegato & Pertegato, 2013; Sandner, 1998;
Schultz-Venrath, 2015). Freud's reluctance certainly inhibited the development of a group-based understanding of shame in the psychotherapeutic
field too. A further reason could be that Freud was exclusively intrapsychic
or dyadic drive orientated rather than intersubjective. The third aspect is
that shame and embarrassment are one of the blind spots in the training run
by many psychoanalytic institutions. Regardless of the question of whether
shame is inherent in psychoanalytic training, we regularly expose ourselves
very deeply both in our analysis and in supervision (Alonso & Rutan, 1988b;
Blaß, 2016). Psychoanalytic and sometimes also group analytic institutions
(Leszcz, 2004) use shame and shame-anxiety, more or less unconsciously,
in order to enforce conformity and cohesion (Küchenhoff, 2018). Shame-
assured conformity is based on group-identification and shared ideals.
Rejection, exile, social exclusion and abandonment are the impending punishments and from a group analytic understanding the worst outcome for
the individual. The cohesion of the psychoanalytic community is still based
on a sense of shame-anxiety, a fear of imminent shame, if someone deviates
from the psychoanalytic mainstream. Whether or not it is always possible to
authentically talk about it in the training analyses between candidates and
training analysts is questionable because of the mutual shame dimensions.
This proves the difficulty in research into supervision of psychotherapeutic
candidates (Grünewald-Zemsch, 2019).

The inclusion of an individual in groups is often accompanied by rituals which target the body. "The pervasive phenomenon of initiation rites commonly involves violence against the bodies of individuals and an incorporation of bodies through dance or other forms of synchronized collective actions" (de Warren, 2017, p. 59f.). By using examples of dance or other forms of synchronized drills and marches of the modern military, the individual is tied into a social group through a ritualized submission of the body to the group. The submission of an individual to pain and shame, for example by completing a hazardous ritual in which new recruits must crawl through mud, marks the person's inclusion in the group through a pledge.

John Bowlby was one of the remarkable pioneers who, with his attachment theory, had discovered a fundamental aspect of psychoanalysis that the rest of institutionalized psychoanalysis had overlooked for a long time. Could it be that the shame of psychoanalytic institutions stems also from the fact that psychoanalysts do not want to be ashamed of not knowing something so important? That shame, well documented by Fonagy and Campbell (2015) is also the "result of an unconscious meeting with others, a kind of alarm system warning when the potential rejection of a group is activated" (Friedman, 2014). When large-group identity is threatened, the result is a shared narcissistic threat, associated with shame, humiliation, helplessness or feelings of revenge. Revenge, exclusion and other forms of humiliation are different attempts to ward off the feeling of institutional shame.

Group analysis and the mentalization model are overlapping in an understanding that the development of the self is intersubjective and group-based and not only the outcome of a dyadic process. This view is far more than an extension of psychoanalytic theory; the group comes prior to the individual or more provocatively put: the baby is born into his or her group. "Since the self only exists in the context of others, self-development is tantamount... to the aggregation of experiences of self in relationships" (Fonagy & Target, 1997, p. 684). From a developmental perspective, the ability of the primary attachment person to make sense of the baby's feeling state is highly influenced by "how she/he feels about herself as a mother", "how supported she is in her relationships", "how her mother felt about her as an infant" and "how her interaction is based on bodily interaction complemented by their communicative interplay", supported by members of her primary group. The early bodily interactions are restaged in group psychotherapies of adults; insofar, therapeutic groups are a mirror of shame dynamics within the family.

When the baby is crying or distressed, non-verbally expressing its discomfort, the caregiver has to resonate, to digest and to express in a marked, congruent manner (for example "motherese") the emotion of the baby/child/patient. These kinds of affect expressions influence "the organizational nucleus of the child's future personality, and ... the representational format of the very young child comprises the mother's faces and vocalizations" (Krause, 2021). Only then are representations of these affects built step by step, which in turn the toddler can increasingly rely on. This is largely congruent with John Bowlby's concept of internal working models (IWMs) and with Daniel Stern's "RIG's" – Representation of Interactions which have been Generalized (Stern, 1992 [1985]). The clinicians only have to prove how stable these representations are and whether they exist at all.

Individuals with complex trauma develop a lack of affect regulation arising from experiences of a "disorganized or traumatic attachment relationship" where the caregiver doesn't respond, sensitively. The situation is further complicated when accompanied by unmarked and/or noncongruent mirroring. In this case, we often encounter patients who either encapsulate or externalize parts of the alien or false self, including unendurable shame. In the latter case, unendurable shame can be transformed into violence, often in response to the massive humiliation of someone and producing existential shame (Thußbas, 2015). These patients, who are shameless when aggressive outbursts are repeated, detached from all limits, often end up in forensic departments, labelled as having an "antisocial personality disorder". They may use their own bodies socially, e.g. as "skinheads" or by "tattooing" to express their emotional states, or medically in the form of somatization or entering dissociative states, because their self-object-differentiations haven't developed.

What is mentalizing?

Mentalizing (or "reflective functioning") is a socio-cognitive capacity to think about oneself and others as psychological beings and to consider underlying mental states and motivations when interpreting behaviours in attachment contexts. The Mentalization model encompasses a wide range of related concepts that are focused on various aspects of social cognition, including empathy, mindfulness, theory of mind (ToM), psychological mindedness, alexithymia and insightfulness (Choi-Kain & Gunderson, 2008). Whereas ToM and empathy focus more on aspects of mentalizing others, mindfulness and alexithymia concern core features of mentalizing the self (Luyten et al., 2020). Concepts such as empathy and mindfulness concern affective components of mentalizing, while ToM focuses on cognitive features of mentalizing (e.g., belief–desire reasoning). Mentalizing is thus a broad concept that refers to processes involved in reflective functioning about self–other and cognition–affect, based on internal and external features. Mentalizing refers to the human capacity to understand the self and others in terms of intentional mental states, such as feelings, desires, wishes, attitudes and goals. Mentalizing is a developmental process that relies on good enough attachment relationships and early attachments in particular, as they reflect the extent to which our subjective experiences were adequately mirrored by a trusted other (Fonagy et al., 2004 [2002]). Whereas earlier formulations focused on the unique role of dyadic attachment in fostering or hindering the development of mentalizing (Fonagy, 2000, Fonagy et al., 1991b), the latest views have evolved to a more comprehensive set of considerations concerning the role of family, peers and sociocultural factors in the development of mentalizing (Luyten et al., 2020). In their overview, Luyten and colleagues emphasize also that "the capacity for parental mentalizing … is determined by and embedded within a broader set of factors influencing child development, including family and neighbourhood, the wider environment, and the general sociocultural context" (Luyten et al., 2020, p. 299).

Transcultural differences in stress and affect regulation seem to have an effect on the development of different affect representations (Otto & Keller, 2018 [2014]). In the well-known African proverb: "It takes a whole village to raise a child" there is the hint that the mother-child dyad does not seem to be as important in many African cultures as the large family group in the sense of "multiple mothering" (with many bodies!) in which a child grows up. Although the relationship may be less focused on the biological mother – the child is provided with "different mothers" (alloparenting) at an early age – emotional regulation between some African caregivers and their children may take place by preference through body contact, and via the skin (Schultz-Venrath, 2021). Keller's (2011, 2019) criticism that the theory of attachment is based predominantly on western educated industrialized rich democratic (WEIRD) people has since been taken up by the researchers of the mentalization model. In all probability, this also means that representations are formed not only dyadically, but also by the family members as a group or in a village as the symbol of a larger group. But there seem to be cultural differences in the development of affect representations: children of a group of ethnocentric German mothers in a particular study by Heidi Keller (2011) showed emotions such as anger, fear, sadness, aversion and pride much earlier than children of the group of African mothers in this study whose children by contrast showed shame and feelings of guilt nearly eight months earlier. She also noted that group socialization and the experience that the individual is always "kept" in the group was observed to lead to less fear.

The experiences with others are important for the development of self and object representations. This is neurobiologically supported by the remarkable discoveries of mirror neurons, first with single cell recordings in monkeys and then with brain imaging studies in humans. When observing others engaged in meaningful actions there is a process of "embodied simulation" or of "body mode" in our brains with automatic, prereflective registrations of the other's actions, linked to intentions and feelings. This prompted Bob Emde (2009) to speak psychoanalytically of "We-Go" rather than of "Ego". While historically shame was ascribed to a conflict between ego and ego-ideal (Piers & Singer, 1953), one can now assume that the different faces of shame are rather an expression of a conflict in group contexts, more in the sense of a conflict between Ego and "We-Go"-Ideal (Klein, 1976, p. 178).

Shame and mentalization-based group therapy (MBT-G)

Mentalization-based Group therapy (MBT-G) is a highly flexible development of psychodynamic group therapy in a day hospital for patients who have experienced extreme early trauma (Bateman & Fonagy, 2008; Karterud, 2015), whereby the focus can also be directed towards promoting mentalizing in psychodynamic group psychotherapies or in group analysis in other settings (Schultz-Venrath & Felsberger, 2016). MBT-G stands out as being radically different from psychodynamic group therapy, from which it originated, for example, by restricting group free associations. On the other hand, it does have a clear psychodynamic focus, in the sense of taking into account multiple motivational levels both for the participating individuals and for the group as a whole, by stimulating spontaneous interaction in the group and utilizing here-and-now events for mentalizing purposes. MBT-G is a further development of psychodynamic group psychotherapy for patients with more severe mental and psychosomatic disorders and has emerged with promising results (Bateman et al., 2019; Morken et al., 2019; Schultz-Venrath & Felsberger, 2016). There is a special focus on emotions, which are deepened and worked through by using an affect focused questioning technique, based on identifying both pre-mentalistic modes of functioning and the dimensions of mentalizing (Luyten et al., 2019). The MBT working group around Bateman, Fonagy, Luyten and Target has so far introduced three developmental, empirically derived pre-mentalistic modes that are assumed to be able to describe the behaviour of every human being under certain conditions: the teleological mode, which dominates in the first six to nine months of life, the equivalence mode, in which the inner and outer worlds are identical, and the pretend mode, in which the inner and outer worlds are not connected. In addition to the three modes, we have introduced a fourth mode – the body mode instead of "embodied mentalizing" – which is the earliest mode in terms of developmental psychology (Diez Grieser & Müller, 2018; Schultz-Venrath, 2021). This is supported by the developmental psychological theory that newborns initially perceive mental states as physiological-physical sensations and automatically express them due to innate tendencies. The modes of experiencing subjectivity reflect ineffective mentalizing that developmentally predates the capacity for full mentalizing. Patients with somatoform disorders, eating disorders, personality disorders, including borderline patients, exhibit numerous phenomena whose specific bodily experiences are associated with the level of the body mode. These patients like to deal concretely with external appearances, such as how they look and what they weigh, and show many misperceptions of their bodies.

Thus a kind of "hyperembodiment" takes place in patients with eating disorders (Skarderud & Fonagy, 2012, p. 360). Shame experiences and all other affects also belong to the body mode.

The therapist's awareness of the diverse nature of shame is crucial in any consideration of shame in psychotherapy. It seems that "therapists who do not work exclusively within a dyadic individual therapy are more used to encountering the experience of shame" (Friedman, 2008, p. 50). The central problem as a group psychotherapist is to notice the many faces of shame in plenty of time. The most well-known shame utterances are heard when the therapist after the first meeting suggests group psychotherapy, and the patient says: "Group? No thanks!". Although it has become relatively well documented, group psychotherapy shows equally good or even better results for almost all clinical issues compared to individual psychotherapy (Burlingame & Strauß 2021), there is a continuing level of mistrust of the group as a psychotherapeutic approach. As Bowden (2002) found in a study on anti-group attitudes in the NHS, group psychotherapy, to some extent still tends to be viewed as second-best by professionals and patients alike (Nitsun, 2006b, p. 4). Relative to individual psychotherapy, Nitsun states that "the perceived lack of safety is frequently given as a reason for devaluing groups", which he thinks is related to the possibility of exposing the most vulnerable and intimate aspects of the self, namely our sexuality. "The problem about revealing the sexual life is often a problem of revealing shame. Hence, the recognition of shame and its expression in the group is a significant aspect of the much-needed sexual discourse" (Nitsun, 2006b, p. 4). In addition, the idea of publicly involving others in their personal problems seems almost inconceivable to some.

Shame acts interactively and is "infectious", and this is understood by both individual and group therapists. Exposed to the gaze of the others triggers feelings of shame. There is a universal fear of being looked at. Incidentally this could be one reason why *only* around 300 group psychotherapists out of 8,500 registered group therapists in Germany offer group therapy in an outpatient setting (Heuft & Knott, 2019). They represent only two to four percent of all psychotherapies in Germany.

In group-sessions, it is possible that the shame-filled group therapist feels as disconnected from others as the shame-filled patient. He "is locked into a temporary private agony" (Livingstone, 2006, p. 308). Because the experience of shame is magnified as public exposure increases, unexpected shame in a therapist can be even more of a problem in the group therapy setting than in individual therapy. When shame is felt by the group leader during a session, those interminable, excruciating moments of self-derogation and separation can disrupt the leader's ability to mentalize, both his or her engagement in the work, and even the therapeutic processes among and within the group members.

Livingstone (2006) is critical of therapists' over-reliance on the concept of projective identification which, he argues, "has tempted us to disavow ownership of our personal shame" Livingstone (2006, p. 308). Gans and Weber (2000) have argued that leaders "who do not detect, confront, and continually work through their own shame may be limited in their capacity to help the group get to deeper layers of such troublesome feelings" (Gans & Weber, 2000, p. 390). Therapists who frequently have not resolved their own feelings of shame may unconsciously collude with patients in avoiding shame within the therapy relationship. Therapists, like early caregivers, may export their shame experiences by "blaming the patient" (or the child) "for 'inducing' feelings in us" (Morrison, 1994, p. 30).

The small group is a place where the individual can practice bearing the gaze of others. Otherwise, if anyone has been exposed to shame in the first interview, he needs someone to cover his nakedness again. My personal recommendation for such patients is the sentence: "If you think about participating in the group, there is one more advantage over individual therapy: you have at least eight to nine therapists". Group therapists know very well that when "shame dominates", there are two clinical particularities: there is a smaller group of severely victimized patients, which "are likely to disclose the most traumatic experience only late in the course of treatment" (Turner et al., 1996, p. 543). However, in in-patient and day-therapy groups, where the patients seem to be of a more homogeneous composition – a sense of sharing and universality develops more quickly, psychotherapists are often confronted with the opposite. Here the trauma associated with shame threatens the limits of the group setting within the first minutes of a session, presenting great technical challenges for psychotherapists in their early years of training. Not only does shame threaten the members' trust in the group and in the leader, but it also goes along with a specific phenomenon, the so-called "incohesion: aggregation/massification" effect described by Hopper (2003). In the centre of traumatic experiences is, for Hopper, the experience of (annihilation) fear. Experiences of loss, abandonment and damage cause psychic fission and fragmentation, then psychic fusion and confusion and finally a defensive oscillation between them, and feelings of shame, envy and humiliation (Hopper, 2003).

Severely traumatized patients often show chronic or malignant shame, and everybody can imagine that sitting in a circle of seven to nine people with this sort of history must be a nightmare for all of them (Hadar, 2008). However, the paradox is: there is no better cure than a group. Experience has shown that the level or severity of shame determines the kind of interventions that are required. Patients with malignant shame need to be well prepared for the group, usually through attending an introductory MBT group known as iMBT (Bateman et al., 2019). Group analysis in the tradition of Foulkes focuses on the importance of understanding events between certain members of the group as a "configuration of disturbance" and "locating the disturbance", for example, understanding the scapegoated patient who is communicating his disturbances to the whole system. This is beautifully illustrated by Montgomery (2006) who describes a group of chronically depressed, shame-prone individuals and traces their development from an initial (safe) denial of difference, through open expression of conflict and rage to final acceptance and integration of shame.

Clinical experiences and the use of personality inventories suggest that patients who score very high on Neuroticism Scales, show high levels of distress, vulnerability to stress and propensity for shame, do poorly in group psychotherapy generally (Ogrodniczuk et al., 2003). For these patients, mentalization-based group therapy was developed (Schultz-Venrath 2020. The central problem for group psychotherapists is to identify the different faces of shame over time, by including the body mode and not just the teleological or equivalence mode (see Figure 6.1). The therapist's awareness of the diverse nature and the different dimensions of shame is absolutely crucial.

Psychosexuality essentially is embodied in sensorimotor experience over the lifespan. There are arousal and pleasure centres in the body which are explored during infancy and growing up, for example thumb sucking and tickling games, or as a child discovers pleasure in their private parts. During infancy and adolescence sensual pleasure is explored including masturbation, phenomena which belong to the body mode. In relation to masturbation, Fonagy states, "this is more evident in boys, but there is ample indication of masturbatory behavior in infant girls" (Fonagy, 2008, p. 21). Depending on society's appreciation of these normative developmental stages and the caregiver's response, shame plays a special role in sexual feelings, which are more often systematically ignored or responded to with repression, inhibition and in cases of sexual abuse are distorted by some caregivers. Fonagy (2008) argues that this may also happen when the caregiver is too directive and misattuned. These observations may explain why themes relating to sexuality are particularly shameful, especially in groups.

The Mentalization model assumes that the primary role of parental mirroring is to bind unintegrated aspects of a constitutional self-state into coherent representations of specific affect states. The infant internalizes the reflection of metabolized affects on the face and on the body of the caregiver as the core of a representation. It is an interesting and also a puzzling result of the work of Iscan and his colleagues (2015), that group participants who discussed their sexual feelings and intimate relationships in greater detail during initial sessions showed less successful therapeutic outcomes than those who were more discreet. In contrast, participants who initially discussed their self-image, expressed shame and guilt, and focused on their ideas and beliefs showed significantly more successful outcomes. Shame has an important place in the therapeutic work – not only with sexuality – in the group. "It stems from the inevitable gap between the private and the public self" (Hadar, 2008, p. 167).

Clinical example of a median in-patient-MBT-G

The median group consisted of sixteen patients with different difficulties arising from early trauma. I welcomed the group asking who would like to tell the newcomers about the rules of the group. This regularly leads to the phenomenon that my third rule, "everybody is allowed to speak about the things which he/she wouldn't like to speak about", is often forgotten. After a minute a thirty-five-year-old man, who was in this group for the first time, said that he was here because he wanted to change his life. He had learned nothing and had earned his money in the last twenty years as a "call boy", mostly for rich women, but sometimes also for older men. Under the heightened attention of the group he talked and talked and talked – I can't remember the details any more, only that I was a little bit ashamed about this strange entrance of a newcomer which I had never experienced before. Suddenly a twenty-year-old young man, whose history included being brought up by a traumatized and difficult mother and a relatively absent father, dramatically fell off his seat, slowly sinking to the ground, with his eyes closed. Immediately, at least eight or nine patients most of them women, leapt to their feet in order to help him get up. Since the patient was sitting right in front of me it was very clear to me that this was a psychogenic dissociative seizure. I recognized this episode from my previous experience as an epileptologist. I remembered Bateman's "mentalizing hand" and called out loudly "stop, please return to your seats, I know that Mr. X. will manage to get back to his seat by himself". The group seemed to mistrust me a little but eventually followed my advice, more or less slowly. Then I asked the group whether anyone had an idea or phantasy about what this seizure was expressing? Some of the women were very angry with me because I hadn't allowed anybody to help this poor young boy, and they asked me furiously whether I would have behaved in this way towards my own children, and so on. I mumbled that I had no son who was falling off seats and asked again for the group's ideas and phantasies. After some time, the group started to work on this question and to my surprise, they linked the seizure to the story of the newcomer, and questioned whether this seizure represented his experiences of sexuality or maybe sexual abuse, even. In the meantime, the young man started to get back onto his seat, the members of the group were astonished, and asked him what had happened to him. After some minutes, he then began to mumble that he had been reminded by the newcomer's story of working as a "call boy" that his father had touched him sexually a long time ago, and he thought now that this had had something to do with why he experienced overwhelming sexual phantasies in relation to both of his parents.

Conclusions

This is an example of the underlying archaic or malignant shame experienced by patients with early trauma which cannot be expressed in words.

As Foulkes (1990, p. 265) wrote: "It is in the hands of the conductor to make this more or less dramatic, not to say traumatic". Mentalizing shame in groups is a generic way of establishing epistemic trust (Fonagy et al., 2019) – trust in the authenticity and personal relevance of interpersonally transmitted information between the patients, the group leader (Foulkes called the leader a conductor!) and the group. Establishing epistemic trust enables people to relinquish the rigidity that characterizes individuals with enduring attachment difficulties originating from a traumatic history. Since shame affects have a high potential for splitting people into groups, it makes sense to combine individual and group therapy in these cases.

The best antidote to neglecting shame is a courageous curiosity to detect and to explore it in the group therapeutic process. If patients in a group remain stuck in one of the pre-mentalistic modes (body mode, teleological mode, psychic equivalence or pretend mode) no psychic development can take place. Patients must therefore be helped to get out of these modes. This is easier said than done since all four modes are states governed by intense emotions resulting either in shame or in shamelessness where emotions are absent. One of the most mentalizing promoting interventions in group therapy are questions to the others in the group, not questions to the person who is revealing feelings of shame. "What might be unbearable in moment?" "Has anyone an idea about when this feeling or expression of emotion started?" All of these are affect focused questions. Sometimes statements by the therapist, such as "I would also be ashamed of this", or "I am also ashamed of this", help to build a bridge for the patient to be able to talk about their unbearable shame.

This approach is, however, only possible if we can get in touch with our own feelings of shame in relation to patients in the group. It is our job to contain the different faces of shame (and other difficult emotions) by being authentic and honest. Shame is the blind spot in many therapies. It is particularly difficult if no light is shed on shame and shamelessness in the therapeutic process, as feelings of malignant shame are central to patients who have experienced early attachment trauma. Patients can only change their troubled interpersonal patterns and be better socially integrated if shame and shamelessness are recognized as a central aspect of their response to their traumatic history and these feelings can then be courageously worked through.

References

Alonso, A., & Rutan, J. S. (1988a). The experience of shame and the restoration of self-respect in group therapy. *International Journal of Group Psychotherapy*, *38*(1), 3–27.

Alonso, A., & Rutan, J. S. (1988b). Shame and guilt in psychotherapy supervision. *International Journal of Group Psychotherapy*, *25*(4), 576–581.

Bateman, A., & Fonagy, P. (2019). Antisocial personality disorder. In A. Bateman & P. Fonagy (Eds.), *Handbook of Mentalizing in Mental Health Practice* (pp. 289–308). Washington, DC: American Psychiatric Publishing.

Bateman, A., Kongerslev, M., & Hansen, S. B. (2019). Group therapy for adults and adolescents. In A. Bateman & P. Fonagy (Eds.), *Handbook of Mentalizing in Mental Health Practice* (pp. 117–133). Washington, DC: American Psychiatric Association Publishing.

Bateman, A. W., & Fonagy, P. (2008). 8-year follow-up of patients treated for borderline personality disorder: Mentalization-based treatment versus treatment as usual. *American Journal of Psychiatry, 165*(5), 631–638.

Bateman, A. W., & Fonagy, P. (Eds.). (2019). *Handbook of Mentalizing in Mental Health Practice.* Washington, DC: American Psychiatric Association Publishing.

Blaß, H. (2016). Sich zeigen und sich verbergen in der psychoanalytischen Supervision. In G. Allert (Ed.), *Scham und Schamlosigkeit. Tagungsband der DPV-Frühjahrstagung* (pp. 413–418). Gießen: Psychosozial-Verlag.

Bowden, M. (2002). Antigroup attitudes at assessment for psychotherapy. *Psychoanalytic Psychotherapy, 16*, 246–258.

Brandes, H. (2018). Response to Robi Friedman's Foulkes lecture: Beyond rejection, glory and the Soldier's Matrix. *Group Analysis, 51*(4), 420–425.

Burlingame, G. M. & Strauss, B. (2021). Efficacy of small group treatments. In L. G. Castonguay, M. Barkham & W. Lutz (Eds.), *Bergin and Garfield's Handbook of Psychotherapy and Behavior Change* (7th ed.). Hoboken, NJ: Wiley (in press).

Choi-Kain, L. W., & Gunderson, J. G. (2008). Mentalization: Ontogeny, assessment, and application in the treatment of borderline personality disorder. *American Journal of Psychiatry, 165*(9), 1127–1135.

Dalal, F. (2002). *Race, Colour and the Process of Racialization. New Perspectives from Group Analysis, Psychoanalysis and Sociology.* London: Routledge.

Darwin, C. R. (1872 [1934]). *The Expression of Emotions in Man and Animals.* London: John Murray.

Dennett, D. (1987). *The Intentional Stance.* Cambridge, MA: MIT Press.

de Warren, N. (2017). We are, therefore i am – i am, therefore we are: The third in Sartre's social ontology. In C. Durt, T. Fuchs, & C. Tewes (Eds.), *Embodiment, Enaction, and Culture – Investigating the Constitution of the Shared World* (pp. 47–63). Cambridge, MA: The MIT Press.

Der Duden. (2009). *Die deutsche Rechtschreibung: Das umfassende Standardwerk auf der Grundlage der neuen amtlichen Regeln.* Berlin: Bibliographisches Institut.

Diez Grieser, M. T., & Müller, R. (2018). *Mentalisieren mit Kindern und Jugendlichen.* Stuttgart: Klett-Cotta.

Elias, N. (1939a). *Über den Prozeß der Zivilisation. Soziogenetische und psychogenetische Untersuchungen. Erster Band. Wandlungen des Verhaltens in den weltlichen Oberschichten des Abendlandes* (Vol. 1). Basel: Verlag Haus zum Falken.

Elias, N. (1939b). *Über den Prozeß der Zivilisation. Soziogenetische und psychogenetische Untersuchungen. Zweiter Band. Wandlungen der Gesellschaft. Entwurf einer Theorie der Zivilisation.* Basel: Verlag Haus zum Falken.

Elias, N. (1994). *The Civilizing Process.* Oxford: Blackwell.

Emde, R. N. (2009). From ego to "We-Go": Neurobiology and questions for psychoanalysis: Commentary on papers by Trevarthen, Gallese, and Ammaniti & Trentini. *Psychoanalytic Dialogues – The International Journal of Relational Perspectives, 19*(5), 556–564.

Fonagy, P. (2000). Attachment and borderline personality disorder. *Journal of American Psychoanalytic Association*, *48*(4), 1129–1146.

Fonagy, P. (2008). A genuinely developmental theory of sexual enjoyment and its implications for psychoanalytic technique. *Journal of American Psychoanalytic Association*, *56*(1), 11–36.

Fonagy, P., & Allison, E. (2014). The role of mentalizing and epistemic trust in the therapeutic relationship. *Psychotherapy*, *51*(3), 372–380.

Fonagy, P., & Campbell, C. (2015). Bad blood revisited: Attachment and psychoanalysis, 2015. *British Journal of Psychotherapy*, *31*(2), 229–250.

Fonagy, P., Gergely, G., Jurist, E. L., & Target, M. (2002 [2004]). *Affect Regulation, Mentalization and the Development of the Self*. London, New York: Karnac.

Fonagy, P., Luyten, P., Allison, E., & Campbell, C. (2019). Mentalizing, epistemic trust and the phenomenology of psychotherapy. *Psychopathology*, *52*, 1–10.

Fonagy, P., & Target, M. (2002). Neubewertung der Entwicklung der Affektregulation vor dem Hintergrund von Winnicott des Konzepts des "falschen Selbst". *Psyche – Zeitschrift für Psychoanalyse und ihre Anwendungen*, *56*, 839–862.

Foulkes, E. F. (Ed.) (1990). *Selected Papers of S.H. Foulkes. Psychoanalysis and Group Analysis*. London: Karnac.

Freud, S. (1900a). *Die Traumdeutung* (Vol. Gesammelte Werke II/III). Frankfurt a.M.: S. Fischer.

Freud, S. (1933 [1932]). Neue Folge der Vorlesungen zur Einführung in die Psychoanalyse. In S. Freud (Ed.), *Gesammelte Werke XV*. Frankfurt a.M.: S. Fischer.

Freud, S. (1985). Briefe an Wilhelm Fließ. 1887–1904. Ungekürzte Ausgabe. Bearbeitung der deutschen Fassung von M. Schröter. In Frankfurt a.M.: S. Fischer.

Frevert, U. (2015). Scham und Beschämung. In Geschichte der Gefühle – Einblicke in die Forschung. https://www.history-of-emotions.mpg.de/texte/scham-und-beschaemung. Last accessed on October 8, 2020.

Frevert, U. (2017). *Die Politik der Demütigung – Schauplätze von Macht und Ohnmacht* (2. Aufl.). Frankfurt am Main: S. Fischer.

Friedman, R. (2008). Courage, dreams and safe space. *International Journal of Counselling and Psychotherapy*, *5*, 45–54.

Friedman, R. (2014). Group analysis today – Developments in intersubjectivity. *Group Analysis*, *47*(3), 194–200.

Friedman, R. (2017). The group analysis of the Akeda: the worst and the best feelings in the matrix. In R. Friedman & Y. Doron (Eds.), *Group Analysis in the Land of Milk and Honey* (pp. 61–74). London: Karnac.

Gans, J. S., & Weber, R. L. (2000). The detection of shame in group psychotherapy: Uncovering the hidden emotion. *International Journal of Group Psychotherapy*, *50*(3), 381–396.

Garfinkle, E. (2012). Shame: The hidden resistance. *Canadian Journal of Psychoanalysis*, *20*, 44–69.

Gatti Pertegato, E. (2014). Foulkes' roots in Trigant Burrow's writings. *Group Analysis*, *47*(3), 312–328.

Gatti Pertegato, E., & Pertegato, G. O. (2013). From psychoanalysis to group analysis. The pioneering work of Trigant Burrow. London: Karnac.

Gleichmann, P. (1979a). Die Verhäuslichung von Harn- und Kotentleerungen. *MEDIZIN MENSCH GESELLSCHAFT MMG*, *4*, 46–52.

Gleichmann, P. R. (1979b). Die Verhäuslichung körperlicher Verrichtungen. In P. Gleichmann, J. Goudsblom, & H. Korte (Hrsg.), *Materialien zu Norbert Elias' Zivilisationstheorie* (pp. 254–278). Frankfurt a. M.: Suhrkamp.

Gleichmann, P. R. (1979c). Städte reinigen und geruchlos machen. Menschliche Körperentleerungen, ihre Geräte und ihre Verhäuslichung. In H. Sturm (Ed.), *Ästhetik und Umwelt.* (pp. 99–132). Tübingen: Gunter Narr.

Grünewald-Zemsch, G. (2019). *Die psychoanalytische Ausbildungssupervision – „Thinking under fire". Geschichte, Methoden und Konflikte.* Gießen: Psychosozial.

Hadar, B. (2008). The body of shame in the circle of the group. *Group Analysis, 41*(2), 163–179.

Haesler, L. (2008). Scham und Intersubjektivität – Ein Beitrag zur Kritik intersubjektivistischer Konzeptualisierung. *Forum der Psychoanalyse, 24*(4), 350–366.

Hell, D. (2018). *Lob der Scham – Nur wer sich achtet, kann sich schämen.* Gießen: Psychosozial-Verlag.

Heuft, G., & Knott, H. (2019) BARGRU-Studie. Welche Barrieren sehen GruppenpsychotherapeutInnen gegenüber der ambulanten Gruppenpsychotherapie? www. D3G.org, last accessed on October 8, 2020.

Hopper, E. (2003). *Traumatic Experience in the Unconscious Life of Groups. The Fourth Basic Assumption: Incohesion: Aggregation/Massification or (ba) I:A/M.* London: Jessica Kingsley.

Iscan, S., Seybert, C., Erhardt, I., Desmet, M., Levy, R. A., & Ablon, J. S. (2015). An empirical comparison of short-term psychodynamic psychotherapy process: Distinctive process factors between successful and unsuccessful therapeutic outcome groups. *Journal of the American Psychoanalytic Association, 63*(4), NP1–NP4.

Karterud, S. (2015). *Mentalization-Based Group Therapy (MBT-G).* Oxford: Oxford University Press.

Keller, H. (2011). *Kinderalltag: Kulturen der Kindheit und ihre Bedeutung für Bindung, Bildung und Erziehung.* Berlin: Springer.

Keller, H. (2019). *Mythos Bindungstheorie: Konzept · Methode · Bilanz.* Kiliansroda: verlag das netz.

Klein, G. S. (1976). *Psychoanalytic Theory: An Exploration of Essentials.* New York: International Universities Press.

Krach, S., Cohrs, J. C., de Echeverria Loebell, N. C., Kircher, T., Sommer, J., Jansen, A., & Paulus, F. M. (2011). Your flaws are my pain: Linking empathy to vicarious embarrassment. *Plos One, 6*(4), e18675. doi:10.1371/journal.pone.0018675

Krause, R. (2021). The development of different selves on the basis of leading maternal affects: Metatheoretical, clinical and technical reflections. *International Forum of Psychoanalysis, 30,* 22–33.

Küchenhoff, J. (2018). Scham und Beschämung – auch in psychoanalytischen Institutionen. *Forum der Psychoanalyse, 34,* 329–342.

Kütemeyer, M., & Schultz, U. (1989). Frühe psychoanalytische Schmerzauffassungen. *PPMP Psychotherapie Psychosomatik Medizinische Psychologie, 39,* 185–192.

Leszcz, M. (2004). Reflections on the abuse of power: Control and status in group therapy and group therapy training. *International Journal of Group Psychotherapy, 54*(3), 389–400.

Livingstone, L. R. P. (2006). No place to hide: The group leader's moments of shame. *International Journal of Group Psychotherapy, 56*(3), 307–323.

Lowenfeld, H. (1976). Notes on shamelessness. *Psychoanalytic Quarterly*, *45*, 62–72.

Luyten, P., Campbell, C., Allison, C., & Fonagy, P. (2020). The mentalizing approach to psychopathology: State of the art and future directions. *Annual Review of Clinical Psychology*, *16*, 297–325.

Luyten, P., Malcorps, S., Fonagy, P., & Ensink, K. (2019). Assessment of mentalizing. In A. Bateman & P. Fonagy (Eds.), *Handbook of Mentalizing in Mental Health Practice* (pp. 37–62). Washington, DC: American Psychiatric Association.

Mikulincer, M., & Shaver, P. R. (Eds.). (2014). *Mechanism of Social Connection: From Brain to Group*. Washington, DC: American Psychological Association.

Montgomery, C. (2006). The virtue of depression in the secret life of shame: A group-analytic perspective. *Group Analysis*, *39*(1), 73–85.

Morken, K. T. E., Binder, P.-E., Arefjord, N. M., & Karterud, S. W. (2019). Mentalization-based treatment from the patients' perspective – What ingredients do they emphasize? *Frontiers in Psychology*, *10*. doi:10.3389/fpsyg.2019.01327

Morrison, A. (1994). The breadth and boundaries of a self–psychological immersion in shame: A one–and–a–half–person perspective. *Psychoanalytic Dialogues*, *4*, 19–35.

Nathanson, D. L. (1994 [1992]). *Shame and Pride: Affect, Sex, and the Birth of the Self: Affect, Sex and the Birth of Self*. New York: Norton.

Nitsun, M. (2006a). *The Anti-Group*. London: Routledge.

Nitsun, M. (2006b). *The Group as an Object of Desire. Exploring Sexuality in Group Psychotherapy*. London: Routledge.

Nummenmaa, L., Glerean, E., Hari, R., & Hietanen, J. K. (2014). Bodily maps of emotions. *PNAS – Proceedings of the National Academy of Sciences of the United States of America*, *111*(2), 646–651.

Ogrodniczuk, J. S., Piper, W. E., Joyce, A. S., McCallum, M., & Rosie, J. S. (2003). NEO-five factor personality traits as predictors of response to two forms of group psychotherapy. *International Journal of Group Psychotherapy*, *53*(4), 417–442.

Otto, H., & Keller, H. (Eds.). (2018 [2014]). *Different Faces of Attachment – Cultural Variations on a Universal Human Need*. Cambridge: Cambridge University Press.

Panksepp, J., & Biven, L. (2012). *The Archaeology of Mind. Neuroevolutionary Origins of Human Emotions*. New York: Norton.

Piers, G., & Singer, M. B. (1953). *Shame and Guilt: A Psychoanalytic and Cultural Study*. Springfield: Thomas.

Roth, B. E. (1989). Critique of A. Alonso and J. S. Rutan "The experience of shame and the restoration of self-respect in group psychotherapy" (January, 1988), and their rejoinder (July, 1988). *International Journal of Group Psychotherapy*, *39*(4), 543–545.

Sandner, D. (1998). Die Begründung der Gruppenanalyse durch Trigant Burrow - Eine eigentümliche Amnesie innerhalb der gruppenanalytischen Tradition. *Luzifer-Amor. Zeitschrift zur Geschichte der Psychoanalyse*, *21*(11), 7–29.

Sartre, J.-P. (2014 [1943]). *Das Sein und das Nichts* (14. Aufl.). Reinbek bei Hamburg: Rowohlt.

Schultz-Venrath, U. (2015). Die Entdeckung der „Gruppenmethode in der Psychoanalyse" (1926) von Trigant Burrow – ein verhinderter Paradigmawechsel? *Gruppenpsychotherapie und Gruppendynamik*, *51*, 7–17.

Schultz-Venrath, U. (2020). Mentalisierungsbasierte Gruppenpsychotherapie (MBT-G). *PiD Psychotherapie im Dialog*, *21*, 1–6.

Schultz-Venrath, U. (2021). *Mentalisieren des Körpers*. Stuttgart: Klett-Cotta.

Schultz-Venrath, U., & Felsberger, H. (2016). *Mentalisieren in Gruppen*. Stuttgart: Klett-Cotta.

Skarderud, F., & Fonagy, P. (2012). Eating Disorders. In A. W. Bateman & P. Fonagy (Eds.), *Handbook of Mentalizing in Mental Health Practice* (pp. 347–383). Washington, DC: American Psychiatric Publishing.

Stern, D. N. (1992 [1985]). *The Interpersonal World of the Infant: A View from Psychoanalysis and Developmental Psychology*. New York: Basic Books.

Thußbas, C. (2015). Kann Gewalt Transformation unaushaltbarer Scham sein? Überlegungen am Beispiel einer Grenzüberschreitung in einer Psychoanalyse. In A. Ebrecht-Laermann, E. Löchel, B. Nissen, & J. Picht (Hrsg.), *Jahrbuch der Psychoanalyse*, Vol. 70 (pp. 47–68). Stuttgart: fromann-holzboog.

Tiedemann, J. L. (2013 [2016]). *Scham (Analyse der Psyche und Psychotherapie)*. Gießen: Psychosozial-Verlag.

Tisseron, S. (2000). *Phänomen Scham*. München: Reinhardt.

Turner, S. W., McFarlane, A. C., & Van der Kolk, B. A. (1996). The therapeutic environment and new explorations in the treatment of posttraumatic stress disorder. In B. A. Van der Kolk, A. C. McFarlane, & L. E. Weisaeth (Eds.), *Traumatic Stress: The Effects of Overwhelming Experience on Mind, Body, and Society* (pp. 537–558). New York: Guilford.

Wille, R. (2014). The Shame of Existing: An Extreme form of Shame. *International Journal of Psychoanalysis*, 95(4), 695–717.

Wurmser, L. (1990). *Die Maske der Scham. Die Psychoanalyse von Schamaffekten und Schamkonflikten*. Berlin: Springer-Verlag.

Chapter 7

The aggressor within

Attachment trauma, segregated systems, and the double face of shame

Adriano Schimmenti

In this chapter, I will discuss how feelings of shame can result from childhood experiences of neglect and abuse within the attachment relationships. I propose that shame arising from early attachment trauma can be defensively organized in multiple layers, from self-conscious feelings to segregated mental states, to paradoxically protect the self from unbearable aloneness and fears of breakdown. Two clinical vignettes will be described that illustrate how shame may weaken the capacities for human relatedness and personal growth of traumatized individuals. However, shame is also shown to be defensively maintained and protected to exclude the awareness of overwhelming feelings related to negative childhood experiences. I go on to discuss the clinical work with traumatized individuals who are trapped by multiple layers of shame, suggesting that the healing process can only develop within safe and trusting attachment relationships, within and outside of therapy.

Attachment trauma

"Attachment trauma" is the name given to emotional states and behaviour derived from childhood experiences of loss, abuse, and neglect within early attachment relationships. Attachment trauma is considered as a key variable for understanding both mental and physical distress.

In fact, meta-analytic findings show that people who were exposed to early attachment trauma are at increased risk for many different psychological difficulties in their adult life. People with troubling "symptoms" arising from early attachment trauma are often diagnosed in the psychiatric field as having psychotic disorders (Varese et al., 2012), bipolar disorders (Agnew-Blais & Danese, 2016), depressive disorders (Infurna et al., 2016), eating disorders (Caslini et al., 2016), borderline personality disorder (Winsper et al., 2016), substance use disorder (Konkolÿ Thege et al., 2017), PTSD (Brewin et al., 2000), and dissociative disorders (Dalenberg et al., 2012). Moreover, a recent meta-analysis by Hughes and colleagues (Hughes

DOI: 10.4324/9781003175612-8

et al., 2017) based on thirty-seven studies and providing risk estimates for twenty-three health outcomes, with a total of 253,719 participants, showed that people who were exposed to severe attachment trauma, defined as being exposed to more than three adverse childhood experiences (ACEs), were at increased risk of many poor health outcomes compared with individuals with no ACEs. Associations between attachment trauma and health outcomes were modest for physical inactivity, being overweight, and diabetes (Odds-Ratio [O-R] < 2); they were moderate for smoking, heavy alcohol use, poor self-rated health, cancer, heart disease, and respiratory disease (ORs between 2 and 3); they were strong for sexual risk taking, mental ill health, and problematic alcohol use (ORs between 3 and 6); and they were even stronger for problematic drug use and interpersonal and self-directed violence (ORs > 7).

The impact of attachment trauma on an individual's biobehavioural functioning is severe. Cook et al. (2017) highlighted seven primary domains of impairment observed in children exposed to attachment trauma. Just to summarize: (a) the attachment system is affected by uncertainties about the reliability and predictability of the world, that generate difficulty attuning to other people's emotional states, social isolation, and interpersonal difficulties; (b) there are biological impairments involving sensorimotor developmental problems, somatization, increased medical problems across a wide spectrum; (c) affect regulation problems emerge, involving difficulty with emotion regulation, difficulty knowing and describing internal states, difficulty communicating wishes, and desires; (d) pathological dissociation arises, and significant alterations in states of consciousness, with amnesia, depersonalization, and derealization, are observed; (e) behavioural control is reduced, with poor modulation of impulses, self-destructive behaviour, aggression against others, and pathological self-soothing behaviours (such as substance abuse and eating disorders); (f) the cognition domain is affected by difficulties in attention regulation and executive functioning, problems with processing novel information, problems with object constancy, difficulty planning, and anticipating, with all their developmental consequences; and (g) self-concept is dramatically damaged, with a poor sense of separateness, disturbances of body image, low self-esteem, shame, and guilt, together with a lack of a continuous, predictable sense of self.

These impairments in a person's life are very troubling and occur because attachment trauma generates significant alterations in the brain. Here are some examples from the research in this field. Brain regions, for example the temporal lobes, can be nearly quiescent and desensitized in children who had been institutionalized from birth. There is evidence that brain scans of severely neglected children show reduced grey matter, enlarged ventricles and cortical atrophy. Empirical observations show that individuals who had been exposed to attachment trauma display alterations in the left temporo-parietal cortex which is critical for information retrieval, emotional stability, explicit memory, and sensory processing, among other functions. In addition there are changes in the right inferior frontal gyrus, which may determine changes in attitudes to risk, in the ventromedial prefrontal cortex, which is implicated in the processing of risk and fear, and also plays a role in the inhibition of emotional responses and in the process of decision-making and self-control. Attachment trauma has an impact on the functioning of the right inferior orbitofrontal cortex which is a critical region for stimulus-outcome associations and the evaluation and possibly reversal of behaviour, and thus has implications for learning from experience and avoiding the compulsion to repeat. There are also changes in the hippocampus which is central, among other brain regions, for the encoding and retrieval of memory (Chalavi et al., 2015; De Bellis, 2005; Gold et al., 2016; Perry, 2009; Schore, 2009; Thomaes et al., 2009). Accordingly, the network of cortical and subcortical interactions that foster the individual's ability to organize mental and behavioural states is damaged in children who have been maltreated and/or have experienced significant failures of care (Schimmenti, 2012).

What happens in the brain of some children who were exposed to attachment trauma seems to reflect what happens in their life and relationships. A dangerous pathway that distorts the individual's development toward atypical trajectories is often observed in the life of these children. Accordingly, in a recent article, I have postulated that early attachment trauma is linked with other trauma occurring later in an individual's life, with empirical findings derived from a sample of traumatized individuals which supports this hypothesis (Schimmenti, 2018). What follows is an example of a traumatic developmental cascade that I have written about elsewhere (Granieri et al., 2018). A child who loses a parent (trauma n. 1) will have an increased probability of being neglected (trauma n. 2) by the other parent (for example, because the living parent struggles to cope with his or her own depressive feelings, and/or because the death of his or her spouse generated financial problems in the family); being neglected at home, in turn, increases the probability that the child will be exposed to abuses (trauma n. 3) outside the family (e.g., being bullied at school), because they lack a loving and protective figure who can help the child to adequately cope with difficulties and problems. This pattern of consecutive exposure to multiple traumatic experiences can continue over and over, with the child being dramatically damaged at multiple levels of functioning by such experiences.

According to this theoretical framework, it is clear that attachment trauma may foster unprocessed feelings of inadequacy, unworthiness, anger, and resentment in the child, among many other dysregulated feelings that cannot be processed within safe and nurturing attachment relationships. So, the child may need to dissociate such feelings from awareness to preserve a positive internal image of the caregiver (Schimmenti, 2017). This is because attachment, from the cradle to the grave, is a motivational system that is embedded in the human species, a biological endowment that allows our species to survive both physically and psychologically. However, the dissociated feelings concerning attachment trauma may surface in the form of other traumatized mental states, disruptive and impulsive behaviours, together with multiple internalizing and externalizing "symptoms" which are communicating the severe distress which has been endured.

Defensive exclusion and segregated systems

All the above considerations are consistent with Bowlby's (1962, 1980) original insights about defensive exclusion and segregated systems. In his paper "Defences that follow loss: Causation and function," Bowlby (1962) observed that "… selective exclusion is an integral and ubiquitous part of the action of the central nervous system." Bowlby also reminded us that the mind can retain some conditional integration in deploying defensive exclusion in response to an experience that would otherwise be overwhelming, though at the price of segregating certain kinds of environmental information (Reisz et al., 2017). Actually, it seems that Bowlby has anticipated the current understanding of dissociation as a normal process of the mind that allows individuals to maintain a conditional sense of integration, by temporarily excluding distressing feelings and mental states that are inconsistent with the present moment, and that becomes pathological instead if the mind is organized in early stages of development around intense and pervasive dissociative needs, exactly because of attachment trauma (Bromberg, 1998). In fact, in the same paper Bowlby argued that "…what characterises a pathological condition is that exclusion acts in such a way that it creates not only the usual temporary barrier but a permanent one. Thereby psychic systems are segregated from one another as though by an iron curtain." Bowlby proposed that prolonged and intense avoidance of mental contents can result in the defensive exclusion of internal or external cues to the individual's relational needs. In this way, defensive exclusion can ultimately undermine integration and shift the mind into a segregated state, because it can inhibit the ability to update representational models of self and other, and thus discrepant experience and information remain segregated and unavailable.

In another paper, "On knowing what you are not supposed to know and feeling what you are not supposed to feel," Bowlby (1988) explicitly wrote that "Children not infrequently observe scenes their parents would prefer they did not observe; they form impressions their parents would prefer they did not form; and they have experiences their parents would like to believe they have not had." Bowlby provided examples of parents who seek to disconfirm their child's observations of events, natural emotional responses to distressing situations, and even the perception of parents' personalities and behaviour. Especially, three situations are believed to render children particularly prone to engaging in defensive exclusion: (a) situations in which children have done or thought about doing something of which they are deeply ashamed; (b) situations that parents do not wish their children to know about, even though the children have witnessed them; and (c) situations in which the children find the parents' behaviour too unbearable to think about. While the first situation is linked with the internal motivation of the children, it should be observed here that the other two situations reflect deep conditions of attachment insecurity, manipulation, deception, cognitive disorientation of the children, and potentially neglect and abuse.

Thus, I would say that what is unthinkable in attachment trauma is that the one who should protect the child is the same individual who damages him or her. This is why the child is exposed, as Main and Hesse (1990) observed, to a "fright without solution" that may disorganize the child's mind. And at this point, the child has only one option, that is, to defensively exclude the information concerning the maltreating parent, and segregate it into a mental system, which is distinct from other accessible mental states and not amenable to psychological processing.

Defensive exclusion leads to a split in the individuals' internal working models (IWMs) of attachment, the cognitive and affective schemata that include the representations of self, other, and the relationship between self and others. One set of IWMs will be accessible to awareness and discussion, and will be based on what a child has been told. This set would represent the parent as good and the parent's neglecting, rejecting, and abusing behaviour as caused by the "badness" of the child. The other model, based on what the child has experienced but has defensively excluded from awareness, will represent the hated or disappointing side of the parents (Bretherton, 1992). That is, the set of the IWMs containing the available information will be retained in the declarative memory, whereas the segregated information will often remain unprocessed within the episodic memory.

The role of shame in attachment trauma

When situations of attachment trauma are on the line, I believe that shame acts to prevent access to the segregated systems and their IWMs. Shame is an aversive state. It is usually a self-conscious emotion accompanied by a feeling of being exposed, ridiculous, and devalued. The experience of shame can arise from many sources, such as a violation of some role or standard, a failure to meet expectations, or a defect of the self that cannot easily be repaired (Lewis, 1992).

Shame is always a relational experience. According to Helen Block Lewis (1987, p. 15), "shame is one's own vicarious experience of the other's scorn. The self-in-the eyes-of-the-other is the focus of awareness." However, shame can arise not only from others' scorn (active shaming), but also from significant non-responding of others (passive shaming) that might lead the individual to feel unworthy and empty.

The root of shame can be traced back to childhood experiences: shame occurs in early stages of life in response to perceived rejection or separation from caregivers. Shame alerts the child to the threat of separation, so that action can be taken to protect the attachment bond (Schore, 1998). Actually, it is because of our capacity to attach that we experience shame. Shame allows us to "fit in" by "excluding" aspects of self, and in most severe cases even the self as a whole (Wille, 2014).

Actually, shame can represent the effect of dysfunctional relationships during childhood: if the attachment figures are not affectively attuned, or if they "disconfirm their child's observations of events [and their child's] natural emotional responses to distressing situations," to maintain Bowlby's (1979) description, the child may feel that his or her own internal experience is unworthy and shameful. As the trust in an attachment figure is betrayed, early trauma creates a template for traumatic shame (Benau, 2017; Schimmenti, 2012).

Such shame is double-faced: on one side, it threatens the individual's self-esteem, fostering a sense of defectiveness, inadequacy, and unworthiness; on the other side, it has the critical function of protecting access to the individual's "psychic pits" (Schimmenti & Caretti, 2010, 2016), i.e. to the segregated systems containing an identification with the aggressor (Ferenczi, 1933/1988, 1933/1949), the "real" perception of the attachment relationships, and the awareness that the deepest attachment needs have not been fulfilled. The double bind is between "I am bad, but I can attach," and "I am good, but I am alone." It should be observed here that the experience of unfulfilled attachment longings is unbearable, and in this case shame can paradoxically fill the void of non-being (Benau, 2017). In other words, the child cannot come too close to the pit of his or her true experiences with the caregiver. Coming too close would bring the child terror, disorganization, disintegration, and dissolution. All that is the opposite of attachment.

In this context, shame offers a way out of these unbearable feelings: it organizes and simplifies what is overwhelming. Self-conscious shame, especially in attachment trauma, may constitute the *facade* (in terms of observable shame behaviours, such as blushing, avoiding eye contact, lowering the head, the desire to hide, or escape) of a deepest and unbearable shame feeling.

I will call this central and unbearable feeling as the Core Shame State. The Core Shame State is the result of a traumatic identification (Schimmenti, 2017) with a neglecting and abusing attachment figure, which is not easily accessible to discussion, processing, and transformation because it is segregated and paradoxically protected by self-conscious shame. In this traumatic identification, the segregated system includes an "alien transplant" (Ferenczi, 1932/1988), in which the individual's representation of self corresponds to that projected onto the child by the abusing and neglecting caregiver (Schimmenti, 2017). In fact, as Ferenczi (1933/1949, p. 228) has sensed many years ago, "the weak and undeveloped personality [of the child] reacts to sudden unpleasure [...] by anxiety-ridden identification and by introjection of the menacing person or aggressor."

This poses a serious question for the way in which we support people who have suffered from attachment trauma and who experience traumatic shame. As I said elsewhere (Schimmenti, 2012, p. 198), "an individual must have developed a sense of security in order to tolerate the painful experience of facing his or her own 'monsters', and that sense of security must be stronger than the fear of succumbing to the monsters." It must be emphasized here that without this internalized other, sometimes there is no sense of connection. From a clinical point of view, that is why the identification with the aggressor is hard to relinquish: not only because the child would have to face the parent's badness, but more importantly he or she would have to face the terror of utter aloneness and annihilation.

The following accounts of my work with two different people aim to illustrate the unbearable nature of the Core Shame State, and why it is critical to work through it when supporting people to recover from early attachment trauma.[1]

Kate

> There's something inside me that pulls beneath the surface
> Consuming, confusing
> This lack of self control I fear is never ending Controlling I can't seem
> To find myself again My walls are closing in
> I've felt this way before So insecure
>
> *Crawling* – Linkin Park (2000)

Kate is a thirty-year-old woman with a master's degree in psychology who has returned to live with her sister and her divorced mother, after ending her marriage of five years. She requested a consultation because of her intense symptoms of anxiety, and also because she knew about my study of dissociation and told me that this could be relevant to her own experience.

In the first consultation, she reported that she had been treated for bulimia and panic attacks before, and then added a puzzling statement that she had always "protected" her former therapists. She attempted suicide at the age of sixteen, for which she had been hospitalized for a couple of weeks. She had also been in psychological treatment for six months for her bulimia nervosa, and later for two and a half years because of her panic attacks. Kate said that these treatments were effective, but did not want to explore why she had felt it necessary to protect her therapists.

Subsequent consultations were devoted to us discovering the detailed issues underlying her difficulties. Kate presented a number of disorders in comorbidity: these included persistent depressive disorder, major depression, generalized anxiety disorder, and post-traumatic stress disorder (dissociative subtype) as assessed by SCID-5-CV (First et al., 2016). She also described experiencing some thought insertion and hallucinatory symptoms, such as olfactory hallucinations (smell) and something crawling in her skin. Moreover, Kate suffered from coeliac disease and was medicated for hyperthyroidism.

This was of course a very complicated clinical picture. However, as Kate explicitly reported that my study on trauma and dissociation could be relevant for her case, I decided to check for her dissociative symptoms with the SCID-D-R (Steinberg, 1994, 2000), and everything became much clearer. She had moderate amnesia (it happened every day, even if she lost only few minutes), high depersonalization (which was very frequent and pervasive), low derealization (which had happened only in few occasions), high identity confusion (she frequently asked herself who she was), and moderate identity alteration (she sometimes felt and behaved as though there were different persons within herself). She also had experience of compartmentalized internal voices. Accordingly, it became evident that Kate had a Dissociative Identity Disorder (DID). In a later consultation, Kate admitted that she already knew she probably had had DID for many years, but was ashamed of it as she thought that having multiple and dissociated self states meant that she was crazy.

There is little doubt that Kate's disorder was the result of severe and enduring attachment trauma. Kate's parents really were "scare-givers," as Orit Badouk Epstein (2015) properly defined such attachment figures, that is they were caregivers who apparently took care of Kate while deeply scaring her because of their unpredictable and sometimes sadistic behaviours. Furthermore, Kate was sexually abused by her older brother for many years; the abuse began when she was only eight years old. As a consequence of attachment trauma, Kate's expectations toward interpersonal relationships were deeply negative, and she was very ashamed, anxious, and sad. She felt responsible for everything bad that had occurred in her life, and she feared that other people (including me) would have judged her as a "morally loose woman" if they knew what had really happened to her. These expectations reflected the damage that Kate's experiences of neglect and abuse had done to her self and relationships.

Apparently, shame was a conscious emotion for Kate. She recognized that she felt shame for many reasons, including her presumed low intelligence (her parents often told her that she was stupid when she was a child, and despite her evident intelligence she was still identified with the parents' depiction of herself as a child), her pervasive anxiety that made it difficult for her to deal with during work and daily activities, her dissociative experiences, and her past and current sexual experiences.

However, I felt that Kate's conscious shame experiences protected her from a deeper feeling of worthlessness related to her overall mental and behavioural functioning. I was aware that Kate hid the true nature of her difficulties from everyone before, including her former therapists. So, it was true that she had always "protected" her therapists by compulsively taking care of them (Bowlby, 1980; Liotti, 2014) and of their potential feelings of shame and inadequacy when treating her. I discovered that compulsive caretaking (Solomon & George, 2011) was a way of feeling worthy for Kate: her love wasn't loved and delighted in, so she had no place to put her love other than into others. Thus, providing care to others, including her abusers, served as an adaptive strategy for maintaining closeness and feelings of belonging for Kate, even though this behaviour fostered further feelings of inauthenticity and indignity, in an endless cycle that led Kate to feel that there was something basically wrong within her.

The aggressor within Kate had been generated in the extremely painful experiences of neglect and abuse that she had lived through during childhood. Accordingly, Kate's Core Shame State included a segregated system in which a dissociated representation of the self revealed a traumatic identification with the aggressor. As one of her identities addressed the issue: "if Kate was not loved and if she was abused, this happened because she does not deserve either love or care. Kate is a bad child, so she deserved to be abused."

In this way, one can better understand Kate's compulsive caretaking of her family problems in later years, including the alcoholism of her father, the depression of her mother, and the outbursts and turmoils of her abusing brother, as an attempt to preserve the attachment bonds by trying to repair her internalized feelings of unworthiness, indignity, and unbearable aloneness. Actually, Kate's deepest feeling of shame did not concern what happened to her in the past, what she did, or how she behaved; she felt an unbearable shame for who she was. The child (now adult) had concluded that there was something terribly wrong with her, rather than what was done to her.

I understood this feeling as an unconscious attempt to make the aggressor go away ("I'm already a nobody") via the internalization of the aggressor ("You don't need to attack me. I've already taken care of that better than you ever can"). In this way, however, shame attaches to everything and attacks everything (character, behaviours, body, relationships, and so on). It is noteworthy that the representation of "I am bad," in lieu of "I was treated badly" gives some clients a way to control, in fantasy, the uncontrollable abuse and neglect, to preserve the parent and the attachment, and to avoid unbearable aloneness and psychic disintegration.

In this context, I think that shame represents the internal solution to an unsolvable dilemma, not just the problem clients and therapists might think at first glance. And in the same vein I think that in many cases of attachment trauma shame is organized in layers, from self-conscious feelings to segregated mental states, so as to protect the attachment bond at any cost.

The Core Shame State, albeit extremely painful, needs to be explored and worked through in therapy. This is because this unbearable and dissociated feeling has a protective function for the human mind that prevents any access to spontaneity in human relationships, and ultimately the possibility of personal and relational growth. In the case of Kate, the segregated Core Shame State protected her from the awareness of being unloved and unwanted, and consequently from attachment disorganization and mental disintegration. This brought Kate to defensively exclude her need to be loved and cared for, and to always protect her abusers and anyone around her instead. This allowed psychic survival, but at the price of fostering further feelings of shame, multiplicity, and severe psychopathology.

So, clinicians must collaborate with their clients in the exploration of the pain that shame defends against, not the shame *per se*, because shame paradoxically represented the traumatized client's solution, not the root of the problem. Kate's Core Shame State was based on a segregated system including a traumatic identification with "the aggressor within": a part of her dissociated IWMs which was identified with the "bad child" who had deserved to be criticized by her mother and abused by her brother. This child saw herself as bad, unworthy, immoral, and actually deserving the abuse. The work with the "bad child" was of course a key to our therapy relationship, but access to the Core Shame State from an attachment-based perspective also included: (a) tolerance of Kate's resistance to becoming attached (while working with clients who suffered from attachment trauma, the clinician should always remember the maxim "the slower you go, the faster you get"); (b) interpersonal validation of feelings, as a way to foster therapeutic alliance and Kate's perception of the consulting room as a safe retreat; (c) "tact" (Ferenczi, 1912) while exploring her internal states; (d) psychoeducation and interpretation when conflict states arose (to increase Kate's "window of tolerance"; (Bromberg, 2011; Siegel, 1999); and (e) supporting Kate's curiosity about how new knowledge in relation to her internal world could promote more adapted and self-consistent behaviours in the external world (to foster Kate's secure base). This provided the internal and relational safety that allowed Kate to recognize and understand the development of the segregated system involving her identification with the aggressor.

This approach then leads to diminishing the power of the internalized aggressors, by offering new ways of being in relationship, with the clinician, with the client's own internal world, and (later) in the world beyond the therapy relationship. It is critical that the exploration and working through of the Core Shame State gets to the terror of aloneness and overcomes it, otherwise this lurking terror becomes unbearable, and the person may even disintegrate emotionally. In fact, especially in the first stages of our work, I feared that Kate might have a breakdown. For example, when she remembered some abusive experiences from her past there was often an abrupt shifting to altered states which frightened her and made her feel ashamed.

Yet, I felt a positive feeling inside me that I did not understand at first, which lasted until the end of her therapy. I later recognized that this feeling was related to Kate's trust in me and our work. She felt sufficiently safe in our relationship to show me who she truly was, something that was almost impossible in her family and in past relationships. So, she might feel alone, but not *so* alone that she couldn't surrender to the experience of her past trauma. Thus, in my relationship with Kate I have seen attachment theory "in action". I experienced how my validation of her feelings and my belief in her capacity to heal and grow was reciprocated by her trust in me and our consultations. Thinking again about the work with Kate always reminds me of a fundamental tenet of attachment theory, that is, trust in relationships is key to effective recovery and healing of early attachment trauma.

Peter

> You're like your father I see right through you
> Just like your father I thought I knew you
> You can't come here
> You can't cry
>
> *In the Garden* – Dolores O'Riordan (2007)

Peter was a smart and creative man, an artist in his early thirties. He came to consult with me about his anxiety symptoms and an almost paranoid delusion that all individuals judged him negatively while he performed his music. Also, he reported in the first consultation that he had recently argued with his fiancée, whom he loves passionately, and during the argument he had hit her on the shoulder and pushed her violently onto the bed, then threatened her by putting his hands over her face. He had never acted this way before; he started crying after this episode and thought the time had come to have a consultation with a clinician.

Peter grew up in a traditional Sicilian family, where physical punishments and criticism of children are common, as they are (wrongly) considered to have positive educational outcomes. His father was physically harsh with him, so that a few episodes in Peter's childhood actually resembled physical abuse, and he was very critical of some of Peter's attitudes. As a result, Peter feared his father's physical and verbal reactions to him as a child. Yet, Peter felt that his father was also loving toward him, and reported many episodes in which his father played with him, appreciated him, and protected him from violent peers. Peter loved his mother a lot when he was a child, and felt that he had to protect her from his father's violent outbursts. As an adolescent, it became clear to him that his mother was so absorbed in the conflict with her husband, that she had pushed Peter into becoming a parentified child, their roles reversed so Peter had to take care of her psychological well-being.

After a few interviews, Peter reported a strange symptom: since he took his driving test at the age of eighteen, he frequently heard a critical internal voice when he was alone in the car, and he always argued angrily with this voice. Peter was aware that this voice came from within himself. It had no particular sound, but was as derogating of him as his father was toward him during his childhood. The voice criticized him severely for all his personal choices including his decision to seek psychotherapy.

Thus, Peter revealed two apparently psychotic symptoms (hearing a critical voice inside his head, and being almost paranoid about people's judgemental reactions to his music), but the diagnostic assessment showed that Peter did not show other psychotic symptoms, nor did he have a clinical disorder. Also, although he presented with some narcissistic features, Peter was very empathetic with almost everyone in his life.

Consequently, it became critical to understand the origins of Peter's unusual pattern of distress. It was easy to observe that Peter talked aloud with the internal voice only when he was in the car, and that his father's work was related to cars: thus, hearing a criticizing voice in his mind while in the car could represent for Peter the internalization of his father's criticism toward him. Peter accepted the hypothesis that the internal voice was a part of him derived from the internalization of his father's criticism, and considered that violently arguing with this voice could represent for him an unconscious strategy to counteract the traumatic shame he had experienced in the relationship with his father during childhood.

It was more difficult to consider in this context – and in fact it took more time to acknowledge it in the consultations – that Peter's father had however also loved him intensely and in an enlivening way, while his mother was supportive but absorbed in her own conflict with her husband. Thus, Peter's psychic survival was tied to recognition from his father, even if his father was harsh. Consequently, Peter had to keep separate the harshness of his father and the loving nature of the relationship, or the love essential to his survival would be spoiled.

Apparently shame was a conscious emotion for Peter. He recognized his shame about needing therapy, about being judged by other people, also in relation to his recent violent reactions during the argument with his fiancée. More generally he was aware of the shame he felt about his need to be appreciated by everyone, which limited his assertiveness and self-confidence. Yet, Peter's most disturbing feelings of shame were hidden. In fact, shame about his behaviour and needs hid his shame for having attachment longings. Peter's conscious feelings of shame protected him from traumatic shame that involved his entire self: he feared that he was weak and cowardly, a "cry-baby," as his father accused him of being when he was a child.

I thought that "the aggressor within" Peter had developed in the form of the internal voice that he heard when he was alone in the car exactly because the car was the symbolic place that represented his relationship with his father. Thus, in Peter's case arguing with the voice had the meaning of complaining to the father for his harsh treatment and for his view of Peter as a crybaby, but at the same time it served to preserve an attachment relationship with the father. So, while it seemed that Peter unconsciously felt that he was worthless, such feelings of worthlessness protected him from a deeper shame concerning his extreme separation anxiety and fear of abandonment.

As Bowlby (1973) discusses in the second volume of his trilogy on attachment and loss, separation from an attachment figure evokes anxiety and anger. Accordingly, Peter's Core Shame State involved him being ashamed of the pride he felt for being autonomous and profoundly different from the other members of his family (e.g., Peter would later become the first member of his large family who got a university degree). Peter was paying a high price for his segregated feelings of pride and for his secret revenge against his father, because his father was his main attachment figure and Peter's IWMs were based on such a figure. In a vicious circle, Peter's Core Shame State dizzily escalated his separation anxiety, and separation anxiety produced further shame. Actually, Peter was ashamed of his attachment longings, of the separation from his family and his individuation as a man.

The segregated Core Shame State reflected Peter's intense separation anxiety. In fact, the awareness of the separation from his family had fostered an intense fear of abandonment in him. Near the end of therapy, it became clear that Peter had defensively excluded his pride about differentiation from his family and pretended, for his psychological survival, to be as "weak" and "fragile" as his father suggested he was when Peter was a child. This "hiding" behind the image of himself as weak possibly did two things: it agreed with his father, which allowed Peter to maintain the attachment and the connection with him, and it was also a submissive response that prevented further attack from the internalized and split image of the abusive father. This allowed Peter to overcome his guilt for being different from his father, but at the price of continually arguing with the internalized voice and protesting against it.

In conclusion, Peter's Core Shame State was based on a segregated system in which the pride of being different from his father (and father's family) was constantly threatened by the feeling that such difference would cause separation from and abandonment by him. This was the reason why Peter was "attached" to the criticizing voice. Actually, Peter was torn and unable to connect with both his hatred of his father and his love for him. Since the shaming attachment object was also the object who gave him the recognition his life depended on, seeking for real improvement in therapy was conflictual for Peter, as it could imply a loss of an internal object which was critical for his attachment system. If Peter gave up his father, whom he loved, then he would have little loving connection to his family.

As shame regulates affect – in this case, the risk of a "loss" of attachment with its consequent sadness and depression (Bowlby, 1980) – Peter's progress in therapy invited contrasting feelings of shame and pride. On the one hand, he was fearful that his traumatic internal state (the criticizing voice) might be lost, as this voice had brought him to an adaptation that had become central for his personal identity. In a traumatic progression (Ferenczi, 1932), he had become a creative artist also *because of* his past relational trauma, since music and arts allowed him to receive attention from father and other family members and to sublimate the negative states concerning harsh treatment as a child. On the other hand, his music was not only "defensive," in the service of attachment, but also "progressive," in the service of his self-aliveness. His music was testimony to his "pro-being" pride (Benau, 2018) in being different from his father and his family, and he felt that it spoke to the heart of who he really was.

As Richard Chefetz (2017, p. 119) wisely and elegantly put it, "dignity is the opposite of shame, and pride is the opposite of guilt." Peter's segregated pride of being different from his father had generated guilt for his need for differentiation, and also the unconscious need of being punished for such "betrayal" (via the internalized criticizing voice). As the attachment needs for closeness, affection, and love had been defensively excluded, Peter was apparently ashamed of being internally as bad and defective as his father pushed him to think during childhood. Actually, it seemed that Peter saw himself as a deceiver who always did the wrong thing either in his musical performances, in his relationships, and now even with his fiancée whom he loved so much. However, we discovered that such shame protected Peter from sensing the separateness from his attachment figures.

Working through the acknowledgement of Peter's attachment needs was critical for his well-being and for restoring his damaged dignity. He first became curious about the role and meaning of this voice in his internal experiences and life. Then, this curiosity concerning his feared internal state in the form of the voice brought him to discover that this voice, even if harsh, was protective toward him and his attachment needs. This fostered his feelings of safety, so that he stopped arguing with the voice, and started laughing and joking with it when it arrived. This new capacity to play with the internal reality (Fonagy & Target, 1996; Winnicott, 1971) was central to the voice reducing its presence and pervasiveness while Peter was in a car. Feelings of security thus developed, and Peter understood the relevance of his attachment needs for his personal and professional life. Peter's mentalizing dramatically improved as he did not fear anymore the content of his segregated mental states and became more able to explore his own internal world and the meaning of his relational experiences. Since then, the success and recognition for his musical performances have increased enormously, he and his fiancée married. Peter continues to feel that he has become a better and more integrated person.

Conclusions

The clinical vignettes of Kate and Peter illustrate how feelings of shame among people who were exposed to attachment trauma can be structured in layers that protect the individual from segregated and unbearable mental contents. I think that the access to these is protected by layers of shame exactly because in this way the traumatized individual will avoid approaching the Core Shame State, as becoming aware of it is predicted to evoke attachment disorganization. In fact, I have specifically highlighted that the unbearable nature of the Core Shame State is defensively excluded, and that a traumatic identification with the abusing and neglecting attachment figure is the bulwark to preserve the mind from the flood of dysregulated feelings derived from the emotional awareness of the attachment trauma, and thus from attachment disorganization.

This is why I believe that the deepest shame feelings can be repaired in the therapy relationship with individuals exposed to attachment trauma only if the clinician recognizes the clients' attachment needs that are expressed also through observed shame behaviours and associated clinical and subclinical symptoms. The dignity of these clients and of their attachment longings must be preserved. As clinicians, we should work with them to foster their safety, security, emotional regulation, mentalizing abilities, and capacity to "play" with reality, including the reality of the therapy relationship.

We should remember that for many clients who have suffered from attachment trauma, shame keeps at bay our two worst fears. First is the internal rage toward the shaming attachment object, with the consequent terror of utter aloneness and the disorganization which that terror warns the person about if the object is destroyed or abandoned. Second, it keeps at bay the causes of this terror, that is the abuse and the feelings of indignity and worthlessness that it had generated.

The repair of shame, and more generally the repair of the wounded self of traumatized individuals with all its segregated systems, lies in the attachment relationship. It is in the clinicians' attempts to foster secure attachment relationships with their clients, even when the clients' childhood attachment relationships have failed or have been grossly damaged, that promotes healing. Recovery can also be found in the clients' efforts to overcome their fears and to learn how to attach to other people and also to relate to all the different parts of self (Schimmenti & Caretti, 2016). The repair is in the attachment relationship, and in how safety and security can positively change this and enable recovery from even the most difficult life experiences.

Note

1   All clinical material has been disguised to preserve clients' confidentiality.

References

Agnew-Blais, J., & Danese, A. (2016). Childhood maltreatment and unfavourable clinical outcomes in bipolar disorder: A systematic review and meta-analysis. *The Lancet Psychiatry, 3*, 342–349. https://doi.org/10.1016/S2215-0366(15)00544-1

Badouk Epstein, O. (2015). Cross the bridge to redefine the pain. *Attachment: New Directions in Psychotherapy and Relational Psychoanalysis, 9*, 290–294.

Benau, K. (2017). Shame, attachment, and psychotherapy: Phenomenology, neurophysiology, relational trauma, and harbingers of healing. *Attachment: New Directions in Psychotherapy and Relational Psychoanalysis, 11*, 1–27.

Benau, K. (2018). Pride in the psychotherapy of relational trauma: Conceptualization and treatment considerations. *European Journal of Trauma & Dissociation, 2*, 131–146. https://doi.org/10.1016/j.ejtd.2018.03.002

Bowlby, J. (1962). Defences that follow loss: Causation and function. In R. Duschinsky & K. White (2020, Eds.). *Trauma and Loss: Key Texts from the John Bowlby Archive* (pp. 17–65). London: Routledge.

Bowlby, J. (1973). *Attachment and Loss, Vol. II. Separation: Anxiety and Anger.* London: Routledge.

Bowlby, J. (1980). *Attachment and Loss, Vol. III. Loss: Sadness and Depression.* London: Routledge.

Bowlby, J. (1988). On knowing what you are not supposed to know and feeling what you are not supposed to feel. In J. Bowlby (Ed.), *A Secure Base* (pp. 111–133). London: Routledge.

Bretherton, I. (1992). Attachment and bonding. In V. B. Van Hasselt & M. Hersen (Eds.), *Perspectives in Developmental Psychology. Handbook of Social Development: A Lifespan Perspective* (pp. 133–155). New York: Plenum Press. http://dx.doi.org/10.1007/978-1-4899-0694-6_6

Brewin, C. R., Andrews, B., & Valentine, J. D. (2000). Meta-analysis of risk factors for posttraumatic stress disorder in trauma-exposed adults. *Journal of Consulting and Clinical Psychology, 68*, 748–766.

Bromberg, P. M. (1998). *Standing in the Spaces: Essays on Clinical Process, Trauma, and Dissociation.* Mahwah, NJ: Analytic Press.

Bromberg, P. M. (2011). *The Shadow of the Tsunami and the Growth of the Relational Mind.* New York: Routledge.

Caslini, M., Bartoli, F., Crocamo, C., Dakanalis, A., Clerici, M., & Carrà, G. (2016). Disentangling the association between child abuse and eating disorders: A systematic review and meta-analysis. *Psychosomatic Medicine, 78*, 79–90. https://doi.org/10.1097/PSY.0000000000000233

Chalavi, S., Vissia, E. M., Giesen, M. E., Nijenhuis, E. R. S., Draijer, N., Cole, J. H., & Reinders, A. A. T. S. (2015). Abnormal hippocampal morphology in dissociative identity disorder and post-traumatic stress disorder correlates with childhood trauma and dissociative symptoms. *Human Brain Mapping, 36*, 1692 1704. https://doi.org/10.1002/hbm.22730

Chefetz, R. A. (2017). Dignity is the opposite of shame, and pride is the opposite of guilt. *Attachment: New Directions in Psychotherapy and Relational Psychoanalysis, 11*, 119–133.

Cook, A., Spinazzola, J., Ford, J., Lanktree, C., Blaustein, M., Cloitre, M., & van der Kolk, B. (2017). Complex trauma in children and adolescents. *Psychiatric Annals, 35*, 390–398. https://doi.org/10.3928/00485713-20050501-05

Dalenberg, C. J., Brand, B. L., Gleaves, D. H., Dorahy, M. J., Loewenstein, R. J., Cardeña, E., & Spiegel, D. (2012). Evaluation of the evidence for the trauma and fantasy models of dissociation. *Psychological Bulletin*, *138*, 550–588. https://doi.org/10.1037/a0027447

De Bellis, M. D. (2005). The psychobiology of neglect. *Child Maltreatment*, *10*, 150–172. https://doi.org/10.1177/1077559505275116

Ferenczi, S. (1912). Transitory symptom-constructions during the analysis. In M. Balint (Ed.), *First Contributions to the Theory and Technique of Psycho-Analysis* (pp. 193–212). London: Karnac.

Ferenczi, S. (1932/1988). *The Clinical Diary*. Cambridge, MA: Harvard University Press.

Ferenczi, S. (1933/1949). Confusion of tongues between the adults and the child: The language of tenderness and of passion. *International Journal of International Journal of Psycho-Analysis*, *30*, 225–230.

First, M. B., Williams, J. B. W., Karg, S., & Spitzer, R. L. (2016). *Structured Clinical Interview for DSM-5 Disorders – Clinician Version (SCID-5-CV)*. Washington, DC: American Psychiatric Association.

Fonagy, P., & Target, M. (1996). Playing with reality: I. Theory of mind and the normal development of psychic reality. *International Journal of Psycho-Analysis*, *77*, 217–233.

Gold, A. L., Shechner, T., Farber, M. J., Spiro, C. N., Leibenluft, E., Pine, D. S., & Britton, J. C. (2016). Amygdala–cortical connectivity: Associations with anxiety, development, and threat. *Depression and Anxiety*, *33*, 917–926. https://doi.org/10.1002/da.22470

Granieri, A., Guglielmucci, F., Costanzo, A., Caretti, V., & Schimmenti, A. (2018). Trauma-related dissociation is linked with maladaptive personality functioning. *Frontiers in Psychiatry*, *9*, 206. https://doi.org/10.3389/fpsyt.2018.00206

Hughes, K., Bellis, M. A., Hardcastle, K. A., Sethi, D., Butchart, A., Mikton, C., & Dunne, M. P. (2017). The effect of multiple adverse childhood experiences on health: A systematic review and meta-analysis. *The Lancet. Public Health*, *2*, e356–e366. https://doi.org/10.1016/S2468-2667(17)30118-4

Infurna, M. R., Reichl, C., Parzer, P., Schimmenti, A., Bifulco, A., & Kaess, M. (2016). Associations between depression and specific childhood experiences of abuse and neglect: A meta-analysis. *Journal of Affective Disorders*, *190*, 47–55. https://doi.org/10.1016/j.jad.2015.09.006

Konkolÿ Thege, B., Horwood, L., Slater, L., Tan, M. C., Hodgins, D. C., & Wild, T. C. (2017). Relationship between interpersonal trauma exposure and addictive behaviors: A systematic review. *BMC Psychiatry*, *17*, 164. https://doi.org/10.1186/s12888-017-1323-1

Lewis, H. B. (1987). Introduction: Shame, the 'sleeper' in psychopathology. In H. B. Lewis (Ed.), *The Role of Shame in Symptom Formation* (pp. 1–28). Hillsdale, NJ: Lawrence Erlbaum.

Lewis, M. (1992). *Shame: The Exposed Self*. New York: Free Press.

Liotti, G. (2014). Overcoming powerlessness in the clinical exchange with traumatized patients. *Psychoanalytic Inquiry*, *34*, 322–336. https://doi.org/10.1080/07351690.2014.899783

Main, M., & Hesse, E. (1990). Parents' unresolved traumatic experiences are related to infant disorganized attachment status. In M. T. Greenberg, D. Cicchetti, & E. M. Cummings (Eds.), *Attachment in the Preschool Years* (pp. 161–181). Chicago, IL: University of Chicago Press.

O'Riordan, Dolores. (2007). *In the Garden* [CD]. London: Sanctuary Records.

Park, Linkin (2000). *Crawling*. [CD]. New York: Warner Music Group.

Perry, B. D. (2009). Examining child maltreatment through a neurodevelopmental lens: Clinical applications of the neurosequential model of therapeutics. *Journal of Loss and Trauma, 14*, 240–255. https://doi.org/10.1080/15325020903004350

Reisz, S., Duschinsky, R., & Siegel, D. J. (2017). Disorganized attachment and defense: Exploring John Bowlby's unpublished reflections. *Attachment & Human Development, 20*, 107–134. https://doi.org/10.1080/14616734.2017.1380055

Schimmenti, A. (2012). Unveiling the hidden self: Developmental trauma and pathological shame. *Psychodynamic Practice, 18*, 195–211. https://doi.org/10.1080/14753634.2012.664873

Schimmenti, A. (2017). Traumatic identification. *Attachment: New Directions in Psychotherapy and Relational Psychoanalysis, 11*, 154–171.

Schimmenti, A. (2018). The trauma factor: Examining the relationships among different types of trauma, dissociation, and psychopathology. *Journal of Trauma & Dissociation, 19*, 552–571. https://doi.org/10.1080/15299732.2017.1402400

Schimmenti, A., & Caretti, V. (2010). Psychic retreats or psychic pits?: Unbearable states of mind and technological addiction. *Psychoanalytic Psychology, 27*, 115–132. https://doi.org/10.1037/a0019414

Schimmenti, A., & Caretti, V. (2016). Linking the overwhelming with the unbearable: Developmental trauma, dissociation, and the disconnected self. *Psychoanalytic Psychology, 33*, 106–128. https://doi.org/10.1037/a0038019

Schore, A. N. (1998). Early shame experience and infant brain development. In P. Gilbert & B. Andrews (Eds.), *Shame: Interpersonal Behaviour, Psychopathology, and Culture* (pp. 57–77). New York: Oxford University Press.

Schore, A. N. (2009). Relational trauma and the developing right brain: An interface of psychoanalytic self psychology and neuroscience. *Annals of the New York Academy of Sciences, 1159*, 189–203. https://doi.org/10.1111/j.1749-6632.2009.04474.x

Siegel, D. J. (1999). *The Developing Mind: How Relationships and the Brain Interact to Shape Who We Are*. New York: Guilford Press.

Solomon, J., & George, C. (2011). *Disorganized Attachment and Caregiving*. New York: Guilford Press.

Steinberg, M. (1994). *Structured Clinical Interview* for *DSM-IV Dissociative Disorders Revised (SCID-D-R)*. Washington, DC: American Psychiatric Press.

Steinberg, M. (2000). Advances in the clinical assessment of dissociation: The SCID-D-R. *Bulletin of the Menninger Clinic, 64*, 146–163.

Thomaes, K., Dorrepaal, E., Draijer, N. P. J., de Ruiter, M. B., Elzinga, B. M., van Balkom, A. J., & Veltman, D. J. (2009). Increased activation of the left hippocampus region in Complex PTSD during encoding and recognition of emotional words: A pilot study. *Psychiatry Research, 171*, 44–53. https://doi.org/10.1016/j.pscychresns.2008.03.003

Varese, F., Smeets, F., Drukker, M., Lieverse, R., Lataster, T., Viechtbauer, W., & Bentall, R. P. (2012). Childhood adversities increase the risk of psychosis: A meta-analysis of patient-control, prospective- and cross-sectional cohort studies. *Schizophrenia Bulletin*, *38*, 661–671. https://doi.org/10.1093/schbul/sbs050

Wille, R. (2014). The shame of existing: An extreme form of shame. *International Journal of Psycho-Analysis*, *95*, 695–717. https://doi.org/10.1111/1745-8315.12208

Winnicott, D. W. (1971). *Playing and Reality*. London: Tavistock.

Winsper, C., Lereya, S. T., Marwaha, S., Thompson, A., Eyden, J., & Singh, S. P. (2016). The aetiological and psychopathological validity of borderline personality disorder in youth: A systematic review and meta-analysis. *Clinical Psychology Review*, *44*, 13–24. https://doi.org/10.1016/j.cpr.2015.12.001

Chapter 8

Personal and professional reflections

Shame and race

Elaine Arnold

In this chapter, I will discuss my understanding of shame and race having been born, and having lived and worked in racialised societies.

Definition of shame

Firstly in trying to get a clear idea of the word shame, I looked at several definitions and they all highlighted the painful feelings which the emotion engenders namely, being defective, bad, being a failure, and an absence of self-esteem. Individuals react to the emotion in a number of ways when caused to feel ashamed. Am I worthy of respect or always wrong in speaking or in doing a task? How am I seen or judged by others? The result of ruminating on these nagging questions may cause them to focus on one or even several becoming self-conscious, embarrassed, unhappy, and pained to the point of withdrawing from social life, severing relationships with family, friends, and colleagues and consequently becoming isolated and depressed. Sometimes there may be a somatised reaction for example, lower back pain, frequent stomach, or chest pain, resulting in the shamed individual seeking medical attention. When there is not a diagnosis of a specific illness and the suggestion made that a psychological or psychiatric service may be helpful, the client may often refuse. People of all ethnic groups I have heard say, "I would be thought of by others as being mad" or "My job would be put at risk as my employer may think it inadvisable to keep me in their employment and decide that I am incapable of doing the tasks assigned to me."

Members of their families may think that if the referral is accepted, they would all be shamed, and therefore would be obliged to keep it a secret.

Medical practitioners several years ago were of the opinion that black and other minority people were incapable of benefitting from "the talking cure". In addition, clients who had been brought up in a society where the doctor (often a white man) was venerated and expected to cure them, were reluctant to believe that any change would occur by "just talking". Another factor which prevented therapeutic help from being offered was that fees

DOI: 10.4324/9781003175612-9

were beyond their reach and the time required over a number of sessions could not be spared.

With various methods of seeking and obtaining change to these racially biased attitudes towards Black, Indigenous, & People of Colour (BIPOC), and with the increase in qualified therapists and counsellors, psychologists, and psychiatrists of all ethnic groups it would seem that currently more referrals are made. Many of these professionals are finally able to recognise that feelings of shame may be related to the many past or ongoing shaming occurrences, often triggered by racism, in their daily lives. Sometimes there were no positive and meaningful relationships in their lives and shame had triggered the terror of loneliness and fear of dissolution.

Recent observations of reactions to being shamed

I decided to write from my personal and professional experiences of seeing people who expressed their feelings of being made to feel ashamed and what actions they took to be relieved of these feelings. On reflection, during this year of the enforced "lock down" caused by the pandemic of Covid-19, I have had more time to observe people whilst standing at the stipulated distance of two metres.

Personal

One very hot day, while standing in a queue waiting the stipulated distance to enter the post office in an area with a high proportion of ethnic minority residents, I observed a young woman pushing a pram with a toddler and two older children a boy and a girl dressed in the uniform of the local nursery school. They stopped about a foot in front of me whilst the children began to unwrap lollipops, excitedly. The toddler began to whimper, and his mother offered him a lollipop, which he pushed away. She then leaned over and checked his disposable nappy which turned out to be wet. She said, in a not unkind but stern voice: "You mean you are wet when I changed you before leaving home!" He covered his face with both hands and cried even more loudly. I said gently to her: "He could not help it." Then to him, "Oh oh is mummy telling you off?" Hearing this stranger's voice, he moved his hands down to see who was speaking to him. I was smiling at him; he stopped crying and looked up to check his mother's reaction. She was smiling whilst replying to me: "I'm not angry with him but I had thought that we would back home before I had to change him again." He stopped crying and was now listening and observing the interchange. We talked about how hot it was and how it was not conducive to walking quickly. Due to the lock down the bus, which was so convenient to their house, now ran infrequently but the children did not mind walking because it gave them the opportunity to stop and buy lollipops! The little boy's sister leaned over and offered him her lollipop which he took and smiled at her. We said goodbye with the children waving, wished each other well and I watched their retreating backs as they walked down the road. I thought they seemed a closely knit family and hoped that there was a dad sharing in this family life, who might help them to feel secure in the community so that they were not exposed to encountering situations in which they would feel ashamed.

Professional

During the pandemic I have engaged in conversations with several people remotely by telephone, and have listened to, and read the narratives of dozens of people through the prolific work of journalists in the press and via other forms of social media. Older people have been recalling some of the times they felt ashamed as children or as young people and how it has affected their personalities. They have eloquently described how they dealt with their feelings of shame. Some had not disclosed how they felt to anyone, whilst others, according to their ages when the incidents occurred, sought the support of siblings, or parents to intervene and stop the negative actions against them. Others became aggressive and often dealt with offenders by winning fights. Some people withdrew, but were able to channel their energies into developing various skills which have led them into careers which give joy and happiness to them, their friends and families at home and abroad and to thousands of others. These were the ones who survived but there must be many who have not; and there may be others who succumbed and have become disturbed emotionally, people who are described as "loners"...

My personal and professional background and the historical links to shame

These narratives triggered memories of my early life in Barbados where I was born and educated to secondary school level.

The island had remained under British rule for nearly 400 years unlike the majority of the other Caribbean islands. It was taken from the Portuguese who did not consider it valuable, without any gold as the Spaniards thought, nor any other precious metals. It was inhabited mainly by two groups of Amerindian Indians (Arawaks and Caribs) who had travelled from the American continents and who lived by cultivating the land and by fishing. The English people who had been transported to the island settled and lived peaceably alongside the Amerindians, cultivating subsistence crops after both had recovered from their initial fear of the difference between them and lack of knowledge of "the ways of being" of each other's culture, essential for building relationships. The white population consisted mainly of men, who for various reasons had been exiled there, by the British Government. Other European powers roamed the seas trading with the populations of the various different Caribbean countries. The Portuguese introduced sugar cane after it was seen to grow profusely in Brazil but in order to be profitably cultivated large portions of land were required, and intensive labour was needed; so those in power divided the island into large plantations but a decreasing population hampered success. The white workers who had served their terms of indenture, returned to England or migrated to North America and other countries.

The Amerindian population decreased; some returned to the Americas, while others fell victim to tropical diseases, and contagious illness contracted from living alongside the white migrants, for which they had no immunity. Others chose suicide rather than work under the conditions of slavery. Following the example of the introduction of black slaves from West Africa into the Americas by the Spanish and other European countries, the English followed and the system of slavery, which forced people to work for no reward, and to live under atrocious conditions, was deemed the solution to the labour problem. In time other crops such as cotton and tobacco which required a large labour force and intensive farming methods were introduced and the slave owners flourished economically. England became a wealthy nation. Historians, formerly mainly white, but now a growing number of whom are black, have researched and written copiously about this (Beckles & Shepherd, 2004; Dookhan, 1971). Currently the social media platforms are helping to inform and to encourage debate among the general public, some in response to The Black Lives Matter movement. How far the information offered will be taken on board to help to change attitudes to issues of race and discrimination, remains to be seen.

With the introduction of black slaves to the Americas, the structure of the society evolved in the form of a colour pyramid with white people at the top in various layers, then those of mixed heritage and black, in various layers, at the base, with little in the way of social mobility. Then, according to Bedford (1972), barring immigration, the only significant scope for social mobility for black people and those from the BIPOC community was through education (Bedford, 1972, p. 62).

This was also the case in the various islands of the Caribbean and so some families worked hard to finance the education of their children. In Barbados, the various parishes instituted scholarship systems, but these were not necessarily awarded by passing the necessary examinations, but by the votes of the white landowners who controlled the public purse of the particular parish (this was akin Local Councils in Britain). Change came about when black and mixed heritage people who had been educated in England mainly at the Universities of Oxford and Cambridge attained middle class status so on their return and with their qualifications in law, history, and politics were able to challenge the existing forms of colonial government and the un-fair and discriminatory practices in the education system. Scholarships then were awarded on merit and not by skin colour. Fortunately, I was the recip-ient of a scholarship from an all age elementary school to a Girls Grammar school built by a newly elected Government. Nevertheless, although school mainly consisted of black children, the teachers were White English, White Barbadian, and two Black teachers. There was very strict discipline and punctuality was insisted upon even though the transport system was erratic and those of us from the rural areas had no other means of travel, until cycling became an acceptable way of travelling and many of us acquired bicycles. We were saved the humiliation of having our names read out to the assembled school, and being placed in detention for being late. Most of us settled down and accepted the punishment while others showed their anger in different ways, by being sullen, or trying to be the clown, or asking permission to be allowed to leave the room frequently in order to go to the toilet! The only reason accepted.

However, if detained for being inattentive in class or for not respecting any rules of the school this would be written about in the end of term report. There would then be punishment by parents for causing shame on the fam-ily. Continuing to tertiary-level education did not seem an option for girls, the two main careers suggested were teaching and nursing. I chose teaching, emulating my cousin, a teacher, who had been selected by the head of her school to teach the younger children in the class and then sent to the island's training college. She had followed the route of the "pupil teacher system" before being trained at the college owned by the Church of England. Bear-ing in mind the stratified nature of the society, on leaving school the girls who were of mixed heritage and so higher up the pyramid, were often ap-pointed without even making an application.

I applied to three schools, which were conveniently near home, and were offering applicants appointments as supply teachers. This was advanta-geous for to me, I would be gaining experience teaching boys and girls in preparation for going to Teachers' Training College and observing how children were treated, and the management styles of men and women in authority. In the three schools, corporal punishment was the accepted form of punishment and children who were slow in learning were often shamed by being told they were dunces. I recalled that I was curious to know more about the home life of these children, but was inhibited by my junior status to question the teachers.

After three years without an appointment, there was a vacancy in another school and a young woman of mixed heritage who had recently left school with a lower qualification to mine and no teaching experience was ap-pointed. I felt angry at being unfairly treated when having worked for three years a younger woman of mixed heritage with less qualification or experi-ence was given a permanent appointment. I discussed this with my family and decided that I would accept the invitation by a family to visit Trinidad where there was a shortage of teachers. Like people of earlier times, though for me it was not a desperate situation of needing an occupation to support my physical needs, I saw immigration as an opportunity to recover from the blatant discriminatory behaviour on the part of the system. I felt secure with a solid educational background, a supportive family which provided a secure base to which I could return at any time. My aim in becoming a qualified a teacher was to be effective in encouraging children to learn and feel proud, helping those who were slow to perform to the best of their ability without being shamed and made to feel unworthy and unacceptable in society.

In Trinidad, I was given the opportunity of living in a cosmopolitan society. The population was made up of various ethnic groups who had been brought by the British Colonial, administration from India and China in order to provide cheap labour. People from various countries of Eastern Europe had also settled. There was immense wealth and also abject poverty among people of African and Indian origins. Here too education was seen as the means of ensuring that their children escaped and became upwardly socially mobile. The Church and other religious bodies provided schools and financed the training of teachers.

There was no difficulty for me to obtain an appointment in a church school and to proceed to enter the Government Training College. The staff were a mix of a white English principal and two white lecturers, but the main subjects were taught by black lecturers who had undergone post-qualifying education in Britain. The curriculum was the one used by English teacher training colleges. There was the beginning of change in the Trinidadian education system, with an adaptation of psychological tests, and the introduction of learning through undertaking projects which gave children opportunities to discover and appreciate their environment. There were more black writers with their work being used in schools.

However, change was not progressing for some sections of the society. Following the British example services for the vulnerable within the society were mostly left to be provided by voluntary charitable organisations. There was a need for the increase and development of other services, especially for children who were deprived of normal home life and having been placed in large institutions by parents too poor to care for them. Others, including mothers with a mental illness, or women deserted by their partners, or children deemed to being beyond control, were being cared for by staff on a shift system in large institutions.

Teaching in the school situated on the compound of one of these institutions I was particularly concerned for babies and toddlers who craved to be held and to feel safe by someone providing sensitive and continuous care. I took action and won a scholarship to study at a university in England to qualify in psychiatric social work specialising in child guidance. At the time John Bowlby was researching the effects of separation on young children cared for in institutions. He was commissioned by the World Health Organisation to explore this as they were concerned about the effects of institutional care on orphans who were left alone at the end of the Second World War in 1945. From his research, Bowlby argued that young children needed a warm, intimate, and continuous relationship with their mother or mother substitute in order to develop satisfactory mental health. The report on his studies entitled *Maternal Care and Mental Health* became required reading on social work courses (Bowlby, 1952). The report generated much heated debate about the detrimental effects of maternal deprivation and the institutionalisation of children. These findings were enlightening and exciting and stimulated new thinking and influenced policy makers to change the practice of placing children in large institutions. Instead small family type homes run mainly by couples were established. My experience working with staff in some of the large children's homes showed me that children in these circumstances exhibited similar care seeking behaviour in trying to have their emotional needs met as those I had observed in Trinidad, West Indies. It became clear that this was a phenomenon that applied to the young of all nations. I also shared my knowledge with managers and staff of the institutions in Trinidad who as a result tried to introduce some changes. For example, they began to put children of different ages into smaller groups with older ones helping to care for younger ones patterned on the cultural norm of their families.

What was difficult to change were the staff's attitudes to the parents of children who needed practical help to rear their children at home where attachment relationships are built in the early years. Some of the parents expressed their feelings of shame and regret that through feeling utterly overwhelmed by the lack of housing, regular income, and support from fathers of the children, they were obliged to leave their children in "The Home" to be brought up by strangers.

Immigration

In Trinidad, people began to imitate the migration by people from other Caribbean islands to England. Formerly, the destinations of migrants were the USA or Canada seduced by the pull of higher salaries, better living accommodation, the variety of jobs. There was also the push to leave which came from losing the "good life" which some people had acquired as a result of enhanced salaries when there was an oil boom for several years and followed by a recession due to a fall in oil prices. Other reasons for migrating were the lowering of standards of behaviour in the community, especially among young men, and the increase in gun and knife crimes which were very often fatal. These reasons were identified in my conversations with a number of people who were leaving the teaching profession, and the civil service at that time.

The majority of migrants were men, some of whom were ex-service men who had returned home but were unable to find employment. Others leaving were in low paid jobs and wanted to raise their economic standards. Some had ideas of furthering their education by working by day and studying at night. There were some women migrants whose aims were to be trained as nurses, others wanted to embrace the opportunity to work and live independent lives for five years coinciding with the time of the expiry date in their passports. The majority left their children with members of their extended families, mainly grandmothers, aunts, older siblings, or family friends. Some travelled with their children. In studying the work of John Bowlby (Bowlby, 1979), I recalled that he had stressed, that just as babies need their mothers, so too do mothers need their children and I wondered how the mothers who had migrated were coping without them. I therefore took action and decided to come to England to research this question.

In my research (Arnold, 2000), I was privileged to meet many of the mothers of the first generation of migrants and to listen to their stories. Some who lived their lives to the full and achieved their aims of seeing their children in the hostile racialised UK. Others did not and there were those who disclosed that they would have liked to have returned home to the West Indies but were too ashamed to do so without achieving their aim as they felt they would be ridiculed and made to feel their failure more keenly. Nevertheless they remained and said that their families and their religious faith had helped them to survive.

Some of them had sought the help of Social Services for places in day nurseries for their young children. However, there was a shortage of places, so their children were sent to residential nurseries which had been built in the Home Counties to house children of English women who had served in the armed services and had been demobbed at the end of the War (1935–1945). More about this story can be found in *The Heart of the Race: Black Women's Lives in Britain* by Bryan, Dadzie, and Scafe (1985). Awarded the Martin Luther King Memorial Prize, it is a socio-historical study looking at the realities of life for black women migrants in the UK after the Second World War recognising that three-quarters of these women were single. It recovers the women's historical agency, situating it in relation to a long tradition of resistance to enslavement. Their participation in the UK labour market, overcoming racist obstacles, was a component of Britain's postwar economic recovery.

The carers in these institutions were white as the Caribbean people were working in the city as cleaners and shop workers and not yet employed as carers. Their children became attached to these white carers and the carers to them. When mothers visited their children they expressed fear and refused to be held by them as they were not now familiar with black people as well as expressing the normal fear response observed in children on reunion after a period of separation from their primary care givers. In my research interviews mothers told me that they were advised that they should not visit as the children were so distressed and afraid of them. Some mothers stopped visiting as they themselves were overwhelmed and understandably unable to witness the distress of their children. Others stopped working and took their children back home and they and their partners shared the care according their hours of work. Some fathers, who had been reared in a cultural background where only women cared for children, were ashamed of being seen by their single friends, pushing a pram or carrying a baby in their arms. But because of the changed conditions of their lives, these men grew into the role of being a nurturer of their children. It is now much more usual to see young black men collecting their children from childminders or from school.

Some mothers left as single parents, were gravely distressed when their children or grandchildren did not achieve in the field of education or had become involved in the criminal justice system, and were deeply saddened by the treatment meted out to younger black people by the police. This was seen as shameful and needed to be kept a secret from family and friends.

Some, who became mentally ill, were wrongly diagnosed as suffering from schizophrenia (Littlewood & Lipsedge, 1997; Burke, 1974). It was much more likely that they were survivors of complex trauma due to separation and loss and the additional impact of living in a racist and unwelcoming environment.

I met many clients who were ashamed of being mentally ill and refused to be treated. Some families were ashamed to have relatives return to their home from hospital when they were discharged from inpatient psychiatric care due to the stigma involved. Many people who are homeless and live on the streets fall into this category; they are left to the ravages of inclement weather and sometimes ill-treatment from others in the community. How many of us feel ashamed and guilty about living comfortably when we meet homeless people on the streets prompting us to give a small donation? There are times when those in authority show their concern and probably feel ashamed of our country, one of the most affluent in the world, where there is such a chasm between the haves and the have nots. It is appalling that people are spending wintry nights sleeping rough on the streets. There needs to be consistency in caring and proper government finances allocated for suitable housing to be provided for this very vulnerable group.

In my experience as a social worker (Arnold, 2012) and as a therapist, many families were known to me with individual members who had not grown into emotional security because their parents grew up in homes where their main carers were unable to provide the necessary consistent and sensitive parenting necessary for the development of secure attachment relationships.

As time moved on I became involved in working at the first intercultural therapy centre called Nafsiyat[1] which was established in London in 1983 where clients from minority ethnic groups were referred or referred themselves. Some of the clients were women of West Indian origin who had been left in the Caribbean for varying periods of time before joining their families, which were often reconstituted, in the UK. In relating their narratives they often voiced the thought that their early separation from their mothers was at the root of their feelings of depression. Some of them expressed guilt that they did not love their mothers as much as they loved their grandmothers, and they found difficulty in sustaining relationships. I invited them to a focus group and when they realised that it was a feeling shared; they thought that the awareness of the phenomenon should be raised among their communities, and all those in the caring professions. The organisation called Separation and Reunion Forum (SRF) was formed in 1998. It held its first conference in June 2000 entitled *The Legacies of Loss* and attracted professionals from education, the caring professions, and the criminal justice system. As the organisation grew in its membership it widened its remit to include people who had experienced loss in circumstances other than migration. These included losses from being "looked after" such as in care or adoption, divorce, bereavement and it changed its name to Supporting Relationships and Families (SRF[2]) and worked in collaboration with Nafsiyat. This provided a secure base for people who felt comfortable in the knowledge that they would be welcomed with patience and understanding.

Some individuals who had been adopted sought help to find their birth families. One such person with whom I worked was Carmen.

Carmen's story

Carmen, a twenty-eight-year-old woman of African Caribbean origin, had requested an appointment as she was feeling depressed. She had heard of the service provided by Nafsiyat from a colleague at work. Carmen was mainly concerned that she seemed unable to make lasting relationships or able to trust people, fearing that they would let her down. She was currently in a relationship with Herman who treated her respectfully and lovingly, but she was unable to trust that it would last, and at times behaved in ways that would deter him from visiting her. If he stayed away as she told him he should, she would take this as evidence that the relationship would not last. She felt ashamed and guilty that she was causing him pain. His family was welcoming of her, but now she felt as though she was unable to accept their kindness and hospitality. She suffered from loss of appetite and was unable to sleep, describing that it was a struggle to get to work at a job which she liked in an office with vibrant and friendly people.

I asked Carmen if she had thought of any possible reasons for her behaviour which I thought to myself was indicative of an ambivalent pattern of attachment.

I shared the view of Acharyya (2000, p. 85) who states that:

> every human being, when suffering distress, initially attempts to find the nature of the distress and what may have caused it and to make sense of it. Once the person has reached a decision (whether this is medically 'correct or incorrect' is immaterial) then the person actively chooses to find appropriate means to alleviate the distress.

In this case, Carmen had felt that her mental well-being was a priority. Her eyes clouded and she began to speak articulately and slowly and told me that as a child she had wondered why her skin colour and her hair were different to that of the other children at her school and different to her mum and dad whom she loved and who loved her and treated her so well. When she was about six years old her adopted mother had told her that she was adopted but she was not sure what it meant, she only knew that they had been able to choose her and that this made her feel special. When she left junior school her parents sent her to a prestigious private secondary school away from the area and the familiar places and faces where she had developed friendships and felt comfortable. She left home early in the mornings and returned late. During weekends, she was fully occupied with homework and so was unable to maintain contact with her former classmates.

This pattern of life resembled the immigration stories of her parents and grandparents which she had read.

Carmen had the darkest skin colour in a group of a few girls who were of mixed heritage, but she was accustomed to living with her parents who were white. She was good at sport but had refused to be pigeon holed in the sports team, and she participated in team games and enjoyed them; however she wanted to pursue an academic career. She excelled in English, mathematics, and geography, and easily obtained the required passes to take her to her first choice of university. After the first parent teacher meeting when her parents attended and showed how proud they were of her attainment, two girls approached Carmen and asked her where her real parents were.

In our session, Carmen stopped speaking and tears rolled down her cheeks, she took a deep breath as if she had been diving and had surfaced to take a breath. I felt very empathic towards her but did not interrupt. She continued:

> I felt so ashamed that there were no members of my parent's family (referring to her birth parents), or any black person who could have helped my mother, and no one who cared for me enough to look after me. It was left to kind white people to rescue me as though I was a stray cat. And in order to make myself feel better, I lied and told them that my parents had gone away to work and I was only being fostered until

they returned, but as I carried the name of my adoptive parents I was not believed. Nevertheless, they did not persist with their questioning.

Carmen, full of sorrow, continued to say:

> I was brought up in a home in which there were very strong moral values and I had been taught that I should always speak the truth but this truth was too painful to be revealed and I felt guilty most of the time. I then felt very uncomfortable wondering if my adoptive mother would ever find out.

At the age of twenty–one, Carmen had discovered from the adoption service that her biological parents were both from the Caribbean and that their marriage relationship had broken down when she was three years old. Her mother had tried to take care of her but found it increasingly difficult as she was working full time and trying to further her education in order to obtain better paid work. She was unable to do all this and had given Carmen up for adoption to ensure that her child would have a better life. Her father had agreed but showed no further interest in her beyond the process of the adoption. The couple had subsequently been divorced and her mother had left the country without a forwarding address. This was at the time when white English couples of mainly Christian backgrounds were eager to make amends for some of the wrongs meted out to black people during days of slavery and the discrimination and the racist views shown to them when they arrived in the UK.

Carmen had left her adoptive family home after years of working and saving in order to purchase her own flat which was in close proximity to them. She had been trying to find her biological mother but without success. She had told her adoptive parents about her search and they were supportive as was her partner. This time she resolved to be honest and not to lie again about the past circumstances of her life.

Her bouts of depression were getting in the way of her being able to build a more sustainable relationships and she felt that finding her mother would assist her in healing from this loss.

Carmen agreed that she would attend six sessions and would request an extension if she needed it. The first four sessions went well. Carmen was always on time and spoke freely about her eagerness to meet her biological mother. There were many unanswered questions. She wondered if physically they looked alike or perhaps was she more like her father. Why did her father not take any interest in her? Would he have preferred a son rather than a daughter? Did her mother go on to have other children?

She said that her adoptive mother had been very supportive and had accompanied her when she first went to obtain her file. Her adoptive father was mildly interested and so they were able to communicate honestly with each other, so she had told her about her thoughts.

On the fourth session, she asked whether I would visit her at home for the last two sessions as her schedule at work had changed and as she had a responsible position there was no one to cover for her. I said would discuss this with the team and let her know. Coming from a social work background, this was not an unusual way of working, and with the team's approval, I rescheduled the appointment. Her address would be available in the office, and I would inform our administrator when I arrived and when I left for issues of safety. Carmen was respectful of boundaries and neither of us overstepped these by behaving as though it were a social occasion. She spoke about her relationship with Herman and asked whether he could be present at the last session. I agreed and he was also respectful and listened and assured me that he was supportive of Carmen. This was the end of the scheduled sessions and the last one ended with Carmen saying that she felt less depressed and was now able to carry on the search herself.

I was mindful of her all of the following week and hoped that she would be successful. Then, I received a letter saying she was very excited because there was a hopeful lead and her mother was now living on another island in the West Indies. Another letter arrived and informed me that me that she was planning to travel there in her vacation and she would let me know the result. She met her mother and it was a successful reunion. I often wonder how and where she is now.

Conclusion

Carmen had chosen a cultural setting familiar to her for help and had been offered the choice of a black counsellor, who had some knowledge of attachment theory and experience of the culture from which her parents had come and thus might be able to understand the issues which were troubling her. She could have chosen a white counsellor if she so desired, yet having been reared in a white family she might have felt a white counsellor would have been superior to the black counsellor, but perhaps she was deterred by still feeling ashamed of having been "rescued" by a white family.

Many black people in our communities who need the help of professionals from the caring services will not have the luxury of having a choice as most of the staff are white. How do they feel about telling their stories to a white worker? Will they feel understood? Do they think that the white worker may be able to meet their needs more effectively than a worker from their ethnic group? Are they ashamed that they have not been as successful in life as the black worker seems to be? Have they internalised racism and think that the white worker is better than the black worker?

How well are white workers prepared to examine their attitudes towards persons who are black? They need to examine the stereotypes they hold about the entire ethnic group and to communicate respectfully. They will need to face their own white fragility and internalised racism. Will they treat people of colour and black people as individuals and be are prepared to give them time to tell their stories and are they accepting of difference? In the words of Jafar Kareem (2000): "In accepting and working with differences in human beings, however, one must try to seek the very universality that exists in diversity" (Kareem, 2000, p. 20). At that time there was only the one centre which was unable to cope with all of the requests from people from the black community who needed to feel safe and secure in a therapeutic setting. They needed therapeutic support without being fearful, and where they would feel a connection that is genuine, from persons who care and who are not fearful or frightening.

It is my firm belief that the time has come for professionals of all ethnicities in the caring services, in health, education, and in the criminal justice system to work together with respect and appreciation of each other's contributions in the healing process. This is necessary if the human race is to survive.

Notes

1   Nafsiyat (Mind, Body and Soul) is a registered charity that provides psychotherapy and counselling for Black, Asian and Ethnic minority people and Refugees in London in the Borough of Islington, where there is a free service for clients who live in the borough. They also accept referrals from Camden, Enfield and Haringey. Website: www.nafsiyat.org.uk
2   Supporting Relationships and Families (SRF) is a registered charity which offers therapeutic counselling services to people living in London boroughs. It is dedicated to raising awareness of the long-lasting traumatic effects on the emotional well-being of young children and families who have experienced broken attachments, separation and loss. We also aim to highlight the need for sensitive counselling and therapeutic services to break the circle of insecure attachments, and the inter-generational nature of attachment patterns in families. Website: www. serefo.org.uk

References

Acharyya S. (1992, 2000). The doctor's dilemma; The practice of psychiatry in multicultural Britain. In J. Kareem & R. Littlewood (Eds.), *Intercultural Therapy: Themes, Interpretation and Practice* (pp. 78–87). Oxford: Blackwell.

Arnold, E. (1992, 2000). Intercultural social work. In J. Kareem & R. Littlewood (Eds.), *Intercultural Therapy: Themes, Interpretation and Practice* (pp. 171–179). Oxford: Blackwell.

Arnold, E. (2012). *Working with Families of African Caribbean Origin: Understanding Issues around Immigration and Attachment.* London: Jessica Kingsley.

Beckles, H. McD, & Shepherd, V. A. (2004). *Liberties Lost: Caribbean Indigenous Societies and Slave Systems.* Cambridge: Cambridge University Press.

Bedford, G. L. (1972). *Persistent Poverty: Underdevelopment in Plantation Economies of the Third World.* Oxford: Oxford University Press.

Bowlby, J. (1952). *Maternal Care and Mental Health.* Geneva: World Health Organisation.

Bowlby, J. (1979). *The Making and Breaking of Affectional Bonds*. London: Tavistock Publications.

Bryan, B., Dadzie, S., & Scafe, S. (1985). *The Heart of the Race; Black Women's Lives in Britain*. London: Virago Press.

Burke, A. (1974). *Mental Illness and Psychiatric Treatment in Relation to Immigrants in Birmingham*. Unpublished Paper, delivered to the Intercultural Group of the British Association of Social Workers, London.

Dookhan, I. (1971). *A Pre-Emancipation History of the West Indies*. London: Collins.

Kareem, J. (1992, 2000). *The Nafsiyat Intercultural Centre: Ideas and Experience in Intercultural Therapy*. In J. Kareem & R. Littlewood (Eds.), *Intercultural Therapy: Themes, Interpretation and Practice* (pp. 14–38). Oxford: Blackwell.

Littlewood, R. (1992, 2000). Towards an Intercultural Therapy. In J. Kareem & R. Littlewood (Eds.), *Intercultural Therapy: Themes, Interpretation and Practice* (pp. 3–13). Oxford: Blackwell.

Littlewood, R., & Lipsedge, M. (1997). *Aliens and Alienists: Ethnic Minorities and Psychiatry*. London: Routledge.

Chapter 9

"Suicide Addict"

The sovereignty of shame in the dissociated mind

Orit Badouk Epstein

Prologue

Through her obsessive artwork of infinite dots, the artist Yayoi Kusama has been expressing her depression and suicidal ideation for over eight decades. To this day, Kusama has chosen to reside by night in a mental hospital in Tokyo while during the day she continues producing her works of art with their infinitude of elaborate repetition which mirrors the loop of her depression and the monotony of her obsession with death. The title of this paper is borrowed from Kusama's book (2005) and poem:

> *Manhattan Suicide Addict*
>
> Swallow antidepressant and it will be gone
> Tear down the gate of hallucinations
> Amidst all the agony, the present never ends
> All the stairs to heaven,
> my heart expires in their tenderness
> Calling from the sky, doubtless,
> transparent in its shades of blue
> Embraced with the shadow of illusion
> Cumulonimbi arise
> Sounds of tears,
> Shed upon eating the colour of cotton rose
> I become a stone
> Not in time eternal
> But in the present that transpires.
> Yayoi Kusama (2005)

Suicide, according to the French philosopher and sociologist Emile Durkheim, is a result of both emotional and social factors and the two are inseparable. In his book *Suicide* (1897), Durkheim concluded that the more socially integrated and connected a person is, the less likely he or she is to commit suicide. He came up with the term *anomie*. Anomie is a state

DOI: 10.4324/9781003175612-10

or condition of instability in individuals or in a society resulting from the breakdown or absence of social norms and values. He associated anomie with the influence of a loss of societal norms that was too sudden and too rigid. When this rigidity becomes normalised and obsolete as a result of the lack of connection to a sense of purpose and belonging to society, an increase in suicide is then predictable. We can see this in times of economic austerity as well as in periods of political and societal upheaval such as the one we are currently facing with the Covid-19 pandemic.

Attachment theory and its main concerns

Post-World War II, the founder of attachment theory, John Bowlby, an avid observer of societal and individual adversity in the face of real-life traumatic events such as war, poverty, childhood neglect and abuse, insisted that separation and loss made these events more difficult to deal with. This was a different approach to other contemporaneous psychoanalytical movements. In an interview he had with Charles Fortune (1991) he said: "In my psychoanalytic training there was an extreme pressure to turn your back on real-life events. But I never swallowed it" ... "Dreadful!" (Fortune, 1991, pp. 71–72).

Being the scientist he was, he therefore selected separation and loss as traumatic factors for study because they lent themselves to empirical research. Separation anxiety he wrote:

> acts as a basic human disposition, it is only a small step to understand why it is that threats to abandon a child, often used as means of control are so very terrifying. Such threats, and also threats of suicide by a parent, are, we now know, common causes of intensified separation anxiety. Their extraordinary neglect in traditional clinical theory is due, I suspect, not only to an inadequate theory of separation anxiety but to a failure to give proper weight to the powerful effects, at all ages of real-life events.
>
> (Bowlby, 1988, p. 30)

In addition to the importance of real-life events, Bowlby's contribution was to see the infant as striving from the start to relate to his mother. Unlike his psychoanalytic colleagues at the time, his assertion meant to give this primordial relatedness an evolutionary foundation to support his theoretical construct. In a nutshell, attachment theory has been concerned with three key issues:

1. **Proximity seeking** – for reasons of survival we need the physical closeness of others.
2. **Proximity maintaining** – irrespective of whether they good or bad caregivers, a child then will attach to those with whom he is familiar.

3.   **Proximity promoting** – are the defences that we develop when conditions for proximity seeking and proximity maintaining have failed.

(Badouk Epstein, 2017, p. 261)

Throughout his work, aggressiveness played an important part in Bowlby's attachment theory. Bowlby saw anger in the child as a reaction to an environment which has failed to adequately meet their needs. In the second volume of his trilogy, *Separation: Anxiety and Anger* (Bowlby, 1973, p. 295), Bowlby also includes Fairbairn's views on aggression:

> Fairbairn addresses himself to the same clinical problem as Klein but proposes a very different solution. In the absence of frustration, he holds, an infant would not direct aggression against his loved object. What leads him to do so is 'deprivation and frustration in his libidinal relationship – and more particularly ...the trauma of separation from his mother.'
>
> (Fairbairn 1952, p. 172)

For the securely attached child, protest is thus part of the child's right to express her unassuaged frustration and needs. It is a sign of a healthy relationship, where the infant feels safe to cry and seek care, while with the unattended infant, the one who doesn't receive an empathic response, instead is left to fend for herself, the inhibition of negative affect develops into a cumulative protest. A frozen scream that eventually becomes an attachment cry, sometimes a silent scream turned into a dissociated self-state that is often engaged in hostility towards the self and other. This Bowlby perceived as the "anger of despair" (Bowlby, 1973, p. 286).

Suicidal ideation

When faced with a client who, at the first meeting, informs us that throughout their adolescence and early adult life they have made various suicidal attempts, may in many cases, elicit fear and panic in us as the therapist. This would be a normal response yet, as Jeremy Holmes points out "we can also attribute this sense of panic to the transference-countertransference matrix re-enacted by the client" (Holmes, 1996, p. 149). Bowlby saw the morbid detachment that we often encounter with a suicidal client, as a form of unresolved chronic or pathological grief. In my experience of working with suicidal clients, this is also the client's silent attachment scream, trying to communicate a profound anguish and a way of both maintaining and seeking proximity. Sometimes it's their only means of communicating with reality. Perceiving and then labelling the suicidal client as "manipulative and attention seeking" can therefore be misleading and counterproductive.

Furthermore, between proximity seeking and proximity maintaining lies the paradox of attachment. While communicating to us this profound sense of despair and internal loneliness, the traumatised client is also implicitly communicating something else, its total opposite, as if wistfully whispering: "look, despite me wishing to die, despite my shame, anger and despair, I still got up this morning and travelled to your office, and now I'm sitting in front of you seeking your kind response and care."

So how can we marry this contrasting dichotomy of despair and detachment versus yearning and searching, all cohabiting in one body?

In a radio programme "Start the Week," the British Journalist Martin Sixsmith, who lost his brother to suicide, said in an interview (Radio 4, 9. 01. 2017) how shocking this had been. He realised that his brother must have had a part which he, Martin, didn't know. "A part he didn't know" is a common testimony we hear from many relatives of people who have committed suicide. This becomes evident when the client continuously presents us with the contradictory behaviours of at least two self-states: the one who wants to live against the one who wants to die.

Attachment, trauma and dissociation

During my twenty years of working with many clients who have suffered complex trauma and suicidal ideation, the narrative I find most helpful in working with this kind of tension, is the one which explores trauma through the lens of attachment theory and dissociative processes, repeatedly expressed through the paradox of attachment. We encounter this most specifically in the clients with disorganised attachment patterns showing us what Bowlby described as "segregated systems of behaviour, thought, feeling and memory." He elaborates this saying "…the governing system and the one having free access to consciousness was a system from which almost every element of attachment behaviour was excluded" (Bowlby, 1980, p. 345).

And perhaps we should also ask, dissociation from what and from whom?

Segregated systems often keep the attachment related information from being integrated into the thoughts and feeling that predominantly influence the individual.

In his poetic way Bromberg explained it thus:

> In order to preserve the attachment connection and protect mental stability, the mind triggers a survival solution, dissociation, that allows a person to bypass the mentally disorganizing struggle to self-reflect without hope of relieving the pain and fear caused by destabilisation of selfhood.
>
> (Bromberg, 2016a, p. 123)

Attachment to a safe caregiver protects the child from predators. From birth the child's need for a primary attachment figure outweighs almost everything else. Therefore, in her plea for proximity seeking a child will be whatever the caregiver wants her to be in exchange for protection. Bowlby (1980) used the word deactivation to describe one of the psychological defences against dis-organisation in the face of attachment's loss. This deactivation involves the exclusion of all affects and thoughts that might activate attachment behav-iour and feelings. We often encounter this defensive exclusion with clients who come from the most insecure of attachment relationships. When the child's needs are at the mercy of their traumatised and traumatising caregiv-ers, then inevitably fear and chronic shame will arise. The researchers Main and Hesse (1990) have classified these children as having a Disorganised (D) attachment pattern of behaviour and concluded that under conditions of threat when a child faces the dilemma of both seeking safety from and fearing the caregiver at the same time, their attachment strategies are likely to collapse. Being stuck in this dilemma creates the paradox of attachment in what Main and Hesse saw as "fright without solution." In order to sur-vive, the maltreated child will have to resort to compartmentalising their unbearable experiences into different pockets of knowing divided from other pockets of un-knowing by amnesic barriers. Not finding out about the carelessness and betrayal at the hand of their caregivers is one of the main purposes of dissociation. This is the realm of implicit procedural knowing and what Antonio Damasio (1999) called "The feeling of what happened", and Liotti (1991) explains as follows:

> If, for instance, the caregiver consistently refuses to listen to the child's statements about their emotional experience or forces the child to accept interpretations of its meaning and cause that radically diverge from his/her first-hand experience, a dissociation will ensue in the child's mem-ory. The episodic memories of the emotional experience the child is not allowed to talk about will not be associated with the explicit seman-tic structures developed through communication with the caregivers. In this case, the early emotional schemata will be segregated in those domains of episodic memory that cannot be easily associated with the verbalizable aspects of self-knowledge.
>
> (Liotti, 1991, p. 219)

Furthermore, in extreme cases of abuse, when fear governs the attach-ment system, dissociation means that the child will have to adapt to the maladaptation previously made to the frightening environment. This is because paradoxically, this unpredictable but adverse experience can gen-erate a greater sense of familiarity and even safety (albeit a false sense of safety) than the unfamiliar, non-abusive one. Thus in their plea for sur-vival, they will also develop parts that know and keep the truth separate, tucked away from conscious reality where the child in her adaptation to the frightening environment has to collude with what I have termed the "scaregiver's" frightening and threatening behaviour, elevating the fear system to practically disremember the abuse that took place (Badouk Epstein, 2015, 2017, 2019a). Some traumatic events are so dark that for the lonely mind, sometimes getting in touch with that certain memory can feel like losing one's mind. Disremembering, according to the philosopher Judith Butler (2004), is a violent attack on the memory, an action that tells the memory to stop, continuously insisting it didn't happen. But then, as we know, that child is forced to lead a double life. In Margaret Hainer's words: "Dissociation is at its essence about both forgetting and remembering. It has the feeling of I can't remember, and I cannot remember" (Hainer, 2016, p. 58).

Thus for the suicidal client, suicidal ideation can be caused by:

1. Severed Proximity seeking – when bonding in the first two years of life between primary caregiver and baby has failed.
2. Proximity maintaining – staying in a familiar and abusive relationship to close relatives ("scaregivers") means existing in hostile-helpless dyadic modes of being, therefore suicidal ideation can be a form of mastery over rage and separateness, an illusion that freedom is available to the person at any time they choose to exit from this world.
3. Proximity promoting – in order to survive, the child will then be forced to compartmentalise their different self-states often expressed through depression, detachment and aggression towards self and other. In some cases, this involves hearing voices such as "go on kill yourself."
4. Socio-economic conditions – during adulthood societal blindness and harsh socio-economic conditions are often an added layer further contributing to a person's profound sense of isolation.

For these reasons, perceiving repetitive suicidal thoughts and other forms of self-harm as a matter of care seeking and dissociation paradoxically acting in conjunction with each other, is a narrative that can better expand our understanding of the client's real-life experiences in a deeper and more helpful way. This improves the chances of therapeutic effectiveness and increases trust between the client and therapist. I always find it fascinating to see how understood the client feels whenever I insist: "It's only one part of you who wants to die, the rest of you has woken up, had breakfast and bravely made your way to my office on time."

The story of Hope

Since we are tiptoeing around matters of hopelessness, I decided to name my client Hope. Hope comes from a hard and dark place. Its hardness is so unbearable that while listening to her trance-like voice, my thoughts sometimes vanish into a dissociative fog trying to protect us both from finding out what really took place in her early life. To begin with, contemplating leaving the haunted museum of her past was impossible as it was the precisely where her suicidal parts resided. In her ordeal, Hope had been suffering from PTSD and many body ailments. She had been diagnosed with a myriad of psychiatric disorders and hospitalised on many occasions.

From birth, Hope was subjected to mind control torture techniques and sadistic abuse at the hands of various family members and other organised criminal groups. In the presence of her highly dissociative mother, Hope learned to cancel herself, and slip away from reality, in her words: "The more I look at my mother, the less I become." "I am a shadow of a shadow, a memory of a memory." "I have been living in a world mirroring reality but never felt a part of it." In not knowing who she was, I slowly learned about Hope's divided system and how she had become in her own words "An unjointed person." This is what Nijenhuis and Van der Hart (2011) define as "Structural dissociation": "Dissociation in trauma entails a division of an individual's personality, which constitute a core feature of trauma" (Nijenhuis & Van der Hart, 2011, p. 418).

Alternation between and co-existence of the trauma and avoidant part (s) that experience "too little" or more specifically:

• Apparently Normal Personality (ANP): the host/ front personality who can function nevertheless is suffering amnesia, conscious and unconscious avoidance strategies.
• Emotional Parts (Ep(s)): trauma fixated part(s) that experience too much or too little, thus constantly reliving and re-enacting the past trauma in the present.

The language of structural dissociation is helpful to understanding extreme abuse and the rigidity and division of mind it creates in the client's general behaviour and interactions. In my efforts to attune to the client's own depiction of their inner lives, I have been open to the client's wish to use their own terminology of choice and define their own state of mind. Some clients like the word parts, some like entities, characters, alters, different modes, personalities, insiders, self-states, people, our way of being and "not-me" and other. From the start, Hope introduced hers as parts.

Hope's terrified gaze was glazed over with what felt like a pained smile. This was her Apparently Normal Personality (ANP) who wasn't fully aware of the existence of all the other embodied emotional parts (EPs) such as, a group of children she named the orphans, a sex slave, a gatekeeper, the boxer, a unicorn character and many other parts. To begin with a tender accommodating voice, emphasising attunement to the exclusion of analytic interpretations, helped Hope to feel safer and parts started appearing and reported their existence describing how they came about. Each part had a story to tell, each part had secrets to reveal. Her system, she would report, had many walls. At times their concreteness did not feel metaphorical (so for example when she said there is a wall between parts it really felt like some kind of a wall was deliberately installed there). Each part had a protective role in "trauma time." Here, they could only be helpful in their futile attempts to communicate something that not many people could comprehend. For example, Hope was subjected to the most sadistic and predatorial attacks one can barely imagine, where she was forced to perpetrate as well as enjoy the abuse. Thus, for Hope having a "sexual slave" part still active in her adult life, meant that sexual re-enactments kept taking over in their paradoxical existence, both seeking care through sex as well as trying to protect her from ever coming intimately closer to men and women alike. Screaming razors in her ears, suicidal parts then would follow that path and plunged her into the depths of depression, preventing her from seeing the light of day. Hope was too traumatised and too ashamed to dream differently to accommodate change. She would regularly leave me messages expressing her wish to die: "Feel numb today – like there is no point to anything, maybe related to baby stuff." "Feel empty, lost, dead inside." "We're in horror time." "Feel totally empty, cold, abandoned, dying." "This is no life, it's a living death – as much as it ever was." "There is a voice screaming go on kill yourself." "Death means nothing just like sex means nothing, if anything it's our only act of freedom."

When profoundly painful and shocking events are so overwhelming to the mind, they tend to hide away and are dissociated from everyday life. Some traumatic events are so dark that getting in touch with that memory is often perceived by many professionals to be an act of fantasy and fabrication. Nonetheless when a traumatic memory appears like the floating wreckage from a sinking ship it can be found and salvaged with the care of an attuned therapist who like a safe shore can provide the safety needed to explore what lies between the client's history and the present moment. The difference now in her witnessed exploration is that the client feels a growing sense of self-worth rather than feeling she is on the brink of losing her mind.

In one particular session Hope described sadistic sexual and violent scenes too overwhelming to the ordinary mind. I remember us staring at each other blankly almost in a trance, my mind wandered off to the image I had of Kusama's infinite dots circling around her. It was not until the sound of a letter slipping through the letter box, that we were both rushed back into the present moment. Hope barely noticed my blushing face, and the shame I felt for my own disappearance. She then collapsed with exhaustion and burst into tears. I held her hands and comforted her with few soothing sounds. She said she felt held in an unfamiliar but longed for way.

As time progressed, we discovered more unbearable realities which little Hope had been through. Her tortured past made sure that the suicidal parts were regularly around, ferociously protecting her from any possible threat. For the severely traumatised person who is not accustomed to sharing their past with anyone, an unspeakable secret must not reveal itself because the risk of opening these wounds not only drips blood (metaphorically) but also exposes their deep shame which tends to brew into self-disgust. Hope's repeated death wish was the only expression of her inhibited rage, still, the proximity to her abusers meant that she was stripped of the capacity to regulate and develop her own subjectivity. Each time she saw a member of her family, her attachment system was activated as Main and Hesse have described:

> when the parent cannot be used as a secure base, then fearful affect will be inadequately regulated where the child's safety had been compromised to fright without solution, resulting in collapse of behavioural attentional strategies.
>
> (Main & Hesse, 1999, p. 172)

Hope would regularly tell me: "I don't know what it is not to live in fear." For those who are imprinted in fear and when the attachment system is aroused and governed by unassuaged fear for long periods, dissociation also means that the child will have to adapt to the maladaptation of her "scaregiver," thus becoming a "scare-seeker." Fonagy (2016) explains and names this state as "inhibited ego destructive shame".

> When the attachment system is activated by fear, the infant seeks the care-giver and reaches out for them when they are still frightened. This vicious cycle of seeking proximity in a state of fear while being frightened goes on to triggering more fear and thus eliciting more proximity and so on.... What happens in the brain is that the system responsible for understanding others in 'mental states' terms is inhibited. This permanent state of activation is what inhibits the capacity for reflective functioning in themselves and others.
>
> (Fonagy, 2016)

Once Hope reduced contact with her abusive family things became a little calmer. Up to that point, therapy felt like a band aid that offered temporary relief and the client's sense of selfhood was frequently erased just by a look from her "scaregiver" (Badouk Epstein, 2015, 2017, 2019b). Nevertheless, triggers around certain dates, anniversaries and more secrets from the past would continue to haunt her. The suicidal part of her then held on desperately to the knowledge that if things ever got bad enough, the option to kill herself was always available, and would repeatedly return almost as her way of expressing her separateness and agency.

For the loved child, the repetition of positive experiences with a caring family, is like a soothing lullaby that moves in a non-linear way and grows into different intersubjective meanings. In direct contrast, for the abused and neglected child, the repetition of frightening experiences, resulting in a profound sense of annihilation and suicidal ideation, is her only expression of rageful defiance against an unmourned life. Paradoxically, suicidal thoughts may also become a stabilising focal point which holds the hope for something better and offers a mastery of one's destiny. Also, because the known is so unbearably painful, so intolerably shameful, the unknown may hold the thought that death is not as painful as life is, and believe it or not, this notion seems to mitigate against the anxiety of that non-nihilistic part, the Anti-Me and the one which is there to protect the US from the YOU.

Also, in the absence of affect tolerance, and the presence of concrete thinking, suicidal parts will sometime take control to compensate for the poor capacity to mentalise. Deeply conditioned with a sense of badness, their fear of conflict may act as a gatekeeper which manages access to the expression of their rage against those who frightened them and didn't protect them in the first place.

So in the face of all that has been mentioned this far, how can we work towards the mobilisation of these frozen terror-states and try to bring some relief to what Bromberg describes as "a total wipe-out of selfhood"? (Bromberg, 2017, personal communication)

Towards recovery

My intensive work with Hope helped a gradual process of moving from disorganisation to organisation and towards some integration.

The intensity of Hope's aloneness and the extent of her self neglect felt like a baby who was left in a cot uncovered and soiled for an unknown period of time. She would report that she would always sleep on the floor even if the most comfortable bed was available to her. During sessions Hope would also choose to lie on the floor of my practice. I would then cover her shivering body with a blanket and a hot water bottle and repeatedly say: "Oh dear, poor you, mmm…mmm.. oh.. oh dear. …" speaking in almost infant direct speech which included authentic yet exaggerated intonation, with repetition and in a high pitch, mirroring her pain back to her with this basic form of preverbal sound and communication (Badouk Epstein, 2019a, p. 352). This is what Beebe and Lachmann (2014), described as "implicit processing" and Bucci (2011) suggests: "The language that the analyst speaks needs to be connected to the patient's affective core: this must be through the analyst experiencing the patient in him/herself" (Bucci, 2011, p. 255). These are the "procedural processes" which include attention process, spatial intensity, facial and vocal emotion. "Through repetition, these action sequences influence organisational process and guide behaviour" (Bucci, 1997, p. 24).

Polyphonic dialogism

But then you may rightly ask and what about all the other parts in her system? Here I want to share an idea which helped me further explore my work with Hope's divided system. In a radio interview, the Nobel Prize winner for literature, the Russian journalist Svetlana Alexievich (2016), said:

> Somebody who has spent their entire life in a concentration camp can't just understand overnight what freedom is. The twentieth century, which might be called the barbarian century with all its murders the holocaust and wars, has undermined our trust in fiction because reality proved much more horrifying, even more fantastic than fiction.

In her book, *Second-Hand Time,* Alexievich describes her travels around Russia interviewing a range of citizens. Like Durkheim, she noticed the huge increase in the numbers of suicides in post-Perestroika Russia. "Suicide" she wrote: "is a night time state when a person weaves on the edge between being and non-being... I want to understand suicide with the rigour of a person in day time" (Alexievich, 2013, p. 32).

Inspired by Dostoyevsky and the Russian Philosopher Mikhail Bakhtin, Alexievich's polyphonic way of recording people's stories in her books is a rich testimony to the multitude of contrasting voices she witnessed in the vastness of traumatised Russia. Here are some of the voices she recorded post Gorbachev:

a   "We were like children discovering a new world, eventually we stopped fainting at supermarkets. Back then books replaced life" (Alexievich, 2013, p. 55). – This I find similar to the voice of the client's (ANP's) describing her move from the abusive past to finding a trauma therapist.

b   "There is only one person who can save us and that's comrade Stalin. If only he'd come back for just two days, he'd have them all shot and then he can be once again laid to rest" (Alexievich, 2013, p. 63). – Similar to the voices of the parts who identify with the idealised abusive father (identification with the aggressor).

c   "I'm a drinking man. Why do I drink, I don't like my life, I want to do an impossible somersault and with the help of alcohol transport myself to another place where everything is good and beautiful" (Alexievich, 2013, p. 65). – Similar to the voices of the self-harming parts.

d   "The last year of the Soviet Union, what I do remember is the ever-present shame. I was ashamed of Brezhnev covering himself in medals and stars" (Alexievich, 2013, p. 85). – Similar to the client's feeling of shame when realising the extent of her trauma.

Polyphonic art and literature have provided me with a mirror from the arts akin to the internal map of my very traumatised clients. It has helped me find an understanding of diversity through their contrasting landscapes.

More so, it has enabled me to develop an ongoing empathic dialogue with the most brutalised parts of a person since in times of survival each part is a helper, even if for the layman their means of helping may come across as skewed and disordered.

Affective responsiveness

For the first three years of regularly attending therapy, Hope's suicidal ideation meant staying with the paradox until the paradox felt understood. It has allowed me to hear the disconnected and suicidal parts travel through the unaccepting social mores repeatedly expressing their wishes to die. Together we sat with the discomfort and tension created by the reckless parts acting out whenever she felt under threat. In not trying to fix them, Hope's ANP also felt less judged, guilty or shamed and her trust in me thus increased. While I hold the light for her lively parts, those who regularly attend therapy, those who send me loving messages and those who like playing with me, I also have learned to hold the darkness of the parts who are too afraid to come out in case they are blinded by that light. In listening to her many contradictory parts opposing each other, the suicidal parts hold the respect and integrity for some meaning. They therefore deserve neutral emphasis which does not assimilate the projection and any form of analytic interpretation, she is simply not ready for that.

A polyphonic approach to dissociation thus tries to amalgamate all the factors I mentioned so far in this paper and not to take a stand too strongly on either side otherwise a greater reaction and chasm will develop. I often tell my supervisees, no matter how difficult it is to hear our clients' attachment screams, try to see them as scare-seekers and yourself as an affective respondent not a fixer, not being too controlling or too invasive. Little by little as conflict between the parts recedes the suicidal parts regularly express their relentless anguish, the other parts, particularly the young ones, begin to better regulate and better relate to people outside the therapy. This will eventually lead to a move from the rigidness of their structured dissociation and an improvement in their intersubjective relatedness.

However, if and when suicidal parts present a real threat to life, it is important for the therapist to:

1. Get in touch with the client's GP and their community care team.
2. Identify the reason for the threat – it can be a nightmare, a triggering date, an existential or practical struggle such as a shortage of money. But what I find are the most prevailing of threats are the feelings arising from the slightest rejection and exclusion which leads to chronic shame, self-loathing and profound sense of unworthiness.
3. Acknowledge and validate the role of the suicidal parts as a protector against life's upheavals and what feel like traumatic disappointments.

4. Remain curious and compassionate about why they want to end life when you the therapist have also witnessed those parts who are eager to stick around – emphasise the power of witnessing these contradictions.
5. Since in its essence, fear is an assault on the senses, talking may not always suffice. Therefore, the unusual conditions presented by clients with complex trauma invite the therapist to act creatively outside the traditional boundaries and I sometimes offer the client a cup of tea, toys, scents, a hot water bottle or play their favourite music for them.

The countertransference with severely traumatised clients is also complex and multi-layered too. If both therapist and client get triggered and dissociate, witnessing between self-states is hardly possible. Nevertheless, when the client reveals her symptoms and the therapist, through her own therapy and supervision, has learned to mentalise and filter out her own symptoms from those of the client, they both can come out of their hiding places to a place of meeting and visible recognition. So, for example, I recall one specific session when my client and I both shed a few tears, this did not destabilise the client rather it brought us closer.

When Sisyphus was condemned by the gods to forever roll the rock up a hill, repetition became free of hope, since life without hope is a life in exile. The ongoingness of repetition in the case of suicidal ideation arises from the client's unresolved grief, an expression of rage and shame against an environment that failed to protect them. Yet repetition with a caring witness can hold the hope needed to dissolve the shame that covers the sorrow beneath. In Chefetz's words: "To be a faithful witness to a person telling the story of their unbearable pain there is no turning away, even if we acknowledge the wish to just do that" (Chefetz, 2015, p. XII). For the therapist to serve as an echo chamber for this polyphonic symphony enables an organic process of feeling known and understood and the client learns to feel a growing sense of internal organisation and better affect regulation. This is part of our trauma work, an effort to hold the constant tension between the different parts, between the night child and the day child and between the knowing and not knowing. This is an ongoing issue. Marked by repetition, negotiation with the suicidal part is necessary yet repetition is part of negotiation. While empathy is the guiding emotion that guarantees the best results, we keep on repeating each other's point of view until we feel understood. In his essay on Edith Stein the philosopher Nikolas Prassas (2015) summarised Stein's (1917/1989) original ideas in her book *Empathy and the Constitution of the Self in the Philosophy of Edith Stein*:

It is through empathy that we constitute as a person…. To understand myself, to be what I truly am; a person inhabiting a world in which I am not identical, I must have another with whom I can empathise, a person with whom we are empathically grounded.

(Prassas, 2015, p. 5)

The therapist's creativity

The "reservoir of love" is a term I devised as a positive mental representation of both explicit and implicit memories that a child has and can draw upon when feeling dysregulated or alone and are such that the child believes that they feel loved, worthy and accepted (Badouk Epstein, 2019b, p. 44). Empathic expression towards the suicidal parts therefore is not collusive, rather it is inclusive and helps stabilise and mitigate the conflict between all parts. In the words of Guntrip (1975):

It is as I see it, the provision of a reliable and understanding human relationship of a kind that makes contact with the deeply repressed traumatized child in the way that enables (the patient) to become steadily more able to live, in the security of a new relationship.

(Guntrip, 1975, p. 150)

When the haunted client has finally found a safe place from which association of her bruised words and her concrete being begins to gain coherence; a mourning process will inevitably unfold and will try to reconcile with her missing life, her traumatic disappointments as well as those arising from everyday life.

My relationship with Hope's different parts vary on three asymmetric and non-linear levels where I try to attune (and of course sometimes I also misattune):

- With the adult part (ANP): we are equal partners, where I offer some psychoeducation.
- With the younger parts (EPs): I have an authentic caregiving rapport, offering some kind of positive parental support.
- With the suicidal and other self-harming parts: I provide an empathic echo-recipient relationship offering containment through a non-judgmental and a non-intrusive approach.

Traumatic experiences tend to rigidify the self, they collapse symbolism. In attachment terms, a rigid internal structure is often the result of putting safety before exploration. Having a continuous and transparent negotiation between these different modes of being, can help the process greatly. In our work with complex trauma, maintaining classical boundaries in itself has proven to be too rigid and ineffective. According to Bowlby, "attachment theory suggests that the therapeutic relationship may be so shaped as to function as a secure base for the exploration of both 'inner' and of 'outer' realities" (Bowlby, 1977, p. 429). Providing the client with a secure base therefore means that the therapist in her role as the attachment figure can offer the client:

- Sensitivity: attune and try to see things from the client's point of view.
- Acceptance: explain the limitations of the therapy rather than blaming the client.
- Cooperation: a non-pathologising approach, respecting separateness and different opinions. Understanding and not shaming the very traumatised parts of the client.
- Accessibility: emotional and psychological availability – the need for non-rigid boundaries. In Bowlby's words: "Depending on the situation each therapist must make his own decision and draw his own lines" (Bowlby, 1988, p. 154).
- Creativity: the therapist's elaborative and playful ideas will add richness to the process of the client's journey towards "earned security."

Some of Hope's abuse took place under water. From a very young age she felt that her body cohabited parts who were "shark like" and who had been trained to make sure she remained loyal to her family and destroy any ways of coming closer to another person, especially her therapist. Attachment to the abuser also means internalizing parts of the abuser in the client's dissociated system, which are expressed through rage and followed by shame. In many cases this is the client's way of mitigating her fear. In trying to communicate with these parts, we constructed a children's story which helped Hope's young parts to make better sense of her inner and outer world. And so, the story goes:

> Once upon a time a little girl was born in a sea full of sharks. Her mother and father showed no care, nor did they love her, instead they left her in the care of a school of very nasty sharks who imprisoned and regularly tortured her. From a very young age, the little girl knew that in order to stay alive she had to learn to swim with those sharks and mimic their ways of being. But while swimming in the big ocean she also noticed that not all the creatures in the sea behaved like sharks. In particular she liked watching the dolphins and the care they offered their calves. She longed to be part of their pod, so from very early on, whenever she could, the little girl would escape and secretly follow the playful dolphins. Alas, the school of sharks kept torturing the little girl until they were satisfied with her developed shark part. This part became so angry almost in an equal measure towards them. One day in late summer, the

girl, who by now was a young woman, managed to break away from the school of sharks. Still curious about the life of dolphins, she was now eager to swim with them but sadly due to her extensive abuse she could barely swim and had to be hospitalised. In hospital she was treated as someone who had lost her mind. This made her feel worse and she felt nothing but anger and shame until one day when a kind doctor encouraged her to leave the hospital to go and find a dolphin therapist. And so, after a while she found one.

The dolphin therapist seemed kind just like the dolphins she once saw in the sea. Slowly, the girl then felt that she could trust her and gradually revealed all the secrets and all the shamed parts that existed inside her. The dolphin therapist welcomed all the parts of her, and the girl felt that they could freely express themselves without too much fear. In particular the very angry shark parts, who for a long time were raging and didn't like the dolphin therapist since they found her kindness to be infuriating. This was a new experience which at times felt unbearably painful but was also comforting because for the first time the girl felt understood.

Little by little she felt better and stronger in herself and her reliance on the dolphin therapist lessened to the point where she could now swim on her own. "This feels new but not necessarily great", said the girl to the dolphin therapist, "not swimming with sharks means no more crises, no more hospitalisation and no more suicide attempts. It's all too quiet, and just swimming with a dolphin doesn't feel safe either, in fact it feels scary and empty and I don't know who is in charge anymore!"

The following week in the most unexpected manner, the girl told the dolphin therapist that the shark part had managed to sneak out and go back to swim with the shark school again. The dolphin therapist's face sank but unlike other times, for the first time the girl noticed the marked sadness on the therapist's face. "Please don't be sad" she said with a newly found compassion, just spending time with the dolphins can feel very shaming, but we will do our best to convince the shark part to see sense and swim with us back to a safe shore. The therapist then added "but perhaps my sadness is about your sadness too, since you may feel that getting better also means ending the therapy." "How did you guess? I was too ashamed to admit this to both myself and you" the girl whispered with tears in her eyes. "Because when we end therapy we don't usually feel this frightened and shamed", replied the dolphin therapist.

Telling this story helped Hope make sense of her recovery process and her newly found narrative towards earned security.

Furthermore, with the help of the digital revolution, we now find ourselves connecting with each other as never before. We have also entered a period where binary thinking has been showing some real flux. In the case of Hope, dialogue and negotiating between me and the suicidal parts has been greatly aided by texting a message a day. Here are some of the text messages between us:

HOPE: "Terror.. terror I cannot survive more, Orit, something is so wrong with me I'm out of touch, still so dissociated – there is no me to save us..."

ORIT: "I'm so sorry to see you suffering like this, I'm thinking of you."

HOPE: "This is no life, Orit. It's a living death – as much as it ever was.. feeling invisible."

ORIT: "I'm really sorry to see you suffering like this. I can see you."

HOPE: "Feeling suicidal.... It's remember and go mad and don't remember and go mad."

ORIT: "Your suffering deserves witnessing and so do your memories."

HOPE: "Thank you for not punishing us for feeling this. Learning that we don't always have to be pleasing."

ORIT: "Keep on being YOU. Love your YOUNESS."

HOPE: "Youness our new word."

In slowly helping Hope tolerate the shock of her experiences, her inner young parts began to feel held and understood, and a new, slightly more hopeful voice started to emerge from the rubble of her demolished self. After four Christmases, during my holiday break, Hope's suicidal parts went quiet for the first time.

However, with the fall of the dissociative barriers, came the daunting realisation of the enormity of loss and the extent of the abuse that had taken place. Buffeted by grief, the suicidal parts then took a new form and Hope's grief was beyond consolable. "It's just too much, how can anyone live life knowing everything that took place?" she exclaimed with apparent pain on her face. When working with this degree of helplessness, often experienced by client and therapist alike, when the abusive past is so extensive, so abhorrent and so unbelievable, there is not yet a language that can remotely describe or convey the enormity of these traumatic experiences. How can a language aptly describe the enormity of the internal carnage, do we have words to describe the kind of violence that strikes an innocent and defenceless child? The Italian philosopher Adriana Cavarero (2008) whose thesis on the ontology of vulnerability, is asking us to reflect upon the way we view the conditions experienced by victims. Her argument is that terror and war describe things from the perspective of warriors. She coined the term "horrorism" which aims to describe the experiences of helplessness and defencelessness of the victims of violent attacks. According to Cavarero, terror is an action which denotes primarily the immediate impact of fear on the body which compels us to take flight, while horror is a state of paralysis that can block speech and excludes the moment of flight – leaving us feeling frozen and repugnant. In not favouring one term over the other, I find Cavarero's emphasis on "horrorism" helps us better expand our awareness whenever words fail us.

Conclusion

Using an attachment and trauma lens, we can see that, for reasons which are conducive to survival, attachment betrayal may always be protected by dissociative processes. As therapists, facing suicidal clients has always been our worst nightmare. In not seeing our client's internal anomie as something the client has had to dissociate from, we remain blind to the client's horror and attachment screams. A relational and adaptive approach means not seeing suicidality as simply something to be rid of but rather as the loudest form of protest that is communicated from the abyss of the client's traumatic early relational world. The mourning process for the client with complex trauma is arduous yet possible. If the demands of mourning are to acknowledge loss, to denounce denial, to remember and to refuse dissociation then how does one go on to recognise the unfathomable loss and shame of life without care?

Here, the therapist's sensitivity and attunement is designed to mediate and to hold the tension between what is grievable and what is not grievable. The therapeutic journey thus far entails maintaining:

- Compassion and curiosity about what really took place in the client's early life.
- Accepting all parts as equal.
- Facilitating a democratic dialogue between all parts.
- Grieving for everything that has been lost and can never be reclaimed.

With the help of attachment and trauma theories, and polyphonic literature, the majority of Hope's internal system began to tolerate the feeling of being alone without feeling lonely. The repetition is what remains, but the frequency of time and space gradually morphs into something new, less acute since it is the intensity of shame which abates. With each suicidal repetition the structure of the dissociation becomes less rigid and the boundaries between what used to be an overtaking entity are now more of a shadow, an echo rather than a persecutory voice, a fleeting thought rather than an idea, a brief self-state rather than a controlling part. In offering Hope teaspoons of love and acceptance, a polyphonic approach allowing a pluralistic dialogue and negotiation between myself and each part seems to have helped her recognise that the suicidal parts like all her other less relational parts, were her "internal helpers" in trauma time while in the present they can only hinder her opportunities for living life in the present.

In seeing the therapy relationship as a safe place and the therapist as an attachment figure who responds affectively, Hope's suicidal parts are more able to take in some of the nourishment on offer and the balance between the life force and death is constantly being redrawn. In the words of Philip Bromberg, "To put it a bit more poetically, a therapist must be constantly negotiating with a range of self-states with different voices, even when the voice of pain is louder than others" (Bromberg, 2016b, personal communication).

Eventually when a glimpse of freedom from the past begins to show, the division of the personality becomes more permeable and the tension between being and becoming begins to unfold. The healing process is never a static structure but a non-linear process of repetitive negotiation between what is lost and what is earned. After all, in life, everything apart from death involves repetition. Yet, with each repetition we gain something new. In attachment terms, earned security is the process of mobilising repetition towards affect regulation, maturation, and renewed trust. Through this reiterative act of empathy, as we collaboratively negotiate things, the frequency and intensity of repetition slowly begins to change shape and meaning. After seven years of seeing Hope twice weekly, while her speech is still in the plural, her actions are increasingly in the singular and our efforts to rebuild an internal community of hope have begun to take root. Hope's suicidal ideation is rarely present. She has settled into a new home and has a new set of friends.

Since there is no dissociation without loss, repetition in Bowlby's terms would be one's natural way of expressing unresolved grief. Depression for Hope is represented by her un-parented internal working model (IWM). In her words: "I was lost but now I'm found." The secure base is there to offer the exchange of fear for safety, anger for tenderness, control for respect of difference and shame for pride, all enabling the development of self and the growth of love.

References

Alexievich, S. (2013). *Second-Hand Time*. London: Fitzcarraldo Editions.

Alexievich, S. (2016). Interview BBC Radio 4 *Today* programme, May 25, 2016, 8:40am.

Badouk Epstein, O. (2015). Cross the bridge to redefine the pain. *Attachment New Directions in Psychotherapy and Relational Psychoanalysis*, 9, 290–294.

Badouk Epstein, O. (2017). The occupied body. *Attachment New Directions in Psychotherapy and Relational Psychoanalysis*, 11, 257–272.

Badouk Epstein, O. (2019a). "The most tender place in my heart is for strangers": Sexual addiction, the fear system and dissociation through an attachment lens. *Attachment New Directions in Psychotherapy and Relational Psychoanalysis*, 13, 43–60.

Badouk Epstein, O. (2019b). Gaslight – Reality distortion by familiar attachment figures. In B. Huppertz (Ed.), *Approaches to Psychic Trauma, Theory and Practice* (pp. 347–363). Washington, DC: Rowman & Littlefield.

Beebe, B., & Lachmann, F. (2014). *The Origins of Attachment.* New York: Routledge.

Bowlby, J. (1973). *Attachment & Loss, Volume 2, Separation, Anger and Anxiety.* London: Pimlico.

Bowlby, J. (1977). The making and breaking of affectional bonds. II. Some principles of psychotherapy. *British Journal of Psychiatry, 130,* 421–431.

Bowlby, J. (1980). *Attachment & Loss, Volume 3, Loss Sadness & Depression.* London: Pimlico.

Bowlby, J. (1988). *A Secure Base: Clinical Applications of Attachment Theory.* London: Pimlico.

Bromberg. P. (2016a). It never entered my mind. In E. Howell & S. Itzkowitz (Eds.), *The Dissociative Mind in Psychoanalysis, Understanding and Working with Trauma* (pp. 118–127). New York: Routledge.

Bromberg, P. (2016b). Personal communication, December 24, 2016.

Bromberg, P. (2017). Personal communication, April 16, 2017.

Bucci, W. (1997). *Psychoanalysis and Cognitive Science: A Multiple Code Theory.* New York: Guildford Press.

Bucci, W. (2011). The role of subjectivity and intersubjectivity in the reconstruction of dissociated schemas: Converging perspective from psychoanalysis, cognitive science and affective neuroscience. *Psychoanalytic Psychology, 28,* 247–266.

Butler, J. (2004). *Precarious Life: The Powers of Mourning and Violence.* London: Verso.

Cavarero, A. (2008). *Horrorism, Naming Contemporary Violence.* New York: Colombia University Press.

Chefetz, R. A. (2015). *Intensive Psychotherapy for Persistent Dissociative Processes.* New York: Norton.

Damasio, A. (1999). *The Feeling of What Happens. Body and Emotion in the Making of Consciousness.* New York: Harcourt.

Fairbairn, W. R. D. (1952). *Psychoanalytic Studies of the Personality.* London: Tavistock.

Fonagy, P. (2016). *Ego-destructive shame* [psychalive.org Video file]. https://www.youtube.com/watch?v=ANdlIJLCcWg. Last accessed on November 28, 2020.

Fortune, C. 1991. Psychoanalytic champion of "real-life experience": An interview with John Bowlby. *Melanie Klein & Object Relations, 9,* 70–86.

Guntrip, H. (1975). My experience of analysis with Fairbairn and Winnicott. *International Review of Psychoanalysis, 2,* 145–156.

Hainer, M. L. (2016). The Ferenczi paradox: His importance in understanding dissociation and the dissociation of his importance in psychoanalysis. In E. Howell & S. Itzkowitz (Eds.), *The Dissociative Mind in Psychoanalysis, Understanding and Working with Trauma* (pp. 57–69). New York: Routledge.

Hesse, E., & Main, M. (1999). Second generation effects of unresolved trauma in non-maltreating parents: Dissociated, frightened and threatening parental behaviour. *Psychoanalytic Inquiry, 19,* 481–540.

Holmes, J. (1996). *Attachment, Intimacy, Autonomy, Using Attachment Theory in Adult Psychotherapy.* London: Jason Aronson

Kusama, Y. (2005). *Manhattan Suicide Addict.* Paris: Les Press Du Reel.

Liotti, G. (1991). Insecure attachment and agoraphobia, In C. M. Parkes, J. Stevenson-Hinde, & P. Marris (Eds.), *Attachment across the Life Cycle* (pp. 216–233). London: Routledge.

Main, M., & Hesse, E. (1990). Parents' unresolved traumatic experiences are related to infant disorganized attachment status: Is frightened and or/frightening parental behaviour the linking mechanism? In M. T. Greeenberg, D. Cicchetti, & E. M. Cumming (Eds.), *Attachment in the Preschool Years: Theory, Research and Intervention* (pp. 161–184). Chicago, IL: University of Chicago Press.

Nijenhuis, E. R. S., & Van der Hart, O. (2011). Dissociation in trauma: A new definition and comparison with previous formulations. *Journal of Trauma and Dissociation, 2*, 416–445.

Prassas, N. (2015). *Empathy and the Constitution of the Self in the Philosophy of Edith Stein.* Oxford: Dalai Lama Centre for Compassion.

Stein, E. (1917/1989). *On the Problem of Empathy.* The Collected Works of Edith *Stein* (vol. 3, 3rd revised ed., W. Stein, Trans.). Washington, DC: ICS Publications.

Index

Note: *Italic* page numbers refer to figures and page numbers followed by "n" denote endnotes.

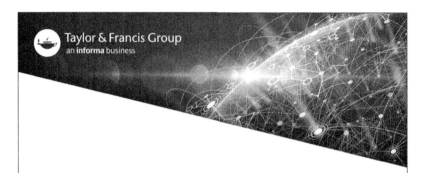

Printed in Great Britain
by Amazon